FOOD PRESERVATION AND SAFETY

FOOD PRESERVATION AND SAFETY

Sumitra N. Pandey

MANGLAM PUBLICATIONS
DELHI-110053 (INDIA)

Published by :
MANGLAM PUBLICATIONS
L-21/1, Street No. 5, Shivaji Marg, Near Kali Mandir,
J.P. Nagar, Kartar Nagar, West Ghonda, Delhi-110053
Phone : 011-22945677, (M.) 9968367559, 9868572512
E-mail: manglam.books2007@rediffmail.com
manglam.publications2007@rediffmail.com

Food Preservation and Safety

First Edition 2010

ISBN 978-93-80013-39-8

PRINTED IN INDIA

Published by Ravindra Kumar Yadav for Manglam Publications, Delhi-110053 Laser Typeset by Amandeep Singh Bansal, (Graphic Era), Delhi- 92, Printed at Sachin Printers, Moujpur Delhi- 53

Preface

The primary purpose of this Book is to serve as a resource for federal and state cooperative extension service staff providing background scientific information on home curing and smoking for food preservation. Knowledgeable home food preservers will find information in this Book that will help them identify hazards that are associated with curing and smoking meats at home, and help them reduce risks of food poisoning associated with these processes. References cited throughout this book will aid the reader in locating additional information. This Book does not specifically address safe practices for commercial or retail establishments.

Home food preservation remains an important and popular cultural activity. Concern has arisen over (1) the emergence of new foodborne diseases that challenge the safety of traditional food preservation methods and (2) the public's desire for variety and healthfulness that leads them to both non traditional foods and non traditional processes that may lack research into their safety.

This Book provides information that is science-based and covers safety hazards associated with home cured and smoked meats only. It does not cover hazards associated with raw meats or cured/smoked non-meats. The principles provided in this Book are recommendations and guidance to home food preservers. No laws govern the home preservation of foods and as such this is strictly a guidance document. This Book is not intended for commercial entities, no matter how small the producer may be. All commercial food preservation must comply with applicable state and federal laws that are beyond the scope of this document.

—Author

Contents

Preface

1. Introduction 1
2. Safety of Jellies, Jams, Spreads 18
3. Home Canning of Low-acid Vegetables 30
4. The Art and Practice of Sausage Making 55
5. Freezing Fruits 73
6. Canning Meat 90
7. Making Pickled Products 99
8. Preserving Fruit Pie Fillings 120
9. Care and Handling of Fish 125
10. Freezing and Food Safety 134
11. Barbecue and Food Safety 213
12. Food Safety in the Kitchen 234

Bibliography 287

Index 288

1

Introduction

PRESERVATI ON OF GAME MEATS AND FISH

Wild game provides wholesome, nourishing food, but it should be handled and preserved carefully to retain quality. Like domestic meat, wild meat is perishable, so care is needed to maintain its safety. The purpose of this publication is to provide recommendations for safely preserving game meats and fish for later enjoyment.

Freezing meat and fish is the most accepted way to maintain top quality. Other methods for preserving game meats include curing and smoking, drying, corning, canning and sausage making. Fish also may be pickled or canned.

FOOD SAFETY GUIDELINES

- Wash your hands for at least 20 seconds with soap and water before beginning to work and after changing tasks or after doing anything that could contaminate your hands, such as sneezing or using the bathroom.
- Start with clean equipment. After using, clean equipment thoroughly with hot soapy water.
- After washing cutting boards, other equipment and surfaces with hot soapy water and rinsing, sanitize with a solution of 1 tablespoon chlorine bleach per gallon of water (or approximately 1 teaspoon per four cups water). After spraying the surface or dipping cutting boards in the solution, allow to air-dry. Remake sanitizing solution daily.

- Keep raw meat separate from other foods on cutting boards and other work surfaces. Consider using color-coded cutting boards.
- If using frozen meat in sausage formulations, thaw it in a refrigerator at 40 degrees Fahrenheit or below on the lowest shelf to avoid dripping of juices on ready-to-eat foods.
- Keep meat as cold as possible (40 F or lower) during sausage processing.
- Use a food thermometer to measure internal temperature of smoked meat and other preserved meat. Use a food thermometer to measure doneness in cooked meat, too.
- Use a pressure canner (not a water bath canner) when canning game meat and fish. Dial gauge pressure canners should be calibrated yearly.

FREEZING GAME MEATS

To ensure good quality in frozen meat:

1. Freeze meat while it is fresh and in top condition.
2. Select proper freezer wrapping materials. To ensure quality, the wrapping material needs to be moisture/vapor resistant. Be sure to use packaging material designed for freezing.
3. Wrap tightly; pressing out as much air as possible.
4. Freeze and store at 0 F or lower.
5. Avoid long storage periods.

Most wild game will keep up to one year frozen without loss of quality. Vacuum packaging of meat before freezing will help maintain excellent quality of the meat.

In most states, hunting laws require that all wild game be used before the next hunting season. Check regulations for the amount of game you can keep and length of time that you can keep it.

Curing and Smoking Game

One purpose in curing meat is to make a high-quality meat product for future use. Only properly butchered and thoroughly cooled meats should be used. Fresh meats can be home-cured by two methods: dry cure or pickle cure (often called sweet pickle cure). Traditionally, dry-cured meats were not injected with sweet pickle; however, when temperature control is difficult or impossible, injecting "pickle" helps to ensure a safe, high-quality product.

The purpose of injecting or pumping is to distribute pickle ingredients throughout the interior of the meat so that curing begins on the inside and cures outward at the same time that curing begins on the outside and works inward. This protects the meat against spoilage and provides a more even curing.

Pumping is usually done with a stitch pump*, an instrument with a hollow needle and holes in the needles through which brine can come out when the needle is inserted in the meat (Figure 1).

***Can use ordinary syringe. Inject into several areas.**

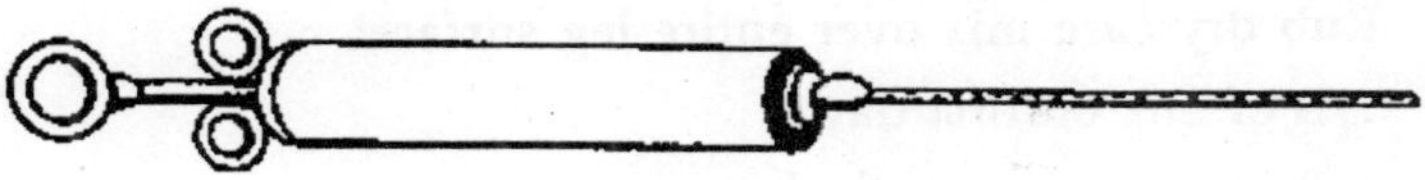

Figure 1

Stitch Pumping

Pickle recipes usually are given on packages of commercial cure. Start by scrubbing the tip pump in warm soap water, then rinse. To keep the pump sanitary while pumping meat, don't touch the needle with hands or lay it down. When not in use, put pump needle-end-down in container that holds the pickle.

To use, draw pump full of pickle and insert needle all the way into the meat. Push with slow even pressure. As pickle is forced into meat, draw the pump toward you to distribute pickle as evenly as possible. Always fill pump full of pickle to prevent air pockets.

Meat will bulge a little and a small amount of pickle will run out of the meat when the pump is withdrawn. To stop the pickle from running out after the needle is withdrawn, pinch the needle holes together with thumb and forefinger for a few seconds. Use three or four pumpfuls of pickle for legs and shoulders that weigh

10 to 15 pounds, and five or six pumpfuls for those that weigh 15 to 25 pounds.

Dry-curing Game

After pumping, apply dry cure using the recipe below or a commercial product.* Rub well over all the meat especially around the bones, hock and the knee joint.

**Freeze-Em-Pickle made by B. Heller and Company; "Morton Tender Quick Cure" or other products are appropriate. Each product has its own recipes.*

Dry cure (for 100 pounds of meat)

6 pounds salt

3 pounds sugar

3 ounces sodium nitrate or 1 ounce sodium nitrite**

*** Sodium nitrate and sodium nitrite (USP Grade) can be obtained at a drug store. Salt peter (potassium nitrate) may be used instead.*

Rub dry cure mix over entire leg surface:

1/3 of mix on first day

1/3 of mix on seventh day

1/3 of mix on fourteenth day

Place on flat surface, uncovered, at 38 F for two days per pound of leg, or approximately four to six weeks. Curing action stops when temperature inside the meat gets below 34 F.

When the meat is cured, let the smaller legs soak for 30 to 40 minutes and larger ones 60 minutes in lukewarm water. Then work and scrub with clean stiff brush to remove grease and salt. Meat is now ready to smoke.

Using Sweet Pickle Cure

Put pumped leg in a container such as a crock, barrel, sealed wooden box or a stainless steel container, or in a USDA-approved plastic container that is approved for food products, such as containers used in the restaurant trade. Do not use other metal containers. Add water to cover the meat. Make up pickle solution just prior to putting in the product. Remove the meat and add enough salt to the water so an egg will float, measuring as you add. If you do not have a specific pickle cure recipe, add sugar to equal one-half the amount of salt used. Add commercial cure to pickle solution according to package directions.

Put leg into pickle solution. Let stand at 38 F for three days per pound of meat (45 days for 15 pounds of meat). If temperature becomes warm and brine becomes ropy, remove meat. Wash the meat. Boil and skim pickle solution or make a new one. The new pickle solution should be as strong as the original. If space is a limiting factor, it might be advantageous to bone out the wild game. Keep the pieces of meat as large as possible and then use one of the procedures described for curing. Smoke after curing is complete.

Smoking

Smokehouses can be as simple as a tarp covering or as sophisticated as a commercial unit. An old refrigerator makes a useful smokehouse.

Caution: For safety, remove the locking device from the door and replace with a simple latch that will lock only from the exterior.

Hardwood such as hickory, maple, chokecherry, oak or apple is best for smoking. Never use a soft wood such as pine because the resin tars will produce off-flavors.

Smoke leg until golden brown at 110° F to 125 °F. Then raise smokehouse temperature to 170 °F until the internal temperature of the meat reaches a minimum of 137 F. Usually the internal temperature is brought up to 141 °F. If you want to have a fully cooked product, then you need to bring the internal temperature to at least 148 °F. Ready-to-eat commercial products are even finished at higher temperatures. Once the desired smoke color is obtained, you want to finish your product in your oven. Always use a calibrated meat thermometer to check temperatures.

DRYING OR "JERKYING"

Drying or "jerkying" meat is an art that has been known since the dawn of civilization. There are many recipes which can be tried, but before you begin check the **jerky maker's checklist** and then adapt these directions to your own circumstances.

A Jerky Maker's Checklist

1. Use fresh lean meat that is free of fat and connective tissue.
2. Slice the meat across the grain.
3. Add the correct amount of seasoning. If you do not have a scale, use approximate equivalent measures for seasonings as follows:
   - Salt.....10.5 ounces (298 grams) = 1 cup
   - ....8.0 ounces (227 grams) = 3/4 cup
   - .... 3.0 ounces (85 grams) = 4 1/2level tablespoons
   - Sugar...5.0 ounces (141 grams) = 2/3 cup
   - .... 3.5 ounces (100 grams) = 1/2 cup
   - .... 1.0 ounce (28 grams) = 2 level tablespoons
   - Ground spices...0.5 ounces (14.3 grams) = 6 level teaspoons
   - ....0.08 ounces (2.4 grams) = 1 level teaspoon
   - Saltpeter (Potassium Nitrate) ....0.3 ounce (8.5 grams) = 2 level teaspoons
4. Cure the meat the correct length of time at 38 F. Salted meat should be placed in wooden, stainless steel or stone containers.
5. Keep the drying or smoking temperature in the smokehouse or oven at 120 F (use a thermometer).
6. If an oven is used, line the sides and bottom with aluminum foil to catch the drippings. Open the door to the first or second stop, or prop open to allow moisture to escape and to lower the oven temperature. A fan will speed air circulation and the drying process.
7. Use hardwood for smoking. (Do not use pine, fir or conifers because they cause off-flavors.)
8. Remove the jerky from the smokehouse or oven before it gets too hard for your taste. Five pounds of fresh meat should weigh approximately two pounds after drying or smoking.
9. Store jerky in clean, airtight containers or plastic bags at room temperature, or wrap it in freezer paper and freeze. Check often during the first month to be sure jerky is dry

enough to keep well. Although jerky will last almost indefinitely at any temperature, its quality deteriorates after a few months.

10. Seasonings and smoking or drying times can be changed to suit individual tastes. Be careful however, to maintain minimum temperatures to avoid bacterial growth.

Large pieces of meat that are pickle-cured make excellent jerky when sliced and dried or smoked. Corned meat pickle solutions are preferred because spices are included in the cure.

Smoked Deer Jerky

Debone hind leg, splitting into individual muscles; top, bottom and tip. Pump with brine* (two pounds commercial saltcure mixture per gallon of water). Place in crock or USDA-approved plastic container. Do not use plastic containers such as garbage cans, plastic bags or supermarket ice cream buckets. Cover completely with brine and weight meat down to keep it submerged.

Store in cooler (38 F) for 10 days.

Every two days, change the position of the meat and weight it down again. After 10 days remove from brine and smoke five hours at 150 F. Hang to dry at room temperature (about two weeks). Cut off to use as needed.

BEEF (OR DEER) JERKY

1. Pre-freeze meat to be made into jerky so it will be easier to slice.
2. Cut partially thawed meat into long slices no more than 1/4 inch thick. For tender jerky, cut at right angles to long muscles (across the grain). Remove as much visible fat as possible to help prevent off-flavors.
3. Prepare two to three cups of marinade of your choice in a large saucepan.
4. Bring the marinade to a full rolling boil over medium heat. Add a few meat strips, making sure they are covered by the marinade. Reheat to a full boil.
5. Remove pan from range. Using tongs, remove strips from hot marinade (work quickly to prevent overcooking) and

place in single non-overlapping layers on drying racks. (Repeat steps four and five until all the meat has been precooked.) Add more marinade if needed.

6. Dry at 140 to 150 F in dehydrator, oven or smoker. Test for doneness by letting a piece cool. When cool, it should crack but not break when bent. There should not be any moist or underdone spots.
7. Refrigerate the jerky overnight in plastic freezer bags, then check again for doneness. If necessary, dry further.

CAUTION: Soaking the strips in marinade before precooking is not advised as the marinade could become a source of bacteria. Putting unmarinated strips directly into the boiling marinade minimizes a cooked flavor and maintains the safety of the marinade.

Hot Pickle Cure Jerky

Yield: Five pounds of fresh meat should weigh approximately two pounds after drying or smoking.

1. Slice 5 lb. of meat (1/4 inch thick strips) with the grain. Use lean meat free of fat and connective tissue.
2. Spread out meat and sprinkle on 3 Tbsp. salt, 2 tsp. ground black pepper, and 2 Tbsp. sugar. Put the meat in a pan or dish and let stand for 24 hours in the refrigerator.
3. Pound the meat on both sides to work in the spice. Optional: Dip strips of meat in a liquid smoke solution (five parts water to one part liquid smoke) for one to two seconds for added flavor.
4. Make a brine by dissolving 3/4 cup salt, 1/2 cup sugar, and 2 Tbsp. ground black pepper in a gallon of water. Stir to dissolve the salt and sugar.
5. Bring the brine to a low to medium boil. Immerse the fresh meat strips (a few at a time) into the boiling brine until they turn gray (one to two minutes). Remove meat from the brine, using clean tongs or other utensils that have not contacted the raw meat.
6. Spread out meat on a clean dehydrator rack or on a clean rack in the top half of a kitchen oven. If you use a kitchen

oven, open the oven door to the first of second stop. Heat at 120 to 150 F (lowest oven temperature) for 9 to 24 hours or until the desired dryness is reached.

7. Remove jerky from oven before it becomes too hard or brittle. Properly dried jerky should crack when bent in half but should not break into two pieces.
8. Store jerky in clean jars or plastic bags, or wrap it in freezer paper and freeze. If kept dry, properly prepared jerky will last almost indefinitely at any temperature, but is quality deteriorates after a few months.

Corning Game

Venison, antelope, moose, bear or beef can be corned following the same method. People who usually do not like wild meats may like them corned, as corning takes out the musky wild flavor and tenderizes the toughest wild meats. A good piece of round is wonderful corned, but less desirable cuts of meat like the brisket can be corned, too.

To make six gallons of corning liquid:

3 pounds (6 3/4c.) salt

10 ounces (1 3/8 c.) sugar

2 ounces sodium nitrate

1/2 ounce sodium nitrite

3 level tsp. black pepper

3 level tsp. ground cloves

6 bay leaves

12 level tsp. mixed pickling spice

For onion flavor, add one medium-size onion, minced. For garlic flavor, add 4 garlic cloves, minced. Put the ingredients into a pickle crock or glass jar and add enough water to make a total of 6 gallons, including the ingredients. Cover the container.

The ideal temperature for corning meat is about 38 F. During the fall or spring months, this is not too difficult to obtain. In the winter, an unheated part of a basement can be used for corning meat. During summer months, it is hard to find a place around 38 F. Higher temperatures need not affect the end result of the corning process at all, if, for every 15 F of temperature above 38 F, you add one-third more salt. At 83 F, add three pounds more salt, making a total of six pounds of salt. Place meat into the liquid. Put a heavy plate on meat; weight plate, if necessary, to keep meat below pickle brine. Leave the meat in corning liquid for 15 days. On the fifth and 10th days, stir the liquid well, remove the meat and put it back so the bottom piece is on top. After the 15th day, remove the meat. Use what you want immediately and store the balance in a cool place refrigerated at 38 degrees. It is recommended that after meat is removed from the corning liquid it should be cooked and consumed within one week or frozen for up to one month. The meat at this stage has a grayish pink color. When cooked, corned meat changes to the characteristic pink color associated with a cured product.

Cooking Corned Meat

Place the corned meat in a pan with a cover. Add cold water to cover meat. Bring to a boil and remove the scum from the water. Reduce the heat and simmer for about five hours or until tender. Season to taste and serve as the main meat dish.

Canning Game

Only good quality, properly cleaned and cooled game should be canned. To ensure safety of canned meats, meat *must* be processed in a pressure canner to reach a sufficiently high temperature for a long enough time to kill all bacteria that cause spoilage or food poisoning. Large game animals are canned like beef. Small game animals and birds are canned like poultry. Either type of meat can be raw packed or hot packed.

SMALL GAME ANIMALS AND BIRDS

Procedure: Choose freshly killed and dressed, healthy animals or birds. Dressed meat should be soaked one hour in water containing 1 tablespoon of salt per quart and then rinsed. Remove excess fat. Cut meat into suitable sizes for canning. Can with or without bone.

Hot pack - Boil, steam or bake meat until about two-thirds done. Add 1 teaspoon salt per quart, if desired. Fill jars with pieces and hot broth, leaving 1 1/4 inch headspace.

Raw pack - Add 1 teaspoon salt per quart, if desired. Fill jars loosely with raw meat pieces, leaving 1 1/4 inch headspace. Do not add liquid.

Procedure: Choose quality chilled meat. Remove excess fat. Soak strong-flavored wild meats for 1 hour in brine water containing 1 tablespoon of salt per quart. Rinse. Remove large bones.

Hot pack - Precook meat until rare by roasting, stewing or browning in a small amount of fat. Add 1 teaspoon of salt per quart, if desired. Fill jars with pieces and add boiling broth, meat drippings, water or tomato juice, leaving 1-inch headspace.

Raw pack - Add 1 teaspoon of salt per quart if desired. Fill jars with raw meat pieces, leaving 1-inch headspace. Do not add liquid.

GROUND OR CHOPPED MEAT

(bear, beef, lamb, pork, sausage, veal, venison)

Procedure: Choose fresh, chilled meat. With venison, add one part high-quality pork fat to three or four parts venison before grinding. Use freshly made sausage, seasoned with salt and cayenne pepper (sage may cause a bitter off-flavor). Shape chopped meat into patties or balls or cut cased sausage into 3- to 4-inch links. Cook until lightly browned. Ground meat may be sautéed without shaping. Remove excess fat. Fill jars with pieces. Add boiling meat broth, tomato juice or water, leaving 1-inch headspace. Add one teaspoon of salt per quart to the jars, if desired.

MAKING SAUSAGE

The lean trimmings from wild game make an excellent meat for sausage production. Try one of your favorite recipes and substitute wild game or fowl trimmings for the beef portions.

Venison Summer Sausage

15 pounds venison

10 pounds pork trimmings (5 pounds lean, 5 pounds fat)

7 ounces (2/3 cup) salt

1 ounce (2 Tbsp.) commercial cure

1 ounce (2 Tbsp.) mustard seed

3 ounces (1/2 cup) pepper

3 ounces (1/2 cup) sugar

1/2 ounce (3 Tbsp.) marjoram

Mix salt and cure with coarsely ground venison and pork trimmings. Pack in shallow pan and place in cooler for 3 to 5 days. Then add rest of ingredients and mix well.

Cure is optional. It is used to develop a pink color and as a preservative.

Note: This sausage recipe is quite spicy. If you like less spice, cut down proportions of spices. Smoke sausage as described in the following method.

Smoking Sausage: Stuff prepared sausage into 3-inch diameter fibrous casings. Smoke at 140 F for 1 hour, 160 F for one hour and 180 F until internal temperature reaches 152 F (insert a calibrated meat thermometer in the thickest part of the sausage to check internal temperature). Remove from smokehouse and rinse/spray with hot water for 15 to 30 seconds. Follow with cold rinse/spray or place in ice water until internal temperature is reduced to 100 F. Let dry 1 to 2 hours. Refrigerate.

Wild Game Polish Sausage

25 pounds 50/50 pork trimmings (50% lean and 50% fat)

20 pounds wild game (lean meat)

1 quart water

14 ounces (1 1/3cups) salt

2 ounces (4 Tbsp.) cure

1/2 ounce (6 tsp.) marjoram

1 1/2 ounces (3 Tbsp.) mustard seed

3 cloves garlic

2 ounces (1/4 cup) pepper

Mix all ingredients together and grind the product through a coarse plate and follow this with a fine grind. Stuff in hog casing and smoke at 120 F for one hour, 150 F for one more hour, then at 170 F two hours or until internal temperature of 141 F is reached.

Follow same procedure as described for smoking venison summer sausage.

Quick Sausage

2 pounds hamburger or deerburger mix

1/2 tsp. pepper

1/8 tsp. garlic powder

1/4 tsp. onion powder

2 Tbsp. curing salt

1 Tbsp. liquid smoke

1 cup water

1 Tbsp. mustard seed (optional)

Pack mixture in a water glass to within ½ inch of the top. Use large glass container or enough glass tumblers. Cover and freeze overnight. Run warm water on glass to release. Plastic containers will not crack and are safer, but may pick up flavors from the sausage. Wrap in cellophane wrap. Tie ends. Simmer 1 hour in water. Slice thin.

Note: Hamburger or pork sausage can be mixed with ground venison.

FREEZING, PICKLING AND CANNING FISH

Freezing Fish

Special care should be taken with fish because it tends to dry out more quickly than other meats. Glazing with ice or freezing in water are good methods of freezing fish.

For ice glazing, place cleaned, eviscerated fresh fish in a tray in freezer. When frozen, dip in near-freezing ice water. Place fish again in freezer to harden the glaze. Repeat dipping fish until about 1/8 inch of ice coating has been formed. Overwrap with film, freezer paper of foil. To freeze in water, fill freezer container (clean milk cartons can be used) with water. Add whole fish or fish fillets. Completely cover fish with water, then seal and freeze. Whole dressed fish probably freezes best this way.

Note: The authors have had good results freezing fish for long periods of time by wrapping dressed fresh fish in plastic wrap and then wrapping again in aluminum foil.

Pickling Fish

While the term "pickled fish" sometimes is used to include fish cured in brine, it should be applied only to those products in which vinegar is used. Only a few types of fish are preserved commercially by pickling, but almost any species may be prepared for home use.

A Pickling Checklist

1. When using the vinegar-spice cure, preserve only the freshest and best quality fish. The flavor, texture, color and keeping quality also are affected by the water, salt, sugar, vinegar, herbs and other miscellaneous ingredients.
2. Use drinking water or water approved under all sanitary codes. "Hard" waters are unsuitable, especially those with a high iron, calcium or magnesium content. The minerals interfere with the curing process and can cause rancidity and off-flavors.
3. Use high-quality white distilled vinegar of 5 percent acidity (50 grain). Acidity is usually listed on the label. Do not use vinegars of unknown acidity. Ciders and other fruit vinegars may give the fish an off-flavor and color.
4. Use a high-quality, pure granulated dairy or canning salt. The salt must be as free as possible from magnesium compounds, as these impurities give a bitter flavor to the cured product and may cause discoloration of the fish. Non-iodized salt is best for pickling.
5. Use table (cane or beet) sugar.
6. Use fresh, high-quality spices. Best results are secured by buying fresh, whole spices, and making up the mixture, by recipe at the time it is to be used. Prepared commercial mixtures are convenient and time-saving if you can obtain the desired amount.
7. Soak fresh fish in a weak brine of 1 cup salt to 1 gallon cold water for 1 hour.
8. Drain and pack fish in a glass, heavy food grade plastic or enamel container with a strong brine (2 1/2 pounds salt to 1 gallon water) for 12 hours. Refrigerate at 40F or lower.

Pickled Fish

(Recipe is spicy*)

10 pounds fish

1 ounce whole allspice

1 ounce mustard seed

2 ounces regular mixed pickling spice

1/2 pound onion, sliced

1/2 ounce bay leaves

1 1/2 quarts distilled (white) vinegar

2 1/2 pints water

1 ounce white pepper

1 ounce hot ground or dried peppers (optional and to taste)

Rinse fish in fresh water. Combine the recipe ingredients in a large pan or kettle. Bring to a boil and add fish. Simmer for 10 minutes, or until fish is easily pierced with a fork. Remove fish from the liquid and place in a single layer on a flat pan and refrigerate for rapid cooling to prevent spoilage. Pack cold fish in a clean glass jar, adding a few spices, a bay leaf, freshly sliced onions and, if desired, a slice of lemon.

Strain the vinegar, bring to a boil, and pour into jars until the fish are covered. Cover jars with lids.

This product must be stored in the refrigerator at 40 F or lower and should be used within 4 to 6 weeks.

*For a less spicy product, use less white pepper and hot or ground pepper.

Pickled Smelt

2 pounds cleaned smelt

3 cups water

1 tsp. salt

1/4 tsp. white pepper

2 bay leaves

1 cup onion, sliced

3 cups white vinegar*

Cook fish in water, salt, pepper and bay leaves and onion in a covered pan for 12 minutes. Drain and measure fish stock; you will need about 2 cups. Add the vinegar to the stock and bring to a boil. Cook 5 minutes and cool in refrigerator at 40 F or lower.

Pour over fish, let stand in refrigerator for several hours. Serves 4 to 6. *If the taste of vinegar is too strong, offset it by adding 1/4 to 1/2 cup sugar.

Norwegian Pickled Herring

3 salted herring
3 Tbsp. sugar
1 1/4 cups water
3/4 cup vinegar
1/3 tsp. white pepper
A few whole peppers
1 red onion

Be sure to use properly salted herring. Clean and cut herring into fillets. Soak in water (to cover completely) 12 to 15 hours. Skin and remove all bones. Dissolve the sugar in water, add vinegar, pepper and thinly sliced onion. Add herring and refrigerate a few hours before serving.

Store in the refrigerator at 40 F or lower and use within 4 to 5 weeks.

Canning Fish

(Blue, mackerel, salmon, steelhead, trout and other fatty fish except tuna)

Although freezing is the easiest way to preserve fish, canning does offer some advantages, particularly if one lacks freezer space. The only safe way to process fish is in a pressure canner. Fish that has been frozen can be safely canned; thaw fish in a refrigerator and can promptly. Follow recommended canning procedures carefully.

Caution: Eviscerate fish within two hours after they are caught. Keep cleaned fish on ice until ready to can.

Fish may be canned with its bones. They add to the flavor and nutritive value of the product; however, it is recommended only pint or smaller containers be used.

CANNING PROCEDURE

Remove head, tail, fins and scales. Wash and remove all blood. Split fish lengthwise, if desired. Cut cleaned fish into 3½-inch lengths. Fill pint jars, skin side next to glass, leaving 1-inch headspace. Add one teaspoon of salt per pint, if desired. Do not add liquid.

"Mock" Salmon

Allow 2 1/4 to 3 pounds of whole fish for each pint of canned fish. Clean and prepare fish. Remove head, fins and tail. Remove skin, if desired. If the fish is slimy, a solution of 1 tablespoon vinegar to 2 quarts water helps remove the slime. The color of some fish can be improved by soaking the fish in cold water containing 1/2 cup salt to 1 gallon water for 30 minutes; *do not reuse salt water*. Rinse fish in clean water. Cut fish into jar-sized lengths. Make sauce.

Sauce

1 cup catsup

1 cup vinegar

1/2 cup water

3 Tbsp salt

1/4 cup minced onion

2 bay leaves, crumbled

Combine and heat the above ingredients. This makes enough sauce for about 8 pints. Pack fish into jars to within 1 inch of the top. Cover with sauce, leaving 1-inch headspace. Remove air bubbles, wipe jar rims, place prepared lids on jars and tighten the screw bands.

Quick Pink Salmon

To each pint of fish add:

1 Tbsp. vinegar

1/4 tsp. salt

2 Tbsp. tomato juice.

2

Safety of Jellies, Jams, Spreads

Sweet spreads are foods with many textures, flavors and colors. They are thickened or jellied to varying degrees. The traditional jellies and jams are preserved primarily by sugar.

INGREDIENTS

For proper texture, jellied fruit products require the correct combination of fruit, pectin, acid and sugar. The fruit gives each spread its unique flavor and color. It also supplies the water to dissolve the other ingredients and furnishes some or all of the pectin and acid. Good quality, flavorful fruits make the best jellied products.

Pectins are substances in fruits that form a gel if they are in the right combination with acid and sugar. All fruits contain some pectin. Apples, crabapples, gooseberries and some plums and grapes usually contain enough natural pectin to form a gel. Other fruits, such as strawberries, cherries and blueberries, contain little pectin and must be combined with other fruits high in pectin or with commercial pectin products to obtain gels. Because fully ripened fruit has less pectin, one-fourth of the fruit used in making jellies without added pectin should be underripe.

The proper level of acidity is critical to gel formation. If there is too little acid, the gel will never set. If there is too much acid, the gel will lose liquid (weep). For fruits low in acid, add lemon juice or other acid ingredients as directed. Commercial pectin products contain acids which help to ensure gelling.

Sugar serves as a preserving agent, contributes flavor and aids in gelling. Cane and beet sugar are the usual sources of sugar for jelly or jam. Corn syrup and honey may be used to replace part of the sugar in recipes but too much will mask the fruit flavor and alter the gel structure. It is best to use tested recipes for replacing sugar with honey or corn syrup. Do not reduce the amount of sugar in traditional recipes. Too little sugar prevents gelling and may allow yeasts and molds to grow.

REDUCED SUGAR SPREADS

A variety of fruit spreads may be made that are lower in sugar and calories than the traditional jellies and jams. These products may use modified pectin, gelatin or gums to thicken them. Noncaloric sweeteners or reduced amounts of sugar provide the sweetness.

Two types of modified pectin are available for home use. One gels with one-third less sugar and is sold as a light or lite fruit pectin. It contains preservatives to help prevent microbial spoilage. The other is a low-methoxyl pectin which requires a source of calcium to form a gel. To prevent spoilage, jars of these reduced sugar products must be processed longer than traditional jellied products in a boiling water bath. Recipes and processing times provided with each modified product must be followed carefully. The proportions of acids and fruits should not be altered, as spoilage may result.

Spreads prepared with gelatin should not be processed or frozen. They should be refrigerated and used within 4 weeks.

Prevent Problems:

- Paraffin or wax seals are no longer recommended for ANY sweet spreads.
- All sweet spreads that will be stored at room temperature should be processed.
- The use of sterile jars and a 5 minute process time is preferred.
- If unsterile jars are used, the process time is 10 minutes. The additional processing time may cause weak gels in some products.
- Sweet spreads which develop mold growth should not be used.

- Overcooking may break down pectin and prevent proper gelling.
- Make one batch at a time. Increasing the quantities often results in soft gels.
- Use the jar size specified in the recipe. Use of larger jars may result in excessively soft products.

General Procedure

Extracting the Juice

One pound of fruit should yield at least 1 cup of clear juice.

Wash all fruits thoroughly before cooking. Cut firm, larger fruits into small pieces. Crush soft fruits or berries. Add water to fruits. Put fruit and water in a large saucepan and bring to a boil. Simmer, stirring occasionally, for the amount of time listed or until the fruit is soft.

Table 1. Measures for preparing jellies without added pectin.

To extract juice

	Cups water to be added per pound of fruit	Minutes to simmer before extracting juice	Add to each cup of strained juice: Sugar (cups)	Lemon juice (optional)	Jelly yield from 4 cups of juice (half-pints)
Apples	1	20 to 25	3/4	1-1/2 tsp	4 to 5
Blackberries	0 to 1/4	5 to 10	3/4 to 1	–	7 to 8
Crabapples	1	20 to 25	1	–	4 to 5
Grapes	0 to 1/4	5 to 10	3/4 to 1	–	8 to 9
Plums	1/2	15 to 20	3/4	–	8 to 9

Making Jelly Without Added Pectin

Use only firm fruits naturally high in pectin when extracting juice for jellies to be prepared without added pectin. Select a mixture of about three-fourths ripe and one-fourth underripe fruit. Do not use commercially canned or frozen fruit juices because their pectin content is too low. Use of peels and cores adds pectin to the juice during cooking of the fruit and increases jelly firmness.

Using no more than 6 to 8 cups of extracted fruit juice at a time, measure and combine the proper quantities of juice, sugar, and lemon juice in Table 1 and heat to boiling. Stir until the sugar is dissolved. Boil over high heat, stirring frequently, until the gelling point is reached.

To test jelly doneness, use one of the following methods:

Temperature test — Use a jelly or candy thermometer and boil to a temperature of 220 degrees Fahrenheit at sea level, 218 F at 1,000 feet, 216 F at 2,000 feet, or 214 F at 3,000 feet of altitude.

Sheet or spoon test — Dip a cool metal spoon into the boiling jelly mixture. Raise the spoon about 12 inches above the pan (out of steam). Turn the spoon so the liquid runs off the side. The jelly is done when the syrup forms two drops that flow together and sheet or hang off the edge of the spoon.

When the jelly is done, remove it from heat and quickly skim off foam. Ladle the jelly into sterile jars, leaving 1/4-inch headspace. Adjust lids and process the jars as recommended.

Making Jam Without Added Pectin

For best flavor, use fully ripe fruit. Wash and rinse all fruits thoroughly before cooking. Do not soak. Remove stems, skins, and pits from fruit; cut into pieces and crush. For berries, remove stems and blossoms, and crush. Seedy berries may be put through a sieve or food mill. Measure crushed fruit into large saucepan, using the ingredients in Table 2. Add sugar and bring to a boil while stirring rapidly and constantly. Continue to boil until mixture thickens. As you test for thickness, remember to allow for thickening during cooling.

Table 2. Measures for preparing Jams without added pectin.

	Cups crushed fruit	Cups sugar	Tbsp lemon juice	Jam yield (half-pints)
Apricots	4 to 4-1/2	4	2	5 to 6
Berries	4	4	0	3 to 4
Peaches	5-1/2 to 6	4 to 5	2	6 to 7

One way to test the thickness is to follow the directions for the temperature test for jelly without added pectin. An alternative method is to remove the jam from the heat. Pour a small amount of boiling jam on a cold plate and put it is the freezing compartment of a refrigerator for a few minutes. If the mixture gels, it is done. When jam is done, remove it from heat and quickly skim off foam. Ladle the jam into sterile jars, leaving 1/4-inch headspace. Adjust lids and process the jars as recommended.

MAKING JELLIES AND JAMS WITH ADDED PECTIN

Fresh fruits and juices may be used with commercially prepared powdered or liquid pectins. The order of combining ingredients depends on the type of pectin used. Complete directions for a variety of fruits are provided with packaged pectin. Jelly or jam made with added pectin requires less cooking, generally gives a larger yield, and has more natural fruit flavor. In addition, using added pectin eliminates the need to test for doneness. The following recipes are usually available with packaged pectins:

Jellies — Apple, crabapple, blackberry, boysenberry, dewberry, currant, elderberry, grape, mint, peach, plum, black or red raspberry, loganberry, and strawberry.

Jams — Apricot, blackberry, boysenberry, dewberry, loganberry, red raspberry, youngberry, blueberry, cherry currant, gooseberry, grape, orange marmalade, peach, pear, plum, and strawberry.

Additional recipes may be available by calling the consumer number listed on the pectin package insert.

Be sure to use Mason canning jars and self-sealing two-piece lids, and be sure to process the jars in boiling water as described in Table 3. Purchase packaged pectins needed each year. Old pectins may result in poor gels.

Processing

Prepare products as described in the following pages. All products should be filled hot into sterile half-pint or pint canning jars, leaving 1/4-inch headspace. To sterilize empty jars, put them open side up on a rack in a boiling-water canner. Fill the canner and jars with hot (not boiling) water to 1 inch above top of jars. Boil jars 10 minutes.

Remove and drain hot sterilized jars one at a time and fill with food. Food residue should be removed from the jar sealing edge with a clean, damp paper towel. New two-piece canning lids prepared according to manufacturer's directions should be applied. After screw bands are tightened, jars should be processed in a boiling water canner.

To process in a boiling water canner, fill canner halfway with water and preheat to 180°F. Load sealed jars into the canner rack and lower with handles; or load one jar at a time with a jar lifter onto rack in canner.

Add water if needed to a level of 1 inch above jars and add cover. When water boils vigorously, lower heat to maintain gentle boil, and process jars of the product for the recommended time.

Table 3. Recommended processing time in a boiling water canner for jellies and jams.

			Process time at altitudes of	
Product	Style of pack	Jar size	0-1000 ft (minutes)	1001-6000 ft (minutes)
All jellies and jams with or without and added pectin pints	Hot	Half-pints	5	10

After Processing

After processing is completed, remove jars from the canner with a jar lifter and place on a towel or rack. Do not retighten screw bands. Air-cool jars 12 to 24 hours. Remove screw bands and check lid seals. If the center of the lid is indented, wash, dry, label and store jar in a clean, cool, dark place. If lid is unsealed, examine and replace the jar if defective, use new lids, and reprocess as before or refrigerate and use. Wash screw bands and store separately.

Jellies, jams and spreads are best if consumed within a year and safe as long as lids remain vacuum sealed.

Freezer or Uncooked Jellies and Jams

These can be made with some fresh or frozen fruits or fruit juices. Commercial pectin and a higher percentage of sugar are used. Uncooked jellies and jams may be stored in the refrigerator for up to three weeks. For longer storage (up to six months), freeze.

One pectin manufacturer notes that it is normal for a few sugar crystals to remain in freezer jellies and jams. If the product is too firm, stir to soften. If it tends to separate, stir to blend. If it is too soft, bring it to a boil. It will thicken on cooling.

Remaking Soft Jelly

Recook a trial batch using 1 cup jelly or jam to see if the recooking will give you the results you'd like. If the trial batch is successful, proceed with no more than 4 to 6 cups at one time.

Powdered Pectin

To remake cooked jelly or jam with powdered pectin: For each cup of jelly or jam, measure 2 tablespoons sugar, 1 tablespoon water and 1-1/2 teaspoons of powdered pectin. (Stir the package contents well before measuring.) Mix the pectin and water and bring to a boil, stirring constantly. Add jelly or jam and sugar. Stir thoroughly.

Bring to a full rolling boil over high heat, stirring constantly. Boil mixture hard for 1/2 minute. Remove from heat, skim and pour into hot sterilized jars leaving 1/4 inch headspace. Cover with new prepared lids and process according to Table 4.

Table 4. Recommended process time for Remade Soft Jellies in a boiling-water canner.

		Process time at altitudes of	
Style of Pack	Jar Size	0-1000 ft	1001-6000 ft
Hot	Half-pints	5 min.	10 min.

Liquid Pectin

To remake cooked jelly or jam with liquid pectin: For each cup of jelly or jam, measure 2 tablespoons sugar, 1-1/2 teaspoons lemon juice and 1-1/2 teaspoons of liquid pectin. Place jelly or jam in a saucepan and bring to a boil, stirring constantly. At once add sugar, lemon juice and liquid pectin. Bring to a full rolling boil, stirring constantly, and boil hard for 1 minute. Remove from heat. Skim and pour into hot sterilized jars.

Without Added Pectin

To remake cooked jelly without added pectin: If the fruit juice was not acid enough, and 1-1/2 teaspoons lemon juice per cup jelly before boiling. Heat the jelly to boiling and boil until the jellying point is reached. Remove jelly from heat, skim, pour immediately into sterilized hot containers and seal and process.

Recipes

Grape plum jelly with pectin

3-1/2 pounds ripe plums

3 pounds ripe Concord grapes

1 cup water

1/2 teaspoon butter or margarine (optional ingredient to reduce foaming)

8-1/2 cups sugar

1 box (1-3/4 oz) powdered pectin

Yield — About 10 half-pints

Preparation. Wash grapes. Wash and pit plums; do not peel. Thoroughly crush plums and grapes, one layer at a time, in a saucepan. Add water. Bring to a boil, cover, and simmer 10 minutes. Strain juice through a jelly bag or double layer of cheesecloth. Measure sugar and set aside. Combine 6-1/2 cups of juice with butter and pectin in a large saucepan. Bring to a hard boil over heat, stirring constantly. Add the sugar and return to a full rolling boil. Boil hard for 1 minute, stirring constantly. Remove from heat, skim off foam, and quickly fill into sterile half-pint jars, leaving 1/4-inch headspace.

Strawberry Rhubarb Jam with Pectin

1-1/2 pounds red stalks of rhubarb

1-1/2 quarts ripe strawberries

1/2 teaspoon butter or margarine (optional ingredient to reduce foaming)

6 cups sugar

6 ounce liquid pectin

Yield — About 7 half-pints

Preparation. Wash and cut rhubarb into 1-inch pieces and blend or grind. Wash, stem and crush strawberries, one layer at a time, in a large saucepan. Add butter, if desired, and sugar, thoroughly mixing into juice. Bring to a boil over high heat, stirring constantly. Immediately stir in pectin. Bring to a full rolling boil and boil hard 1 minute, stirring constantly. Remove from heat, and quickly skim off foam, and fill into sterile half-pint jars, leaving 1/4-inch headspace. Adjust lids and process the jars as given in Table 3.

Chokecherry Jelly with Liquid Pectin

Extract the juice as described under General Procedure using enough water to cover the washed fruit and cook about 15 minutes or until fruit is soft. Do not crush or grind the seeds which contain a cyanide forming compound which can be toxic.

3 cups chokecherry juice

6-1/2 cups sugar

2 pouches liquid pectin

1/4 teaspoon almond extract (optional)

Table 5.

			Process Time at Altitudes of	
	Style of Pack	**Jar Size**	**0-1,000 ft**	**1,001-6,000 ft**
Chokecherry				
jelly	Hot	Half-pints	5 min.	10 min.
Syrup	Hot	Half-pints	10 min. or pints	10 min.

Pour juice into large heavy kettle. Add sugar and stir to mix. Place over high heat. Bring to a boil, stirring constantly. Stir in pectin. Bring to a full, rolling boil and boil hard for 1 minute, stirring constantly. Remove from heat. Stir and skim 5 minutes. Add almond extract.

Pour into hot, sterilized half-pint jars; leave 1/4 inch headspace. Use two-piece lids and process in boiling water bath according to Table 5.

Chokecherry Jelly with Powdered Pectin

Extract juice as described under General Procedure.

3-1/2 cups chokecherry juice

4 cups sugar

1 box powdered pectin

Stir pectin into juice. Bring this mixture to a rolling boil (one that does not stop when stirred) over high heat, stirring constantly. Quickly add sugar to juice mixture. Bing to a full rolling boil and boil 1 minute, stirring constantly. Remove from heat. Skim off any foam. Pour into hot, sterilized half-pint jars; leave 1/4-inch headspace. Cover with two-piece lids and process in boiling water bath according to Table 5.

Syrups Made with Juice

4 cups juice

4 cups sugar

1/4 cup lemon juice (if desired)

1/2 package or less powdered pectin (if desired)

Mix juice, sugar, lemon juice and pectin. Bring to boil and boil 2 minutes. Remove from heat, skim off foam, and pour into 1/2 pint or 1 pint canning jars to within 1/2 inch of top. Adjust lids and process in boiling water bath canner according to Table 5. Remove from canner and cool. Check lids, label, and store in cook, dry place.

The following recipes use reduced amounts of sugar.

Grape Jelly with Gelatin

2 tablespoons unflavored gelatin powder

1 bottle (24 ounce) unsweetened grape juice

2 tablespoons bottled lemon juice

2 tablespoons liquid artificial sweetener (Saccharin is acceptable)

Yield — half-pints

Preparation. In a saucepan, soften the gelatin in the grape and lemon juices. Bring to a full rolling boil to dissolve gelatin. Boil 1 minute and remove from heat. Stir in sweetener. Fill quickly into hot sterile half-pint jars, leaving 1/4-inch headspace. Adjust lids. Do not process or freeze — store in refrigerator and use within 4 weeks.

Apple Jelly with Gelatin

2 tablespoons unflavored gelatin powder

1 quart bottled unsweetened apple juice

2 tablespoons bottled lemon juice

2 tablespoons liquid Saccharin sweetener

Food coloring, if desired

Yield — 4 half-pints

Preparation. In a saucepan, soften gelatin in apple and lemon juices. To dissolve gelatin, bring to a full rolling boil and boil 2 minutes. Remove from heat. Stir in sweetener, and food coloring, if desired. Pour into sterile half-pint jars, leaving 1/4-inch headspace. Adjust lids. Do not process or freeze — store in refrigerator and use within 4 weeks.

Variation: For Spiced Apple Jelly, add two 3-inch sticks of cinnamon and four whole cloves to mixture before boiling. Remove both spices before adding the sweetener and food coloring.

Peach Pineapple Spread

4 cups drained peach pulp

2 cups drained, unsweetened crushed pineapple

1/4 cup bottled lemon juice

2 cups sugar (optional)

Yield — 5 to 6 half-pints

This recipe may be made with any combination of peaches, nectarines, apricots and plums.

This recipe may be made without sugar or with up to 2 cups, according to taste or preference. Non-nutritive sweeteners may be added. If aspartame (a low-calorie nutritive sweetener) is used, the sweetening power may be lost within 3 to 4 weeks.

Preparation. Thoroughly wash 4 to 6 pounds of firm, ripe peaches. Drain well. Peel and remove pits. Grind fruit flesh with a medium or coarse blade, or crush with a fork. Do not use a blender. Place ground or crushed fruit in a 2-quart saucepan. Heat slowly to release juice, stirring constantly, until fruit is tender. Place cooked fruit in a jelly bag or strainer lined with four layers of cheesecloth. Allow juice to drip about 15 minutes. Save the juice for jelly or other uses. Measure 4 cups of drained fruit pulp for making spread. Combine the 4 cups of pulp, pineapple, and lemon juice in a 4-quart saucepan. Add up to 2 cups of sugar, if desired, and mix well. Heat and boil gently for 10 to 15 minutes, stirring often. Fill quickly into jars, leaving 1/4-inch headspace. Adjust lids and process.

Table 6. Peach-pineapple spread — Recommended processing time in a boiling water canner.

		Process times at altitudes of		
Style of pack	**Jar size**	**0-1,000 ft**	**1,001-3,000 ft**	**3,000-6,000 ft**
Hot	Half-pints	15 min.	20 min.	20 min.
	Pints	20 min.	25 min.	30 min.

NUTRITION INFORMATION

Table 7. Average content of a tablespoon serving of jam or jelly.

	Canned jam	**Canned Jelly**
Calories	54	49
Carbohydrates, g	14	12.7
Fats, g	—	—
Sodium, mg	2	3

3

Home Canning of Low-acid Vegetables

The method used for canning a product is determined primarily by the acidity of the food or mixture of foods being canned. Low-acid foods must be processed in a pressure canner to be free of botulism risks.

Pressure does not destroy microorganisms, but high temperatures applied for an adequate period of time do kill microorganisms. Successfully destroying all microorganisms capable of growing in canned food is based on the temperature obtained in pure steam, free of air, at sea level. At sea level, a canner operated at a gauge pressure of 10 pounds provides an internal temperature of 240 degrees Fahrenheit.

All fresh vegetables except for most tomatoes are low-acid foods. Most mixtures of low-acid and acid foods also are low-acid products unless their recipes include enough lemon juice, citric acid or vinegar to make them acid foods. Other low-acid foods are red meats, seafood, poultry and milk.

General Canning Procedures

Jars and Lids

Use Mason-type canning jars no larger than what is recommended for the specific food being canned. Use two-piece self-sealing lids. Buy only the quantity of lids that will be used in a year and follow the manufacturer's directions for preparing the lids.

Filling Jars

After filling jars with food, release air bubbles by inserting a flat plastic (not metal) spatula between the food and the jar. Slowly turn the jar and move the spatula up and down to allow air bubbles to escape. Salt may be added if desired. In vegetables, salt seasons the food but is not necessary to ensure their safety. Add salt substitutes, if desired, when serving. Adjust the headspace and then clean the jar rim (sealing surface) with a dampened paper towel. Place the lid, gasket down, onto the cleaned jar-sealing surface. Uncleaned jar-sealing surfaces may cause seal failures.

Next fit the metal screw band over the flat lid. Follow the manufacturer's guidelines enclosed with or on the box for tightening the jar lids properly.

The Pressure Canner

Two serious errors in temperatures obtained in pressure canners occur because:

1. **Internal canner temperatures are lower at higher altitudes.** To correct this error, canners must be operated at the increased pressures specified in this publication for appropriate altitude ranges.
2. **Air trapped in a canner lowers the temperature obtained at 5,10, or 15 pounds of pressure and results in underprocessing.** The highest volume of air trapped in a canner occurs in processing raw-packed foods in dial-gauge canners. These canners do not vent air during processing. To be safe, *all types of pressure canners must be vented 10 minutes before they are pressurized.*

To vent a canner, leave the vent port uncovered on newer models or manually open petcocks on some older models. Heating the filled canner with its lid locked into place boils water and generates steam that escapes through the petcock or vent port. When steam first escapes, set a timer for 10 minutes. After venting 10 minutes, close the petcock or place the counterweight or weighted gauge over the vent port to pressurize the canner.

Weighted-gauge models exhaust tiny amounts of air and steam each time their gauge rocks or jiggles during processing. They control pressure precisely and need neither watching during processing nor checking for accuracy.

The sound of the weight rocking or jiggling indicates that the canner is maintaining the recommended pressure. The single disadvantage of weighted-gauge canners is that they cannot correct precisely for higher altitudes. At altitudes above 1,000 feet, they must be operated at canner pressures of 10 instead of 5, or 15 instead of 10, PSI.

Check dial gauges for accuracy before use each year and replace if they read high by more than 1 pound at 5, 10, or 15 pounds of pressure. Low readings cause over-processing and may indicate that the accuracy of the gauge is unpredictable. Gauges may be checked at most county offices of the NDSU Extension Service.

Handle canner lid gaskets carefully and clean them according to the manufacturer's directions. Nicked or dried gaskets will allow steam leaks during pressurization of canners. Keep gaskets clean between uses.

Gaskets on older model canners may require a light coat of vegetable oil once per year. Gaskets on newer model canners are pre-lubricated and do not benefit from oiling. Check your canner's instructions if there is doubt that the particular gasket you use has been pre-lubricated.

Lid safety fuses are thin metal inserts or rubber plugs designed to relieve excessive pressure from the canner. Do not pick at or scratch fuses while cleaning lids. Use only canners that have the Underwriter's Laboratory (UL) approval to ensure their safety.

Replacement gauges and other parts for canners are often available at stores offering canning equipment or from canner manufacturers. When ordering parts, give your canner model number and describe the parts needed.

Using Pressure Canners

Follow these steps for successful pressure canning:

1. Put 2 to 3 inches of hot water in the canner. Place filled jars on the rack, using a jar lifter. Fasten canner lid securely.

2. Leave weight off vent port or open petcock. Heat at the highest setting until steam flows from the petcock or vent port.
3. Maintain high heat setting, exhaust steam 10 minutes, and then place weight on vent port or close petcock. The canner will pressurize during the next 3 to 5 minutes.
4. Start timing the process when the pressure reading on the dial gauge indicates that the recommended pressure has been reached, or when the weighted gauge begins to jiggle or rock.
5. Regulate heat under the canner to maintain a steady pressure at or slightly above the correct gauge pressure. Quick and large pressure variations during processing may cause unnecessary liquid losses from jars. Weighted gauges on Mirro canners should jiggle about two or three times per minute. On Presto canners, they should rock slowly throughout the process.
6. When the timed process is completed, turn off the heat, remove the canner from heat if possible, and let the canner depressurize. Do not force-cool the canner. Forced cooling may result in food spoilage. Cooling the canner with cold running water or opening the vent port before the canner is fully depressurized will cause loss of liquid from jars and seal failures. Force-cooling may also warp the canner lid of older model canners, causing steam leaks. Depressurization of older models should be timed. Standard-sized heavy-walled canners require about 30 minutes when loaded with pints and 45 minutes with quarts. Newer thin-walled canners cool more rapidly and are equipped with vent locks. These canners are depressurized when their vent lock piston drops to a normal position.
7. After the canner is depressurized, remove the weight from the vent port or open the petcock. Wait two minutes, unfasten the lid, and remove it carefully. Lift the lid away from you so that the steam does not burn your face.
8. Remove jars with a lifter, and place on towel or cooling rack.

Do not retighten lids after processing jars.

COOLING JARS

Cool the jars at room temperature for 12 to 24 hours. Jars cooled on racks or towels minimize heat damage to counters. The food level and liquid volume of raw-packed jars will be noticeably lower after cooling. Air is exhausted during processing and food shrinks. If a jar loses excessive liquid during processing, do not open it to add more liquid. Check for sealed lids as described below.

Testing Jar Seals

After cooling jars for 12 to 24 hours, remove the screw bands and test seals in one of the following ways.

Option 1: Press the middle of the lid with a finger or thumb. If the lid springs up when you release your finger, the lid is unsealed.

Option 2: Tap the lid with the bottom of a teaspoon. If it makes a dull sound, the lid is not sealed. If food is in contact with the underside of the lid, it will also cause a dull sound. If the jar is sealed correctly, it will make a ringing, high-pitched sound.

Option 3: Hold the jar at eye level and look across the lid. The lid should be concave (curved down slightly in the center). If center of the lid is either flat or bulging it may not be sealed.

Reprocessing Unsealed Jars

If a lid fails to seal on a jar, remove the lid and check the jar-sealing surface for tiny nicks. If necessary, change the jar, add a new, properly prepared lid, and reprocess within 24 hours using the same processing time.

Headspace in unsealed jars may be adjusted to 11/2 inches and jars could be frozen instead of reprocessed. Foods in single unsealed jars could be stored in the refrigerator and consumed within several days.

RECIPES

Asparagus Spears or Pieces

An average of 3-1/2 pounds per quart.

Quality: Use tender, tight-tipped spears, 4 to 6 inches long.

Procedure: Wash asparagus and trim off tough scales. Break off tough stems and wash again. Cut into 1-inch pieces or can whole.

Hot pack — Cover asparagus with boiling water. Boil 2 or 3 minutes. Loosely fill jars with hot asparagus, leaving 1-inch headspace.

Raw pack — Fill jars with raw asparagus, packing as tightly as possible without crushing, leaving 1-inch headspace.

Beans or Peas Shelled, Dried

All varieties

An average of 3/4 pounds per quart.

Quality: Select mature, dry seeds. Sort out and discard discolored seeds.

Procedure: Place dried beans or peas in a large pot and cover with water. Soak 12 to 18 hours in a cool place. Drain water. To quickly hydrate beans, you may cover sorted and washed beans with boiling water in a saucepan. Boil two minutes, remove from heat, soak one hour and drain. Cover beans soaked by either method with fresh water and boil 30 minutes. Add 1/2 teaspoon of salt per pint or one teaspoon per quart to the jar, if desired. Fill jars with beans or peas and cooking water, leaving 1-inch headspace. Adjust lids and process according to #2 on Table I or II.

Beans, Baked

Procedure: Soak and boil beans and prepare molasses sauce according to directions for beans with sauce that follows. Place seven 3/4-inch pieces of pork, ham, or bacon in an earthenware crock, a large casserole, or a pan. Add beans and enough molasses sauce to cover beans. Cover and bake four to five hours at 350 F. Add water as needed — about every hour. Fill jars, leaving 1-inch headspace. Adjust lids and process according to #3 on Table I or II.

Beans, Dry, With Tomato or Molasses Sauce

An average of 3/4 pounds per quart.

Quality: Select mature, dry seeds. Sort out and discard discolored seeds.

Procedure: Sort and wash dry beans. Add three cups of water for each cup of dried beans or peas.

Boil two minutes, remove from heat and soak one hour and drain. Heat to boiling in fresh water, and save liquid for making sauce. Make your choice of the following sauces:

Tomato Sauce — Option #1. Mix 1 quart tomato juice, 3 tablespoons sugar, 2 teaspoons salt, 1 tablespoon chopped onion, and 1/4 teaspoon each of ground cloves, allspice, mace, and cayenne pepper.

Heat to boiling. **Option #2.** Mix 1 cup tomato ketchup with 3 cups of cooking liquid from beans. Heat sauce to boiling.

Molasses Sauce — Mix 4 cups water or cooking liquid from beans, 3 tablespoons dark molasses, 1 tablespoon vinegar, 2 teaspoons salt, and 3/4 teaspoon powdered dry mustard. Heat to boiling.

Fill jars three-fourths full with hot beans. Add a 3/4-inch cube of pork, ham, or bacon to each jar, if desired. Fill jars with heated sauce, leaving 1-inch headspace. Adjust lids and process according to #3 on Table I or II.

BEANS, SNAP AND ITALIAN — PIECES

Green and Wax

An average of 2 pounds per quart.

Quality: Select filled but tender, crisp pods. Remove and discard diseased and rusty pods.

Procedure: Wash beans and trim ends. Leave whole or cut or snap into 1-inch pieces.

Hot pack — Cover with boiling water; boil five minutes. Fill jars, loosely leaving 1-inch headspace .

Raw pack — Fill jars tightly with raw beans, leaving 1-inch headspace. Add 1 teaspoon of salt per quart to the jar, if desired. Add boiling water, leaving 1-inch headspace. Adjust lids and process according to #4 on Table I or II.

BEETS WHOLE, CUBED, OR SLICED

An average of 3 pounds per quart.

Quality: Beets with a diameter of 1 to 2 inches are preferred for whole packs. Beets larger than 3 inches in diameter are often fibrous.

Procedure: Trim off beet tops, leaving an inch of stem and roots to reduce bleeding of color. Scrub well. Cover with boiling water. Boil until skins slip off easily, about 15 to 25 minutes depending on size. Cool, remove skins, and trim off stems and roots. Leave baby beets whole. Cut medium or large beets into 1/2-inch cubes or slices. Halve or quarter very large slices. Add 1 teaspoon of salt per quart to the jar, if desired. Fill jars with hot beets and fresh hot water, leaving 1-inch headspace. Adjust lids and process according to #5 on Table I or II.

CARROTS SLICED OR DICED

An average of 2-1/2 pounds per quart.

Quality: Select small carrots, preferably 1 to 11/4 inches in diameter. Larger carrots are often too fibrous.

Procedure: Wash, peel and rewash carrots. Slice or dice.

Hot pack — Cover with boiling water; bring to boil and simmer for five minutes. Fill jars, leaving 1-inch of headspace.

Raw pack — Fill jars tightly with raw carrots, leaving 1-inch headspace.

Add 1 teaspoon of salt per quart to the jar, if desired. Add hot cooking liquid or water, leaving 1-inch headspace. Adjust lids and process according to #6 on Table I or II.

CORN — CREAM STYLE

An average of 2-1/4 pounds per pint

Quality: Select ears containing slightly immature kernels, or of ideal quality for eating fresh.

Procedure: Husk corn, remove silk, and wash ears. Blanch ears 4 minutes in boiling water. Cut corn from cob at about the center of kernel. Scrape remaining corn from cobs with a table knife.

Hot pack — To each quart of corn and scrapings, add two cups of boiling water. Heat to boiling. Add 1/2 teaspoon salt to each jar, if desired. Fill pint jar with hot corn mixture, leaving 1-inch headspace.

Adjust lids and process according to #7 on Table I or II.

CORN — WHOLE KERNEL

An average of 4-1/2 pounds per quart.

Quality: Select ears containing slightly immature kernels or of ideal quality for eating fresh. Canning of some sweeter varieties or too immature kernels may cause browning. Can a small amount, check color and flavor before canning large quantities.

Procedure: Husk corn, remove silk, and wash. Blanch three minutes in boiling water. Cut corn from cob at about three-fourths the depth of kernel.

Caution: Do not scrape cob. Scraping the cob would make this product too dense to process at the times given.

Hot pack — To each quart of kernels in a saucepan, add 1 cup of hot water, heat to boiling and simmer 5 minutes. Add 1 teaspoon of salt per quart to the jar, if desired. Fill jars with corn and cooking liquid, leaving 1-inch headspace.

Raw pack — Fill jars with raw kernels, leaving 1-inch headspace. Do not shake or press down. Add 1 teaspoon of salt per quart to the jar, if desired.

Add fresh boiling water, leaving 1-inch headspace. Adjust lids and process according to #8 on Table I or II.

MIXED VEGETABLES

6 cups sliced carrots

6 cups cut, whole kernel sweet corn

6 cups cut green beans

6 cups shelled lima beans

4 cups whole or crushed tomatoes

4 cups diced zucchini

Optional mix — You may change the suggested proportions or substitute other favorite vegetables except leafy greens, dried beans, cream style corn, winter squash and sweet potatoes.

Yield: 7 quarts

Procedure: Except for zucchini, wash and prepare vegetables as described for each vegetable. Wash, trim and slice or cube zucchini; combine all vegetables in a large pot or kettle, and add enough water to cover pieces. Add 1 teaspoon salt per quart to the jar, if desired. Boil 5 minutes and fill jars with hot pieces and liquid, leaving 1-inch headspace. Adjust lids and process according to #9 on Table I or II.

PEAS, GREEN — SHELLED

An average of 4-1/2 pounds per quart.

It is recommended that sugar snap and Chinese edible pods be frozen for best quality.

Quality: Select filled pods containing young, tender, sweet seeds. Discard diseased pods.

Procedure: Shell and wash peas. Add 1 teaspoon of salt per quart to the jar, if desired.

Hot pack — Cover with boiling water. Bring to a boil in a saucepan, and boil 2 minutes. Fill jars loosely with hot peas, and add cooking liquid, leaving 1-inch headspace.

Raw Pack — Fill jars with raw peas, add boiling water, leaving 1-inch headspace. Do not shake or press down peas. Adjust lids and process according to #10 on Table I or II.

PEPPERS

An average of 1 pound per pint.

Hot or sweet, including chiles, jalapeno and pimiento.

Quality: Select firm yellow, green or red peppers. Do not use soft or diseased peppers.

Procedure: Select your favorite pepper(s). Caution: If you choose hot peppers, wear plastic gloves while handling them or wash hands thoroughly with soap and water before touching your face. Small peppers may be left whole. Large peppers may be quartered. Remove cores and seeds. Slash two or four slits in each pepper and either blanch in boiling water or blister using one of the following methods.

Oven or broiler method. Place peppers in a hot oven (400 F) or broiler for 6 to 8 minutes until skins blister.

Range-top method. Cover hot burner, either gas or electric, with heavy wire mesh. Place peppers on burner for several minutes until skins blister.

Allow peppers to cool. Place in a pan and cover with a damp cloth. This will make peeling the peppers easier. After several minutes, peel each pepper. Flatten whole peppers. Add 1/2 teaspoon of salt to each pint jar, if desired. Fill jars loosely with peppers and add fresh boiled water, leaving 1-inch headspace. Adjust lids and process according to #11 on Table I or II.

PUMPKINS AND WINTER SQUASH — CUBED

An average of 2-1/4 pounds per quart.

Quality: Pumpkins and squash should have a hard rind and stringless, mature pulp of ideal quality for cooking fresh. Small size pumpkins (sugar or pie varieties) make better products.

Procedure: Wash, remove seeds, cut into 1-inch-wide slices, and peel. Cut flesh into 1-inch cubes. Boil 2 minutes in water. Caution: Do not mash or puree. Fill jars with cubes and cooking liquid, leaving 1-inch headspace. Adjust lids and process according to #12 on Table I or II.

For making pies, drain jars and strain or sieve cubes.

SOUPS

Vegetable, dried bean or pea, meat, poultry or seafoods

Procedure: Select, wash, and prepare vegetables, meat and seafoods as described for the specific foods. Cover meat with water and cook until tender. Cool meat and remove bones. Cook vegetables. For each cup of dried beans or peas, add 3 cups of water, boil 2 minutes, remove from heat, soak 1 hour, and heat to boil. Drain and combine with meat broth, tomatoes, or water to cover. Boil 5 minutes. Caution: Do not thicken before canning. Salt to taste, if desired. Fill jars halfway with solid mixture. Add remaining liquid, leaving 1-inch headspace. Adjust lids and process according to #13 on Table I or II.

***Caution: Process 100 minutes if soup contains seafoods.**

SPINACH AND OTHER GREENS

An average of 4 pounds per quart.

Quality: Can only freshly harvested greens. Discard any wilted, discolored, diseased, or insect-damaged leaves. Leaves should be tender and attractive in color.

Procedure: Wash only small amounts of greens at one time. Drain water and continue rinsing until water is clear and free of grit. Cut out tough stems and midribs. Place 1 pound of greens at a time in cheesecloth bag or blancher basket and steam 3 to 5 minutes or until well wilted. Add 1/2 teaspoon of salt to each quart jar, if desired. Fill jars loosely with greens and add fresh boiling water, leaving 1-inch headspace. Adjust lids and process according to #14 on Table I or II.

ADJUST FOR ALTITUDE

As altitudes increase air becomes thinner, and this affects both pressures and boiling points in home canning. Using the process times for canning food at sea level may result in spoilage if you live at altitudes of 1,000 feet or more. Water boils at lower temperatures as altitude increases. Lower boiling temperatures are less effective for killing bacteria. Increasing the processing time or canner pressure compensates for lower boiling temperatures. Select the proper processing time or canner pressure for the altitude where you live.

The altitude in North Dakota varies from 800 feet above sea level in the east to 3,000 feet in the west. The map below shows the approximate altitude of areas of North Dakota.

CANNING OF FRUIT AND FRUIT PRODUCTS

Processing is essential to ensure safety when canning fruits. Fruits, being acid foods, can be safely processed in a boiling water bath. However, some people prefer to pressure-process fruits. This is also an acceptable method. Organisms that cause food spoilage — molds, yeasts and bacteria — are always present in the air, water and soil. Also, enzymes that may cause undesirable changes in flavor, color and texture are present in raw fruits. Use recommended processing methods and times when canning fruits to destroy spoilage organisms and stop the action of enzymes.

SQUASH, WINTER — CUBED

Prepare and process according to instructions for "Pumpkin."

Table I. Recommended Process Times in a Dial-Gauge Pressure Canner.

	Style of Pack	Jar Size	Process Time	Canner Pressure (PSI) at Altitudes of 0-2,000 ft.	2,001-4,000 ft.	4,001-6,000 ft.
1) Asparagus	Hot and Raw	Pints	30 min.	11 lb.	12 lb.	13 lb.
		Quarts	40 min.	11 lb.	12 lb.	13 lb.
2) Dried Beans and Peas	Hot	Pints	75 min.	11 lb.	12 lb.	13 lb.
		Quarts	90 min.	11 lb.	12 lb.	13 lb.
3) Beans, dry, baked or with tomato or molasses sauce	Hot	Pints	65 min.	11 lb.	12 lb.	13 lb.
		Quarts	75 min.	11 lb.	12 lb.	13 lb.
4) Beans, snap and Italian	Hot and Raw	Pints	20 min.	11 lb.	12 lb.	13 lb.
		Quarts	25 min.	11 lb.	12 lb.	13 lb.
5) Beets	Hot	Pints	30 min.	11 lb.	12 lb.	13 lb.
		Quarts	35 min.	11 lb.	12 lb.	13 lb.
6) Carrots	Hot and Raw	Pints	25 min.	11 lb.	12 lb.	13 lb.
		Quarts	30 min.	11 lb.	12 lb.	13 lb.

7) Corn, cream style	Hot	Pints	85 min.	11 lb.	12 lb.	13 lb.
8) Corn, whole kernel	Hot and Raw	Pints	55 min.	11 lb.	12 lb.	13 lb.
		Quarts	85 min.	11 lb.	12 lb.	13 lb.
9)Mixed Vegetables	Hot	Pints	75 min.	11 lb.	12 lb.	13 lb.
		Quarts	90 min.	11 lb.	12 lb.	13 lb.
10)Peas	Hot and Raw	Pints or Quarts	40 min.	11 lb.	12 lb.	13 lb.
11)Peppers	Hot Half-pints or Pints		35 min.	11 lb.	12 lb.	13 lb.
12)Pumpkin and Winter Squash - cubed	Hot	Pints	55 min	11 lb.	12 lb.	13 lb.
		Quarts	90 min.	11 lb.	12 lb.	13 lb.
13)Soups	Hot	Pints	60* min.	11 lb.	12 lb.	13 lb.
		Quarts	75* min.	11 lb.	12 lb.	13 lb.
		*Caution: Process 100 minutes if soup contains seafoods.				
14)Spinach and Other Greens	Hot	Pints	70 min.	11 lb.	12 lb.	13 lb.
		Quarts	90 min.	11 lb.	12 lb.	13 lb.

Table II. Recommended Process Times in a Weighted-Gauge Pressure Canner.

				Canner Pressure (PSI) at Altitudes of	
	Style of Pack	**Jar Size**	**Process Time**	**0-1,000 ft.**	**Above 1,000 ft.**
1) Asparagus	Hot & Raw	Pints	30 min.	10 lb.	15 lb.
		Quarts	40 min.	10 lb.	15 lb.
2) Dried Beans and Peas	Hot	Pints	75 min.	10 lb.	15 lb.
		Quarts	90 min.	10 lb.	15 lb.
3) Beans, dry, baked or with tomato or molasses sauce	Hot	Pints	65 min.	10 lb.	15 lb.
		Quarts	75 min.	10 lb.	15 lb.
4) Beans, snap and Italian	Hot & Raw	Pints	20 min.	10 lb.	15 lb.
		Quarts	25 min.	10 lb.	15 lb.
5) Beets	Hot	Pints	30 min.	10 lb.	15 lb.
		Quarts	35 min.	10 lb.	15 lb.
6) Carrots	Hot & Raw	Pints	25 min.	10 lb.	15 lb.
		Quarts	30 min.	10 lb.	15 lb.
7) Corn, cream style	Hot	Pints	85 min.	10 lb.	15 lb.
8) Corn, whole kernel	Hot & Raw	Pints	55 min.	10 lb.	15 lb.
		Quarts	85 min.	10 lb.	15 lb.
9) Mixed Vegetables	Hot	Pints	75 min.	10 lb.	15 lb.
		Quarts	90 min.	10 lb.	15 lb.
10) Peas	Hot & Raw	Pints or Quarts	40 min.	10 lb.	15 lb.
11) Peppers	Hot	Half-pints or Pints	35 min.	10 lb.	15 lb.
12) Pumpkin and Winter Squash-cubed	Hot	Pints	55 min.	10 lb.	15 lb.
		Quarts	90 min.	10 lb.	15 lb.
13) Soups	Hot	Pints	60* min.	10 lb.	15 lb.
		Quarts	75* min.	10 lb.	15 lb.
	*Caution: Process 100 minutes if soup contains seafoods.				
14) Spinach and Other Greens	Hot	Pints	70 min.	10 lb.	15 lb.
		Quarts	90 min.	10 lb.	15 lb.

GENERAL CANNING PROCEDURES

Jars and Lids

Mason-type canning jars are the best choice. The standard jar mouth is about 2-3/8 inches. Widemouth jars have openings of about 3 inches, making them more easily filled and emptied. Half-gallon jars may be used for canning very acid juices only.

Most commercial pint- and quart-size mayonnaise or salad dressing jars may be used with new two-piece lids for canning acid foods. However, you may expect more sealing failures and jar breakage. These jars have a narrower sealing surface and are tempered less than Mason jars. Mayonnaise-type jars are not recommended for use with foods that will be processed in the pressure canner.

Use two-piece self-sealing lids. Buy only the quantity of lids that will be used in a year and follow the manufacturer's directions for preparing the lids.

Sterilize Jars

To sterilize empty jars, put them right side up on the rack in a boiling-water canner. Fill the canner and jars with hot (not boiling) water to 1 inch above the tops of the jars. Boil 10 minutes, at altitudes of less than 1,000 feet. At higher elevations, boil one additional minute for each additional 1,000 feet elevation. Remove and drain hot sterilized jars one at a time just before filling. Save the hot water for processing filled jars. Fill jars with food, apply lids, and tighten screw bands.

It is unnecessary to presterilize jars for fruits that will be processed 10 minutes or longer in a boiling water canner.

Filling Jars

After filling jars with food, release air bubbles by inserting a flat plastic (not metal) spatula between the food and the jar. Slowly turn the jar and move the spatula up and down to allow air bubbles to escape. Adjust the headspace and then clean the jar rim (sealing surface) with a dampened paper towel.

Place the lid, gasket down, onto the cleaned jar sealing surface. Uncleaned jar-sealing surfaces may cause seal failures.

Then fit the metal screw band over the flat lid. Follow the manufacturer's guidelines enclosed with or on the box for tightening the jar lids properly.

Prevent Darkening

Follow these guidelines to ensure that your canned foods retain optimum colors and flavors during processing and storage:

- Use only high-quality foods which are at the proper maturity and are free of diseases and bruises.
- Use the hot-pack method, especially with acid foods to be processed in boiling water.
- Don't unnecessarily expose prepared foods to air. Can them as soon as possible.
- While preparing a canner load of jars, keep peeled, halved, quartered, sliced, or diced apples, apricots, nectarines, peaches, and pears in a solution of ascorbic acid. This procedure is also useful for preventing stem-end discoloration in cherries and grapes. You can get ascorbic acid in several forms:

Pure powdered form — seasonally available among canners' supplies in supermarkets. One level teaspoon of pure powder weighs about three grams. Use one teaspoon per gallon of water as a treatment solution.

Vitamin C tablets — economical and available year-round in many stores. Buy 500-milligram tablets; crush and dissolve six tablets per gallon of water as a treatment solution.

Commercially prepared mixes of ascorbic and citric acid — seasonally available among canners' supplies in supermarkets. Sometimes citric acid powder is sold in supermarkets, but it is less effective in controlling discoloration. If you choose to use these products, follow the manufacturer's directions.

- Fill hot foods into jars and adjust headspace as specified in recipes.
- Store the jars in a relatively cool, dark place, preferably between 50 degrees and 70 degrees Fahrenheit.
- Can no more food than you will use within a year.

Sweetening Fruit

Adding syrup to canned fruit helps to retain its flavor, color and shape. It does not prevent spoilage of these foods. The guidelines in Table 1 for preparing and using syrups offer a new "very light" syrup, which approximates the natural sugar content of many fruits. Quantities of water and sugar to make enough syrup for a canner load of pints or quarts are provided for each syrup type.

Procedure: Heat water and sugar together. Bring to a boil and pour over raw fruits in jars. For hot packs, bring water and sugar to boil, add fruit, reheat to boil, and fill into jars immediately.

Canning Without Sugar

In canning regular fruits without sugar, it is very important to select fully ripe but firm fruits of the best quality. Prepare these as for hot-packs but use water or regular unsweetened fruit juices instead of sugar syrup. Juice made from the fruit being canned is best. Blends of unsweetened apple, pineapple and white grape juice are also good for filling over solid fruit pieces. Adjust headspaces and lids and use the processing recommendations given for regular fruits. Add sugar substitutes, if desired, when serving.

Water Bath Canners

Water-bath canners are made of aluminum or of porcelain-covered steel. They have removable perforated racks and fitted lids.

The canner must be deep enough so that at least 1 inch of briskly boiling water will be over the tops of jars during processing. Some boiling-water canners do not have flat bottoms. A flat bottom must be used on an electric range. Either a flat or ridged bottom can be used on a gas burner. To ensure uniform processing of all jars with an electric range, the canner should be no more than 4 inches wider in diameter than the element on which it is heated.

Using Boiling Water Canners

Follow these steps for successful boiling-water canning:

1. Fill the canner halfway with water.

2. Preheat water to 140 F for raw-packed foods and to 180 F for hot-packed foods.
3. Load filled jars, fitted with lids, into the canner rack and use the handles to lower the rack into the water; or fill the canner, one jar at a time, with a jar lifter.
4. Add more boiling water, if needed, so the water level is at least 1 inch above jar tops. Cover canner.
5. Turn heat to its highest position until water boils vigorously.
6. Set a timer for the minutes required for processing the food.
7. Lower the heat setting to maintain a gentle boil throughout the process schedule.
8. Add more boiling water, if needed, to keep the water level above the jars.
9. When jars have been boiled for the recommended time, turn off the heat and remove the canner lid.
10. Using a jar lifter, remove the jars and place right side up on a towel, leaving at least 1-inch spaces between the jars during cooling.

Do not retighten lids after processing jars.

COOLING JARS

Cool the jars at room temperature for 12 to 24 hours. Jars may be cooled on racks or towels to minimize heat damage to counters. The food level and liquid volume of raw-packed jars will be noticeably lower after cooling. Air is exhausted during processing and food shrinks. If a jar loses excessive liquid during processing, do not open it to add more liquid. Check for sealed lids as described below.

Testing Jar Seals

After cooling jars for 12 to 24 hours, remove the screw bands and test seals by one of the following options:

Option 1: Press the middle of the lid with a finger or thumb. If the lid springs up when you release your finger, the lid is unsealed.

Option 2: Tap the lid with the bottom of a teaspoon. If it makes a dull sound, the lid is not sealed. If food is in contact with the underside of the lid, it will also cause a dull sound. If the jar is sealed correctly, it will make a ringing, high-pitched sound.

Option 3: Hold the jar at eye level and look across the lid. The lid should be concave (curved down slightly in the center). If center of the lid is either flat or bulging, it may not be sealed.

Reprocessing Unsealed Jars

If a lid fails to seal on a jar, remove the lid and check the jar-sealing surface for tiny nicks. If necessary, change the jar, add a new, properly prepared lid, and reprocess within 24 hours using the same processing time. Headspace in unsealed jars may be adjusted to 1-1/2 inches and jars could be frozen instead of reprocessed. Foods in single unsealed jars could be stored in the refrigerator and consumed within several days.

DIRECTIONS FOR CANNING FRUITS

Apple Butter

Use Jonathan, Winesap, Stayman, Golden Delicious, Macintosh or other tasty apple varieties for good results.

8 pounds apples

2 cups cider

2 cups vinegar

2-1/4 cups white sugar

2-1/4 cups packed brown sugar

2 tablespoons ground cinnamon

1 tablespoon ground cloves

Yield: About 8 to 9 pints

Procedure: Wash, remove stems, quarter, and core fruit. Cook slowly in cider and vinegar until soft. Press fruit through a colander, food mill or strainer. Cook fruit pulp with sugar and spices, stirring frequently. To test for doneness, remove a spoonful and hold it away from steam for two minutes. It is done if the butter remains mounded on the spoon. Another way to determine when the butter is cooked adequately is to spoon a small quantity onto a plate. When a rim of liquid does not separate around the edge of the butter, it is ready for canning. Fill hot into sterile half-pint or pint jars, leaving 1/4-inch headspace. Quart jars need not be presterilized. Adjust lids and process according to Table 3.

Apple Juice

Quality: Good quality apple juice is made from a blend of varieties.

Procedure: Refrigerate juice for 24 to 48 hours. Without mixing, carefully pour off clear liquid and discard sediment. Strain clear liquid through a paper coffee filter or double layers of damp cheesecloth. Heat quickly, stirring occasionally, until juice begins to boil. Fill immediately into sterile pint or quart jars or fill into clean half-gallon jars, leaving 1/4-inch headspace. Adjust lids and process according to Table 3.

Apples — Sliced

Quantity: An average of 2-3/4 pounds per quart.

Quality: Select apples that are juicy, crispy and preferably both sweet and tart.

Procedure: Wash, peel and core apples. To prevent discoloration, slice apples into water containing ascorbic acid (see "Prevent Darkening" under General Canning Procedures). Raw packs make poor quality products. Place drained slices in large saucepan and add 1 pint water or very light, light or medium syrup (see Table 1) per 5 pounds of sliced apples. Boil 5 minutes, stirring occasionally to prevent burning. Fill jars with hot slices and hot syrup or water, leaving 1/2-inch headspace. Adjust lids and process according to Table 3, 4 or 5.

Applesauce

Quantity: An average of 3 pounds per quart.

Quality: Select apples that are sweet, juicy and crisp. For a tart flavor, add 1 to 2 pounds of tart apples to each 3 pounds of sweeter fruit.

Procedure: Wash, peel and core apples. If desired, slice apples into water containing ascorbic acid to prevent browning (see "Prevent Darkening" under General Canning Procedures). Place drained slices in an 8- to 10-quart pot. Add 1/2 cup water. Stirring occasionally to prevent burning, heat quickly until tender (5 to 20 minutes, depending on maturity and variety). Press through a sieve or food mill, or skip the pressing step if you prefer chunk-style sauce. Sauce may be packed without sugar. If desired, add 1/8 cup sugar per quart of sauce. Taste and add more, if preferred. Reheat sauce to boiling. Fill jars with hot sauce, leaving 1/2-inch headspace. Adjust lids and process according to Table 3.

Spiced Apple Rings

12 pounds firm tart apples (maximum diameter, 2-1/2 inches)

12 cups sugar

6 cups water

1-1/4 cups white vinegar (5%)

3 tablespoons whole cloves

3/4 cup red hot cinnamon candies

or 8 cinnamon sticks and 1 teaspoon red food coloring (optional)

Yield: About 8 to 9 pints

Procedure: Wash apples. To prevent discoloration, peel and slice one apple at a time. Immediately cut crosswise into 1/2-inch slices, remove core area with a melon baller, and immerse in ascorbic acid solution (see "Prevent Darkening" under General Canning Procedures). To make flavored syrup, combine sugar, water, vinegar, cloves, cinnamon candies, or cinnamon sticks and food coloring in a 6-quart saucepan. Stir, heat to boil and simmer three minutes. Drain apples, add to hot syrup and cook five minutes. Fill jars (preferably widemouth) with apple rings and hot flavored syrup, leaving 1/2-inch headspace. Adjust lids and process according to Table 3.

Apricots — Halved or Sliced

Quantity: An average of 2-1/4 pounds per quart.

Quality: Select firm, well-colored mature fruit of ideal quality for eating fresh.

Procedure: Follow directions for peaches except the boiling water dip and removal of skin is optional. Wash if skins are not removed. Either hot or raw pack, and use the same process time on Table 3, 4 or 5.

Berry Syrup

Juices from fresh or frozen blueberries, cherries, grapes, raspberries (black or red), and strawberries are easily made into toppings for use on ice cream and pastries.

Yield: About 9 half-pints.

Procedure: Select 6-1/2 cups of fresh or frozen fruit of your choice. Wash, cap and stem fresh fruit and crush in a saucepan. Heat to boiling and simmer until soft (five to ten minutes). Strain hot through a colander and drain until cool enough to handle. Strain the collected juice through a double layer of cheesecloth or jelly bag.

Discard the dry pulp. The yield of the pressed juice should be about 4-1/2 to 5 cups. Combine the juice with 6-3/4 cups of sugar in a large saucepan, bring to boil, and simmer 1 minute. To make a syrup with whole fruit pieces, save 1 or 2 cups of the fresh or frozen fruit, combine these with the sugar, and simmer as in making regular syrup.

Remove from heat, skim off foam, and fill into clean half-pint or pint jars, leaving 1/2-inch headspace. Adjust lids and process according to Table 3.

Berries — Whole

Blackberries, blueberries, currants, dewberries, elderberries, gooseberries, huckleberries, loganberries, mulberries, raspberries.

Quantity: An average of 1-3/4 pounds per quart.

Quality: Choose ripe, sweet berries with uniform color.

Procedure: Wash 1 or 2 quarts of berries at a time. Drain, cap and stem if necessary. For gooseberries, snip off heads and tails with scissors. Prepare and boil preferred syrup (see Table 1), if desired. Add 1/2 cup syrup, juice or water to each clean jar.

Hot pack — For blueberries, currants, elderberries, gooseberries and huckleberries. Heat berries in boiling water for 30 seconds and drain. Fill jars and cover with hot juice, leaving 1/2-inch headspace.

Raw pack — Fill jars with any of the raw berries, shaking down gently while filling. Cover with hot syrup, juice or water, leaving 1/2-inch headspace.

Adjust lids and process according to Table 3, 4 or 5.

Nectarines — Halved or Sliced

Quantity: An average of 2-1/2 pounds per quart.

Quality: Choose ripe, mature fruit of ideal quality for eating fresh or cooking.

Procedure: Follow directions for peaches except do not dip in hot water or remove skins, wash, either hot or raw pack, and use the same process time.

Peaches — Halved or Sliced

Quantity: An average of 2-1/2 pounds per quart.

Quality: Choose ripe, mature fruit of ideal quality for eating fresh or cooking.

Procedure: Dip fruit in boiling water for 30 to 60 seconds until skins loosen. Dip quickly in cold water and slip off skins. Cut in half, remove pits and slice if desired. To prevent darkening, keep peeled fruit in ascorbic acid solution (see "Prevent Darkening" under General Canning Procedures). Prepare and boil a very light, light or medium syrup (see Table 1) or pack peaches in water, apple juice or white grape juice. Raw packs make poor quality peaches .

Hot pack — In a large saucepan place drained fruit in syrup, water, or juice and bring to boil. Fill jars with hot fruit and cooking liquid, leaving 1/2-inch headspace. Place halves in layers, cut side down.

Raw pack — Fill jars with raw fruit, cut side down, and add hot water, juice or syrup, leaving 1/2-inch headspace.

Plums — Halved or Whole

Quantity: An average of 2 pounds per quart.

Quality: Select deep-colored, mature fruit of ideal quality for eating fresh or cooking. Plums may be packed in water or syrup.

Procedure: Stem and wash plums. To can whole, prick skins on two sides of plums with fork to prevent splitting. Freestone varieties may be halved and pitted. If you use syrup, prepare very light, light or medium syrup.

Hot pack — Add plums to hot syrup and boil two minutes. Cover saucepan and let stand 20 to 30 minutes. Fill jars with hot plums and cooking syrup, leaving 1/2-inch headspace.

Raw pack — Fill jars with raw plums, packing firmly. Add hot syrup, leaving 1/2-inch headspace.

Rhubarb — Stewed

Quantity: An average of 1-1/2 pounds per quart.

Quality: Select young, tender, well-colored stalks from the spring or late fall crop.

Adjust for Altitude

As altitudes increase air becomes thinner, and this affects both pressures and boiling points in home canning. Using the process times for canning food at sea level may result in spoilage if you live at altitudes of 1,000 feet or more. Water boils at lower temperatures as altitude increases. Lower boiling temperatures are less effective for killing bacteria. Increasing the processing time or canner pressure compensates for lower boiling temperatures. Select the proper processing time or canner pressure for the altitude where you live.

4

The Art and Practice of Sausage Making

HISTORY

The origin of meat processing is lost in antiquity but probably began when mankind learned that salt is an effective preservative. Sausage making evolved as an effort to economize and preserve meat that could not be consumed fresh at slaughter. In sausage making, quality standards are maintained while using most parts of the animal carcass.

Good sausage makers are as discriminating about what goes into sausage as winemakers are about selecting grapes. Early sausage makers found that a wide range of raw ingredients could be used. The primary ingredients of sausage were the parts of the animal carcasses that could not be used in other ways. Today many primal parts are used in the production of sausage; however, the less tender cuts, organ meats and even blood can be made delicious when ground, spiced and cased.

The procedure of stuffing meat into casings remains basically the same today, but sausage recipes have been greatly refined and sausage making has become a highly respected culinary art. Any product can be made from a wide range of raw materials exposed to rather extreme conditions of temperature and time schedules and be consumer acceptable.

Sausage grew in popularity and brought fame and fortune to many sausage makers and to various cities. Today more than 250 varieties are sold, and many of these can be traced back to the town and country of origin. The contemporary role of sausage fits conveniently into our modern lifestyles as an elegant appetizer for entertaining as well as the main course in "quick-and-easy" meals. Furthermore, sausages are a relatively safe product to consume because of the added effects of salt, pH, cure, drying and cooking to preserve the product and eliminate harmful bacteria.

Sausage is a convenient food available in a great number of varieties and flavors. Sausages are an excellent source of high quality protein, containing all the essential amino acids in appropriate amounts necessary for growth, maintenance and repair of body tissue. Sausage also provides significant amounts of vitamins and minerals.

Types of Sausage

Sausages are made from beef, veal, pork, lamb, poultry and wild game, or from any combination of these meats. Sausage making has become a unique blend of old procedures and new scientific, highly-mechanized processes. Traditionally, sausage was formed into a symmetrical shape, but it now can be found in a variety of shapes and sizes to meet consumers' needs. Many sausage products are vacuum packed, freshness dated and 100% edible.

Sausages can be classified in a variety of ways, but probably the most useful is by how they are processed (Table 1). Processing methods give sausages easily recognizable characteristics.

Equipment

It only requires a grinder, a good meat thermometer and some general household items to make excellent sausage. If you do not have a grinder, you can purchase ground meat from the store. Many products do not need to be smoked, but liquid smoke can be added to give the smoky flavor desired, or you may add a small portion of a cooked, smoked product like bacon to produce the smoky flavor.

You can purchase a household smoker or make one. An old refrigerator converted to a smokehouse works quite well if you need to smoke the product. Smokehouses can be as simple as a tarp covering or as sophisticated as a commercial unit.

Procedure

Sausage making is a continuous sequence of events. Each step in the proper sequence is important to a successful operation.

It is not practical to consider each step separately or to assign more importance to one phase or operation, but for convenience and illustration, we can break sausage production down into four basic processes: selecting ingredients, grinding and mixing, stuffing, and thermal processing.

Selecting Ingredients

The finished product is only as good as the ingredients it contains. Meat should be fresh, high quality, have the proper lean-to-fat ratio and have good binding qualities. The meat should be clean and not contaminated with bacteria or other microorganisms. In other words, meat used in sausage production should be as safe as any meat you would prepare in your kitchen. Selecting spices and seasonings and combining them in proper amounts is important. They must complement each other to create a satisfying product.

Cure, an essential part of some formulations, is sodium nitrite (usually 6 percent) on a salt base. It usually can be purchased at a local locker plant. Sodium nitrite is very necessary to inhibit production and growth of the deadly toxin produced by the microorganism *Clostridium botulinum*. It also gives the characteristic cured color to a sausage product and improves flavor. Commercial products such as Freeze Em Pickle, Tender Quick and saltpeter can be found in markets and at drugstores. If these are used, be sure to follow directions on the packages.

Grinding and Mixing

For safety, keep the temperature of the meat as cold as possible during grinding and mixing. The usual procedure is to grind the various meats coarsely and then add the rest of the ingredients, mixing thoroughly.

A slurry is made of the spices and salt using two cups of water. (Water is added to dissolve the curing ingredients, to facilitate the mixing and to give the products their characteristic texture and taste.)

The product is then ground again to the desired consistency. Mixing should be done before the final grind. Grinding improves the uniformity of the product by distributing the ingredients and making the particles the same size. Unless you have special equipment, it is desirable to work with small batches (up to 25 pounds) so the cure and seasoning can be more evenly distributed. If you don't have a grinder, buy ground meats, add the seasonings and mix thoroughly by hand.

Stuffing

It is not necessary to stuff fresh sausage meat. It can be left in bulk form or made into patties. Most sausage, however, is made by placing the ground ingredients in some type of forming device to give them shape and hold them together for thermal processing. The casing materials may be natural or manufactured. Natural casings are the gastrointestinal tracts of cattle, sheep and hogs. Generally, hog casings are the most suitable for home use and work quite well for Polish and breakfast-type sausages. They are digestible and are very permeable to moisture and smoke.

All casings preserved in salt must be soaked in lukewarm water for at least 30 minutes before use. Flush each casing under cold water, running cold water through the casing. This removes excess salt from the casing. Unused casings can be drained, covered with salt and frozen.

Fibrous casings are more suitable for summer sausage and similar products because of their greater strength and the variety of sizes available. They are permeable to smoke and moisture and can easily be removed from the finished product. These casings should be soaked before use in 80 to 100 degrees Fahrenheit water for at least 30 minutes, but not more than four hours before use. If the casings are not pre-stuck they should be punctured with a knife point or pin to eliminate air and fat pockets in the finished sausage.

Collagen casings contain the attributes of both natural and fibrous casings. They have been developed primarily for use in products such as fresh pork sausage and pepperoni sticks. They are uniform in size, relatively strong and easy to handle. These casings also are used for the manufacture of dry sausages, because they are permeable and will shrink. For cooked products that are generally water-cooked (like braunschweiger), plastic casings impermeable to water are used.

Thermal Processing

Sausage is smoked and heated in order to pasteurize it and extend its shelf life, as well as to impart a smoky flavor and improve its appearance. Smoking and heating also fixes the color and causes protein to move to the surface of the sausage so it will hold its shape when the casing is removed.

A few products, such as mettwurst, are smoked with a minimum of heating and are designed to be cooked at the time of consumption. Others, such as liver sausage, are cooked but not smoked.

Procedure for smoking polish sausage: After stuffing in hog casings (pre-flushed), let hang and dry. Smoke at 120 F for one hour, 150 F for one more hour, then at 170 F for two hours or until an internal temperature of 141 F is reached. Remove from smokehouse and spray with hot water for 15 to 30 seconds. Follow with cold shower or dip in a slush tank until internal temperature reaches 100 F. Let dry for one to two hours. Place in a cooler.

Procedure for smoking summer sausage: After stuffing in casing, smoke at 140 F for one hour, 160 F for one more hour, then at 180 F for two hours or until the internal temperatures reach 155 F. Remove from the smokehouse and follow the same procedure as for polish sausage.

Procedure for making cooked sausage: After stuffing the ground ingredients into an impermeable casing, put the sausage into a pan of water. Heat water to 170 F and hold it there until the sausage reaches 155 F. A thermometer is essential for obtaining proper temperature. The water should not boil, as this will ruin the product. If you are making a sausage product using cooked meat, be sure the meat was cooked with low heat.

FOOD SAFETY GUIDELINES

Bacteria can spread throughout a work area and contaminate equipment and work surfaces. To reduce your risk of foodborne illness:

- Wash your hands for at least 20 seconds with soap and water before beginning to work and after changing tasks or after doing anything that could contaminate your hands such as sneezing or using the bathroom.
- Start with clean equipment and clean thoroughly after using. Be sure all surfaces that come into contact with meat are clean.
- Sanitize surfaces with a solution of 1 tablespoon chlorine bleach per gallon of water. Allow to air dry.
- If using frozen meat in sausage formulations, thaw it in a cooler on the lowest shelf to avoid dripping of juices on ready-to-eat foods. Keep raw meat separate from other foods.
- Marinate raw meat in the refrigerator.
- Keep meat as cold as possible (40 F or lower) during processing.
- If dehydrating meat, don't rely on the dial settings. Measure the temperature of the dehydrator with a calibrated thermometer.

SAUSAGE FORMULATIONS

The following sausage formulations have been used for classroom work and tested:

Beef Jerky*

5 pounds lean beef

1 1/2tablespoons salt

1 tablespoon black pepper

1 1/2 teaspoons cardamon

2 teaspoons marjoram

1 1/2 teaspoons cure (pink color)

2 teaspoons monosodium glutamate

2 teaspoons cayenne pepper

1 tablespoon garlic powder

1/2 cup liquid smoke

1/2 cup water

Mix all spices together with meat. Mix well until meat is tacky. Grind and press into a loaf pan lined with foil. Put in cooler or freezer to firm product for slicing. Slice as thin as desirable and lay on oven racks. Spray oven racks with oil, than lay slices on the racks. Spray with liquid smoke and garlic mixture. Dry in oven at 170 F for two to three hours.

*NOTE: Temperature is very important when making jerky. The USDA Meat and Poultry Hotline's current recommendation for making jerky safely is to heat meat to 160 F before the dehydrating process to assure that any bacteria present will be destroyed by wet heat.

Recent work at the University of Wisconsin demonstrated that the following time-temperature combinations are effective at killing *E. coli* 0157:H7 in jerky products. **Although the lower temperatures are considered effective at killing bacteria, it is recommended that dehydrator temperatures of 145 For higher be used.** Monitor the temperature of the dehydrator by placing the metal stem of a dial thermometer between dehydrator trays, or create an opening for the stem by drilling a hole through the side of the tray.

Drying Temperature	Minimum Drying Time
125 F	10 hours
135 F	8 hours
145 F	7 hours
155 F	4 hours

There are special considerations when making homemade jerky from venison or other wild game, since venison can be heavily contaminated with fecal bacteria depending on the skill of the hunter in dressing the animal and location of the wound. While fresh beef is usually rapidly chilled, deer carcasses are typically held at ambient temperatures, potentially allowing bacteria multiplication.

Hot Pickle Cure Jerky**

This recipe uses a pre-cook phase.

Yield: Five pounds of fresh meat should weigh approximately 2 pounds after drying or smoking.

1. Slice 5 pounds of meat (1/4-inch strips) with the grain, not crosswise. Use fresh lean meat free of fat and connective tissue. Spread out meat and sprinkle on 3 Tbsp. salt, 2 tsp. ground black pepper, and 2 Tbsp. sugar. Put the meat in a pan or dish and let stand for 24 hours in the refrigerator.
2. Pound the meat on both sides to work in the spice. *Optional*: Dip strips of meat in a liquid smoke solution (five parts water to one part liquid smoke) for one to two seconds for added flavor.
3. Make a brine by dissolving 3/4 cup salt, 1/2 cup sugar, and 2 Tbsp. ground black pepper in a gallon of water. Stir to dissolve the salt and sugar.
4. Bring the brine to a low to medium boil. Immerse the seasoned meat strips (a few at a time) into the boiling brine until they turn gray (approximately one to two minutes). Remove meat from brine, using clean tongs or other utensils that have not contacted raw meat.
5. Spread out meat on a clean dehydrator rack or on a clean rack in the top half of a kitchen oven. If you use a kitchen oven, open the oven door to the first or second stop. Heat at 120 to 150 F (lowest oven temperature) for nine to 24 hours or until the desired dryness is reached. Remove jerky from oven before it gets too hard or brittle. Properly dried jerky should crack when bent in half but should not break into two pieces.
6. Store jerky in clean jars or plastic bags, or wrap it in freezer paper and freeze. If kept dry, properly prepared jerky will last almost indefinitely at any temperature, but its quality deteriorates after a few months.

Sweet Italian Sausage

90 pounds pork trim (70 percent lean)

3 quarts water

3 cups salt

1 cup sugar

6 tablespoons cure

7 tablespoons plus 3 teaspoons cracked fennel seed

3 ounces paprika

1/3 cup black pepper

1/3 cup cayenne pepper

1/3 cup garlic powder

2 tablespoons oregano

1 tablespoon sweet basil

Coarse-grind meat trimmings. Add salt, water, sugar, cure and spices. Regrind through 1/4-inch diameter plate and stuff into pork casings. As this is a fresh sausage, no smoking is necessary. Product must be cooked before serving.

Dried Beef

100 pounds lean beef

9 cups salt

6 3/4cups sugar

3 1/2tablespoons nitrate

Using 1-1 1/2 ounces per pound of meat, rub the salt, sugar and nitrate mixture onto the beef, making sure all areas are well covered. Rub the beef twice at three to five day intervals. Allow two days per pound of meat for the cure to complete. This may also be calculated by using seven days of curing time per inch of thickness of the cut.

After the beef is cured, rinse it with cold water several times; then hang it and allow to dry for 24 hours. Apply a light or heavy smoke as desired. Hang in a dry, well-ventilated room for further drying. NOTE: Lamb or venison can be substituted for beef. Use large lean pieces, such as the round or legs, and separate into top, bottom and tip.

Braunschweiger

10 pounds 50/50 pork trim

10 pounds pork liver

1 pound fat bacon

2/3 cup salt (7 ounces)

4 tablespoons white pepper

3 ounces soy protein (70 percent) (optional)

1 medium size onion

1 teaspoon nutmeg

1 1/2 teaspoon ginger

1 tablespoon cure (6 percent)

2 1/2 teaspoons monosodium glutamate (optional)

Grind pork trimmings, liver and other ingredients to a very fine consistency. Mix in spices, salt and cure. Stuff in moisture-proof fibrous casing and cook in 165 °F water bath for 1 1/2 hours or until internal temperature of sausage reaches 155° F. Chill rapidly in water. NOTE: Fat bacon gives smoky flavor.

Haggis

5 pounds pork hearts

3 pounds pork liver

2 pounds beef suet

21 cups oatmeal (3 1/2 pounds)

2-3 medium onions

1/3 cup salt

2 1/2 tablespoons white pepper

1 tablespoon nutmeg

Cook hearts and liver in 180-190° F water until tender; do not boil. Remove cooked items. Reserve broth, and grind hearts and liver with beef suet through 1/4-inch plate. Chop onions to a fine pulp. Bring the broth to a boil and sprinkle in oatmeal. Stir vigorously. To the hot mass add the cooked meats, onions, salt and spices. Stuff in moisture-proof casing and cook for about 3 hours in 170° F water, or until internal temperature reaches 160° F. Chill in ice water and keep at 30-34° F. NOTE: Quite perishable. You may want to cut down on the amount of oatmeal.

Blood Sausage (Klub)

1 pint blood

1 pint milk or water

1/2 teaspoon pepper

1/4 teaspoon nutmeg

1 1/2 teaspoons ground cloves

1 1/2 teaspoons ground allspice

1 tablespoon salt

1 cup quick cooking rolled oats

5-6 cups flour — enough to make a fairly stiff dough

Mix above ingredients together. Drop by large spoonfuls (about 1/2 cup) into a large kettle of salted boiling water. Cook until brown throughout. Remove from water. May be eaten hot with butter and syrup.

To heat up with gravy: cut into small pieces (like potatoes in potato salad) into a kettle or frying pan. Add 1 tablespoon of shortening, sugar to taste and milk. Cook until milk forms a light brown gravy. Serve hot. Additional milk may be added as necessary.

Italian Hot Sausage

5 pounds pork trim 60/40

5 pounds lean beef trim

20 cloves garlic, crushed

4 teaspoons red pepper

4 teaspoons fennel seeds, crushed

2 teaspoons thyme

8 bay leaves

3 tablespoons salt

1 tablespoon black pepper

1/2 teaspoon nutmeg

Grind meat through a coarse plate, then add spices and mix thoroughly. Grind again through a medium plate. Stuff into hog casing. Smoke at 140 °F for proper color development and then raise temperature to 170 °F until internal temperature of product reaches 155 °F.

NOTE: This is a very hot, spicy product. Excellent on pizza and will substitute for pepperoni.

German Grits

1 beef heart

1 beef tongue

5 pounds neck bones or short ribs

1 large onion (chopped)

2 cloves garlic (chopped)

1 teaspoon salt

1/2 teaspoon black pepper

1/4 teaspoon mustard seed

2 cups pearled barley (1 pound)

Old-fashioned oatmeal

Cook heart and tongue in one kettle. Cook neck bones in another kettle. Add enough water to cover meat and simmer until tender (2 to 3 hours). Skim off any extra fat from broth. Remove meat from broth, remove meat from bones and skin tongue. Grind meat through fine plate. To each kettle of broth add the spices and herbs and simmer for 1 hour. Strain broth and add pearled barley. Simmer until barley becomes plump. Mix in cooked ground meat. Add enough old-fashioned oatmeal to soak up excess broth. Season to taste with salt and pepper.

NOTE: If a beefier taste is desired, add beef bouillon cubes to broth, form grits into patties and fry.

Fresh Pork Sausage

45 pounds fresh pork trimmings (70 percent lean)

2 1/2 quarts water

1 1/3 cups salt

15 1/2 tablespoons white pepper

1/4 cup rubbed sage

1/2 cup sugar

Coarse-grind pork; mix in seasonings; grind product to desired size. Stuff into sheep casing. NOTE: May also smoke product for 2 hours at 120° F for smoky flavor. Product must be cooked before serving.

Venison Garlic Sausage

12 pounds pork trim 60/40

10 pounds venison trim

2 pounds beef trim

1 pint water

1 1/2 tablespoons cure

2/3 cup salt

4 tablespoons black pepper

2 teaspoons marjoram

5 1/2 teaspoons mustard seed

2 cloves garlic or 1/2 teaspoon garlic powder

Use same procedure as for Polish sausage.

Polish Sausage

40 pounds lean pork trimmings (80 percent lean)

3 pounds lean beef trimmings (80 percent lean)

1 quart water

3 tablespoons cure

1 1/3 cups salt

1/2 cup black pepper

4 tablespoons mustard seed

4 teaspoons marjoram

3 cloves garlic or 3/4 teaspoon garlic powder

Coarse-grind meat trimmings. Add salt, water, cure and spices; mix thoroughly. Regrind through 1/4-inch diameter plate and stuff into pork casings. Smoke product to desired color and heat to an internal temperature of 141° F. Product must be cooked before serving.

Lar's Super Garlic Sausage

17 pounds beef or venison trim

33 pounds pork trim (50/50)

1 1/2 cups Tender Quick

2/3 cup salt

1 cup brown sugar

1/2 cup black pepper

6 tablespoons garlic powder

2 teaspoons sage

1 teaspoon allspice

1 tablespoon coriander

1 gallon warm water

Grind meat through coarse plate. Mix spices in water and pour over meat. Mix thoroughly. Grind through coarse plate again and stuff in hog casing. Using a cool smoke (90 F), smoke for 12 hours. Product must be cooked before serving. NOTE: If you don't like garlic flavor, cut back on amount. Also could fine-grind the product, if desired.

Venison Summer Sausage

15 pounds venison

10 pounds 50/50 pork trimming

2/3 cup salt

1 1/2 tablespoons cure

2 1/2 tablespoons mustard seed

1/2 cup black pepper

1/2 cup sugar

1 tablespoon marjoram

1 tablespoon monosodium glutamate (optional)

3 tablespoons garlic powder

Mix salt and cure with coarse-ground product. Pack in shallow pan and place in cooler for three to five days. Mix in remainder of spices, regrind and stuff in 3-inch fibrous casings. Smoke at 140 F for 2 hours; raise temperature to 160 F for 2 hours, and finish product at 170 F until internal temperature reaches 155 F.

NOTE: Can substitute lamb or beef for the venison.

Smoked Bratwurst

90 pounds pork trim (70 percent lean)

3 quarts water

3 cups salt

1 to 1 1/3 cups sugar

6 tablespoons cure

3/4 cup white pepper
1/4 cup cayenne
2 tablespoons nutmeg
2 tablespoons thyme
2 tablespoons ginger
1 tablespoon rosemary
1 tablespoon mace

Coarse-grind meat trimmings. Add water, salt, sugar, cure and spices. Mix thoroughly. Regrind through 1/4-inch diameter plate. Stuff into pork casings. Smoke product to desired color and heat to an internal temperature of 141 °F. Product must be cooked before serving.

Smoked Turkey and Pork Sausage

50 pounds turkey trim (90 percent lean)
40 pounds pork trim (50 percent lean)
3 quarts water
3 cups salt
1 cup to 1 cup and 2 tablespoons dextrose
6 tablespoons cure
1 cup white pepper
1/2 cup sage
1/4 cup cayenne
1 tablespoon thyme
1 tablespoon nutmeg
1 tablespoon ginger
1 tablespoon mace
10 tablespoons monosodium glutamate (optional)

Coarse-grind meat trimmings. Add water, salt, dextrose, cure and spices. Regrind through 1/4-inch diameter plate. Stuff into pork casings. Smoke product to desired color and heat to an internal temperature of 141° F. Product must be cooked before serving.

Emulsified Products

30 pounds bull meat
25 pounds 50/50 beef trim
20 pounds 60/40 pork trim

10 quarts water
5 pounds flavorings*
***5 pounds of flavorings consists of:**

	Ounces	Pounds	%
salt	40	2.5	50
corn syrup solids	16	1.0	20
mustard	11.2	.70	14
cure	3.2	.20	4
ground black pepper	3.2	.20	4
coriander	2.2	.14	2.75
nutmeg	2.2	.14	2.75
dehydrated onion and garlic	1.4	.09	1.75
sodium erythorbate	.6	.04	.75

From the above formulation, different products can be made. These differ in texture and taste.

- Wieners — stuff in sheep casing; smoke and cook to 155 F internal temperature.
- Dinner franks — stuff in hog casings; smoke and cook to 155 F internal temperature.
- Ring bologna — stuff in beef casing; form into a ring; smoke and cook to 155 F internal temperature.
- Bologna — stuff in 6-inch diameter fibrous casings; smoke and cook to 155 F internal temperature.
- Leona — add 20 pounds cooked, diced and skinned hog jowls plus 1/3 cup garlic powder to the emulsion; stuff into 2-inch diameter fibrous casings; smoke and cook to 155 F internal temperature.
- Pickle and pimento loaf — add 5 pounds sweet pickles and 5 pounds pimentos. Stuff into parchment-lined metal molds or waterproof fibrous casing. Can be water-cooked or baked to internal temperature 155 F.
- Macaroni and cheese loaf — add 5 pounds cheese and 5 pounds cooked macaroni. Proceed as with pickle and pimento loaf.

NOTE: Monosodium Glutamate (MSG) intensifies and enhances flavor but does not contribute a flavor of its own.

It is the sodium salt of glutamic acid, an amino acid.

One to two percent of the population may be sensitive to MSG and have mild to transitory reactions in some circumstances when they consume significant amounts, such as would be found in heavily enhanced foods.

FDA believes that MSG is a safe food ingredient for the general population.

Weights & Measures Table

Equivalents:

4 cups = 1 quart = 950 ml

2 pints = 1 quart = 950 ml

16 ounces = 1 pint = 500 ml

2 cups = 1 pint = 500 ml

2 cups = 16 fluid ounces = 500 ml

16 tablespoons = 1 cup = 240 ml

8 liquid ounces = 1 cup = 240 ml

4 tablespoons = 1/4 cup = 60 ml

1/4 cup = 2 liquid ounces = 60 ml

1 liquid ounce = 2 tablespoons = 30 ml

3 teaspoons = 1 tablespoon = 15 ml

1 cc = 1 ml

1 ounce = 28 g

Weight Conversions of Common Ingredients

1 pound salt = 1 1/2 cups

1 pound sugar = 2 1/4 cups

1 ounce cure = 1 1/2 tablespoons

1 ounce MSG = 2.2 tablespoon

Spice Weights and Measures

This table is for approximate weights and measures of various spices and is intended as a handy compilation in estimating quantities.

Conversion from OUNCES

	1/4	1/2	3/4	1	2	3	4
Name of Spice			To TABLESPOONS				
Allspice	1.25	2.5	3.75	5	10	15	20
Basil	1.5	3	4.5	6	12	18	24
Caraway	1.25	1.75	2.66	3.5	7	10.5	14
Cardamom	1	2	3	4	8	12	16
Celery, ground	1	2	3	4	8	12	16
Cinnamon	0.88	1.75	2.63	3.5	7	10.5	14
Cloves, ground	1	2	3	4	8	12	16
Coriander, ground	1	2	3	4	8	12	16
Cumin	1	2	3	4	8	12	16
Dill, whole	1	2	3	3.9	7.8	11.7	15
Fennel, whole	1	2.25	3.33	4.5	9	13.5	18
Garlic powder	0.75	1.5	2.25	3	6	9	12
Ginger	1.25	2.5	3.75	5	10	15	20
Mace, ground	1.33	2.75	4 5.	5	11	16.5	22
Marjoram	1.5	3	4.5	6	12	18	24
MSG	0.5	1	1.66	2.2	4.4	6.6	9
Mustard	1	2	3	4	8	12	16
Nutmeg	1	2	3	4	8	12	16
Onion powder	1	2	3	4	8	12	16
Oregano	2	4	6	8	16	24	32
Paprika	1	2	3	4	8	12	16
Parsley flakes	3	6	12	16	32	48	64
Pepper, black	1	2	3	4	8	12	16
Pepper, ground	0.93	1.85	2.75	3.7	7.4	11.1	15
Rosemary, ground	1.75	3.5	5.25	7	14	21	28
Sage, ground	2.5	5	7.5	10	20	30	40
Salt	0.5	1	1.5	2	4	6	8
Savory	1.33	2.75	4	5.5	11	16.5	22
Thyme	1.75	3.5	5.25	7	14	21	28
Tumeric, ground	1.17	1.75	2.66	3.5	7	10.5	14

Example: If a recipe calls for one ounce of Allspice, then you would use 5 level tablespoons.

5

Freezing Fruits

Freezing is one of the easiest methods of preserving foods. Following the guidelines in this circular will help ensure that your frozen fruits remain nutritious and high in quality. Most fruits can be frozen satisfactorily, but the quality of the frozen product will vary with the kind of fruit, stage of maturity and type of pack. Select fruits with a firm texture and well-developed flavor and then treat them with respect. Wash small quantities (2 to 3 quarts) at a time to avoid bruising. Wash through several changes of cold water, lifting produce out of the water each time so that dirt will not settle back on the fruit. Do not let produce soak.

Fruits are prepared for freezing in about the same way as for serving. It is best to prepare enough fruit for only 2 to 3 quarts at one time. If a fruit is to be crushed, suit the method to the fruit. A wire potato masher, pastry fork or slotted spoon may be used to crush soft fruits. Firm fruits may be crushed more easily with a food chopper. A colander, food press or strainer is useful for making purees. Blenders and food processors tend to liquefy the fruit too much. Do not use galvanized ware with fruit or fruit juices because the acid in fruit dissolves the zinc, which is poisonous. Metallic off-flavors may result from the use of iron utensils, chipped enameled ware or tinware that is not well tinned.

PREVENTING DISCOLORATION

Some fruits, such as apples, apricots, peaches, nectarines and pears, darken during preparation for freezer storage and darken very rapidly when thawed unless treated to retard darkening. Several ways to prevent darkening of fruit are used because all fruits are not protected equally well by all treatments.

Ascorbic acid (vitamin C) is effective in preventing darkening in most fruits. Not only does it preserve natural color and flavor, but it adds nutritive value. Ascorbic acid in crystalline or powdered form is available at drugstores or where canning supplies are sold. Ascorbic acid tablets are available and may be used. They are less expensive, but more difficult to dissolve (½ teaspoon ascorbic acid = 1500 mg). Also, filler in the tablets may make the syrup cloudy. To use, dissolve ascorbic acid in a little cold water. Use the amount specified for the fruit being frozen. If using tablets, crush them so they will dissolve more easily.

For syrup pack, add the dissolved ascorbic acid to the cold syrup shortly before using. Stir it in gently so you won't stir in air. Solutions of ascorbic acid should be made up as needed. Keep syrup in the refrigerator until used.

For sugar or dry pack, dissolve the ascorbic acid in 2 to 3 tablespoons of cold water and sprinkle the mixture over the fruit just before adding the sugar.

For unsweetened pack, sprinkle dissolved ascorbic acid over the fruit and mix thoroughly just before packing. If fruit is packed in water, dissolve the ascorbic acid in the water.

For fruit juices, add ascorbic acid directly to the juice. Stir only enough to dissolve the ascorbic acid.

For crushed fruits and fruit purees, add dissolved ascorbic acid to fruit preparation and mix. Ascorbic acid mixtures — special anti-darkening preparations, usually made of ascorbic acid mixed with sugar or with sugar and citric acid — are on the market. Follow the manufacturer's directions for use. Lemon juice or citric acid is used sometimes instead of ascorbic acid. These ingredients are usually not as effective in preventing darkening as ascorbic acid. When used in large quantities, they often mask natural fruit flavors. Steaming for a few minutes before packing is enough to control darkening in some fruits. Steaming works best for fruits that will be cooked before use.

Choosing a Pack

There are several types of fruit packs suitable for freezing: syrup pack, unsweetened pack, sugar pack, dry pack, tray pack and sugar replacement pack. Whichever method you choose, be sure to leave the appropriate head space.

Most fruits have a better texture and flavor if packed in sugar or syrup. Some can be packed satisfactorily without sweetening, but losses of vitamin C are greatest when fruits are packed without sugar. The type of pack will depend on the intended use. Fruits packed in syrup are generally best for serving uncooked; those packed in dry sugar or unsweetened are best for most cooking purposes because there is less liquid in the product. Unsweetened packs and sugar replacement packs often are used by people on special diets.

Syrup pack: The proportion of sugar to water used depends on the sweetness of the fruit and the taste preference of the user. A 40 percent syrup is recommended for most fruits. Lighter syrups are desirable for mild-flavored fruits to prevent masking the flavor. Heavier syrups may be used for very sour fruits.

To make syrup, dissolve the sugar in lukewarm water until the solution is clear. Cool syrup before using.

Use just enough cold syrup to cover the prepared fruit after it has been settled by jarring the container (about ½ to ¾ cup of syrup per pint). To keep the fruit under the syrup, place a small piece of crumpled waxed paper or other water-resistant wrapping material on the top and press the fruit down into the syrup before closing, sealing and freezing.

Table 1.Syrups for use in freezing fruits.

Type of Syrup	Sugar Cups*	Water Cups	Yield of Syrup Cups
10 percent syrup	½	4	4¼
20 percent syrup	1	4	4¾
30 percent syrup	1¾	4	5
40 percent syrup	2¾	4	5a
50 percent syrup	4	4	6

*** In general, up to one-fourth of the sugar may be replaced by corn syrup or mild-flavored honey. A larger proportion of corn syrup may be used if a very bland, light-colored type is selected.**

* In general, up to one-fourth of the sugar may be replaced by corn syrup or mild-flavored honey. A larger proportion of corn syrup may be used if a very bland, light-colored type is selected.

Pectin syrup: This can be used to prepare syrups for freezing berries, cherries and peaches. With pectin, less sugar is needed, and fresh-fruit flavor, color and texture are retained. Pectin syrups are prepared as follows:

Combine 1 box of powdered pectin with 1 cup of water in a saucepan, and stir and boil 1 minute. Stir in ½ cup sugar and dissolve. Remove the pan from the heat and add cold water to make 2 cups of syrup. Chill. Put cleaned and prepared fruit in a 4- to 6-quart bowl; add enough pectin syrup to glaze the fruit with a thin film. Gently fold fruit to coat each piece with the syrup. Then package, seal and freeze promptly.

Unsweetened pack: Fruit can be packed dry, covered with water containing ascorbic acid or packed in unsweetened juice. For fruit packed in water or juice, submerge fruit by using a small piece of crumpled water-resistant material as for syrup and sugar packs. Seal tightly and freeze. Unsweetened packs generally yield a lower quality product than packs with sugar. However, some fruits, such as raspberries, blueberries, scalded apples, gooseberries, currants, cranberries and rhubarb, maintain good quality without sugar.

Sugar pack: Put fruit in a bowl or shallow pan. Sprinkle sugar over the fruit and mix gently until the juice is drawn out and the sugar is dissolved. Use a large spoon or pancake turner for mixing. Soft, sliced fruits, such as peaches, strawberries, plums and cherries, will yield sufficient syrup for covering if the fruit is layered with sugar and allowed to stand for 15 minutes. Some whole fruits may be coated with sugar and frozen. Pack fruit and juice into container. Place a small piece of crumpled water-resistant paper on top to hold fruit down in the juice. Seal and freeze.

Dry pack: The dry pack is good for small whole fruits, such as berries, that give a good quality product without sugar. Simply pack the fruit into a container, seal and freeze.

Tray pack: This is a good pack for the fruits mentioned above in the unsweetened pack section. Spread a single layer of prepared fruit on shallow trays. Freeze and package in freezer bags promptly. The fruit pieces remain loose. Later the bag may be opened, the needed amount taken out and the bag re-closed and returned to the freezer.

Sugar replacement pack: Sugar substitutes, such as aspartame, can be used when freezing fruits. They will give a sweet taste but do not furnish the beneficial effects of sugar, such as color protection and thick syrup. Fruits frozen with sugar substitutes generally will freeze harder and thaw more slowly than those preserved with sugar. Follow directions on the label of the sweetener to determine the amount of sweetener needed. Sweeteners can be added at serving time instead of during the freezing process.

Packing

Choose containers that are made for freezer storage and label with contents and date. Containers should be moisture-vapor resistant, durable and leak-proof to preserve the quality of the fruits by keeping moisture in and air out. Loss of moisture causes brownish-white spots on food known as freezer burn. Freezer burn actually does not spoil the food but can cause toughness and often results in off-flavors. Plastic freezer bags and rigid freezer containers are convenient for freezing foods. Plastic sandwich bags, bread wrappers and cartons from dairy products such as cottage cheese, sour cream or milk are not suitable for long-term freezer storage.

Table 2.Head space.

	Container with wide top opening*		**Container with narrow top opening****	
Type of Pack	**Pint**	**Quart**	**Pint**	**Quart**
Liquid Pack *(fruit packed in juice, syrup or water)*	½ inch	1 inch	¾ inch	1½ inch
Juice	1½ inch	1½ inch	1½ inch	1½ inch
Dry Pack *(fruit or vegetable packed without sugar or syrup)*	½ inch	½ inch	½ inch	½ inch

* This is head space for tall containers either straight or slightly flared.
** Glass canning jars may be used except for a water pack.

* This is head space for tall containers either straight or slightly flared.** Glass canning jars may be used except for a water pack.

Allow head space between packed food and closure because most fruits expand during freezing. Put no more unfrozen food into the home freezer than it will freeze within 24 hours. This is about 2 to 3 pounds per cubic foot of freezer capacity. Leave space for air circulation between unfrozen food packages. Store at 0 F or lower.

Freezer Storage Life

For best quality, use frozen fruits within 12 months. Maintain freezer temperatures at 0 F or lower.

Thawing Fruits

Allow fruit to thaw in the unopened package. Fruits packed in dry sugar thaw faster than those in syrup. Fruits packed without sugar take longer to thaw. Fruit to be served in salads, shortcakes, fruit sauce and fruit cups should be only partially thawed. Thaw fruits for pies until able to separate. Completely thawed fruit will become flabby and may darken upon standing.

Preparation of Fruits for Freezing

For syrup recipe, refer to Table 1; for headspace required, see Table 2.

APPLES

Apple slices _ Select firm, crisp full-flavored apples. Wash, peel and core. Slice medium apples into twelfths, large sizes into sixteenths. Pack in one of the following ways:

Syrup pack: Use 40 percent syrup. For a better quality frozen product, add ½ teaspoon crystalline ascorbic acid to each quart of syrup. Slice apples directly into cold syrup in container, starting with ½ cup syrup to a pint container. Press fruit down in containers and add enough syrup to cover. Leave head space. Seal and freeze.

Sugar pack: To prevent darkening of apples during preparation, dissolve ½ teaspoon ascorbic acid in 3 tablespoons water. Sprinkle over the fruit. To retard darkening, place slices in a single layer in steamer; steam 1½ to 2 minutes, depending on thickness of slice. Cool in cold water; drain. Over each quart (1¼ pounds) of apple slices, sprinkle evenly ½ cup sugar and stir. Pack apples into containers and press fruit down. Leave head space. Seal and freeze.

Unsweetened pack: Follow directions for sugar pack, omitting sugar.

For pies _ Follow directions for sugar pack, omitting sugar. Arrange steamed slices in a pie plate as for a pie. Put the filled plate into a plastic bag and freeze. The solid chunk of slices may be removed from the plate when frozen. Wrap it tightly and return to the freezer. At pie-making time, lay the pie-shaped chunk of slices in your pastry. Put on the sugar and seasonings, top with a crust and bake.

Applesauce _ Select full-flavored apples. Wash apples, peel if desired, core and slice. To each quart of apple slices, add a cup water; cook until tender. Puree and add ½ cup sugar, if desired, for each quart of hot puree, stirring until dissolved. Cool and package. Seal and freeze.

Apple juice _ Place freshly made juice in rigid containers. Leave head space. Seal and freeze.

Apricots

Halved _ Select firm, ripe, uniformly yellow apricots. Sort, wash, halve and pit. Peel and slice if desired. Unpeeled apricots are satisfactory for pies. If apricots are not peeled, heat them in boiling water ½ minute to keep skins from toughening during freezing. Then cool in cold water and drain. Pack into containers in one of the following ways:

Syrup pack: Use 40 percent syrup. For a better quality frozen product, add ¾ teaspoon crystalline ascorbic acid to each quart of syrup. Pack apricots directly into containers. Cover with syrup. Leave head space. Seal and freeze.

Sugar pack: Before combining apricots with sugar, give the fruit the following treatment to prevent darkening:

Dissolve ¼ teaspoon crystalline ascorbic acid in 3 tablespoons of cold water and sprinkle over 1 quart (f pound) of fruit.

Mix ½ cup sugar with each quart of fruit. Stir until sugar is dissolved. Pack apricots into containers and press down until fruit is covered with juice, leaving head space. Seal and freeze.

Crushed or puree: Select fully ripe fruit. For crushed apricots, dip in boiling water for ½ minute and cool in cold water. Peel the apricots. Pit and crush them coarsely.

For puree, pit and quarter the apricots. Press through a sieve; or heat to boiling point in just enough water to prevent scorching and then press through a sieve.

For each quart (2 pounds) of prepared apricots, mix with 1 cup sugar. For a better product, dissolve ¼ teaspoon crystalline ascorbic acid in ¼ cup of water and add to the fruit just before adding the sugar.

Pack into containers, leaving head space. Seal and freeze.

Avocados

Select avocados that yield to gentle pressure with rinds free from dark blemishes. Peel fruit, cut in half and remove pit. Avocados are best frozen as puree — unsweetened for salads and sandwiches, sweetened for other uses. Avocados are not satisfactorily frozen whole or sliced.

For a better quality product, add ¼ teaspoon ascorbic acid to each quart of puree or add 1 tablespoon lemon juice for each two avocados. Pack into container, leaving head space. Seal and freeze.

Bananas

Select firm, ripe bananas. Peel; mash thoroughly while adding 1 teaspoon ascorbic acid per cup of mashed banana. Pack, leaving head space. Seal and freeze. Satisfactory for baking purposes.

Berries, most firm *(blueberries, elderberries, huckleberries)*

Whole _ Select full-flavored, ripe berries all about the same size, preferably with tender skins. Sort, wash and drain. If desired, steam for 1 minute and cool immediately. Preheating in steam tenderizes skin and makes a better flavored product. Use one of the following packs:

Syrup pack: Pack berries into containers and cover with cold 40 percent syrup. Leave head space. Seal and freeze.

Unsweetened pack: Tray pack or pack berries into containers, leaving head space. Seal and freeze.

Crushed or puree: Select fully ripened berries. Sort, wash and drain. Crush or press berries through a fine sieve for puree. To 1 quart (2 pounds) crushed berries or puree, add 1 to 1c cups sugar, depending on tartness of fruit. Stir until sugar is dissolved. Pack into containers, leaving head space. Seal and freeze.

Berries, most soft (*blackberries, boysenberries, dewberries, loganberries, youngberries*)

Select firm, plump, fully ripe berries with glossy skins. Green berries may cause off-flavor. Sort and remove any leaves and stems. Wash and drain. Use one of the following packs:

Syrup pack: Pack berries into containers and cover with cold 40 percent or 50 percent syrup, depending on the sweetness of the fruit. Leave head space. Seal and freeze.

Sugar pack: To 1 quart (1a pounds) berries, add ¾ cup sugar. Turn berries over and over until most of the sugar is dissolved. Fill containers, leaving head space. Seal and freeze.

Unsweetened pack: Pack berries into containers, leaving head space. Seal and freeze.

Crushed or puree: Prepare for packing in the same way as whole berries. Then crush or press through a sieve for puree. To each quart (2 pounds) of crushed berries or puree, add 1 cup sugar. Stir until sugar is dissolved. Pack into containers, leaving head space. Seal and freeze.

Cherries, Sour

Select bright red, tree-ripened cherries. Stem, sort and wash thoroughly. Drain and pit. Use one of the following packs:

Syrup pack: Pack cherries into containers and cover with cold 50 percent syrup, depending on tartness of the cherries. Leave head space. Seal and freeze.

Sugar pack: To 1 quart (1a pounds) cherries, add ¾ cup sugar. Mix until sugar is dissolved. Pack into containers, leaving head space. Seal and freeze.

Cherries, Sweet

Select well-colored, tree-ripened fruit with a sweet flavor. Sort, stem, wash, drain and pit. Pack cherries into containers.

Cover with cold 40 percent syrup. For a better quality product, add ½ teaspoon ascorbic acid to each quart of syrup. Leave head space. Seal and freeze.

With sour cherries, use half sweet, half sour. Pack as above, using 50 percent syrup. Ascorbic acid may be added, but is not essential as it is for sweet cherries alone.

Fresh Coconut

Shred coconut meat or put it through a food chopper. Pack into containers and if desired, cover with coconut liquid. Leave head space. Seal and freeze.

Cranberries

Whole _ Choose firm, deep red cherries with glossy skins. Stem and sort. Wash and drain.

Unsweetened pack: Tray pack or pack into containers without sugar. Leave head space. Seal and freeze.

Syrup pack: Pack into containers. Cover with cold 50 percent syrup. Leave head space. Seal and freeze.

Puree: Prepare cranberries as for freezing whole. Add 2 cups of water to each quart (1 pound) of berries. Cook until skins have popped. Press through a sieve.

Add sugar to taste, about 2 cups for each quart (2 pounds) of puree. Pack into containers, leaving head space. Seal and freeze.

Currants

Select plump, fully ripe, bright red currants. Wash in cold water and remove stems.

Dry pack: Pack currants into containers, leaving head space. Currants also can be frozen first on a tray and then packed into containers as soon as they are frozen. Seal containers and freeze.

Syrup pack: Pack currants into containers and cover with cold 50 percent syrup, leaving head space. Seal containers and freeze.

Sugar pack: To each quart (1a pounds) of fruit, add ¾ cup sugar. Stir until most of the sugar is dissolved. Pack currants into containers, leaving head space. Seal and freeze.

Dates

Select dates with good flavor and tender texture. Wash and split to remove pits. Leave whole or press through a sieve for puree.

Dry pack: Pack into containers, leaving head space. Seal and freeze.

Figs

Select fully ripe fruit, wash and peel if desired.

Syrup pack: Use 40 percent syrup. For a better product, add ¾ teaspoon ascorbic acid or ½ cup lemon juice to each quart of syrup. Pack figs into containers and cover with cold syrup, leaving head space. Seal and freeze.

Dry pack: To prevent darkening of light-colored figs, dissolve ¾ teaspoon of ascorbic acid in 3 tablespoons of cold water and sprinkle over 1 quart of fruit. Pack figs into containers, leaving head space. Figs also can be frozen first on a tray and then packed into containers as soon as they are frozen. Seal containers and freeze.

Gooseberries

Choose fully ripe berries if freezing for pie — berries a little underripe for jelly making. Sort, remove stems and blossom ends and wash.

Unsweetened pack: Tray pack or pack into containers without sugar. Leave head space. Seal and freeze.

Syrup pack: Pack into containers. Cover with 50 percent syrup. Leave head space. Seal and freeze.

Grapefruit, Oranges

Sections or slices _ Select firm tree-ripened fruit heavy for its size and free from soft spots. Wash and peel. Divide fruit into sections, removing all membranes and seeds. Slice oranges if desired. For grapefruit with many seeds, cut fruit in half, remove seeds; cut or scoop out sections. Pack fruit into containers. Cover with cold 40 percent syrup made with excess fruit juice and water if needed. Leave head space. Seal and freeze.

Juice _ Select fruit as directed for sections. Squeeze juice from fruit, using squeezer that does not press oil from rind. Sweeten, if desired, with 2 tablespoons sugar for each quart of juice, or pack without sugar. Pour juice into containers immediately. To avoid development of off-flavors, pack juice in glass jars. Leave head space. Seal and freeze.

Grapes

Choose fully ripe, firm, sweet grapes. Sort, stem and wash. Leave seedless grapes whole; cut table grapes with seeds in half and remove seeds.

Syrup pack: Pack into containers and cover with cold 40 percent syrup. Leave head space. Seal and freeze.

Puree: Wash, stem and crush the grapes. Heat to boiling. Drain off free juice and freeze it separately. Remove seeds and hulls with a colander. To 1 quart (2 pounds) puree, add ½ cup sugar. Pack into containers, leaving head space. Seal and freeze.

Juice: For beverages, select as for whole grapes. For jelly making, select as recommended in specific jelly recipe. Crush grapes. Add 1 cup water per gallon of crushed grapes. Simmer for 10 minutes. Strain juice through a jelly bag. To remove tartrate crystals, let stand overnight in refrigerator or other cool place. Pour off clear juice for freezing. Discard sentiment. Pour juice into containers, leaving head space. Seal and freeze. If tartrate crystals form in frozen juice, they may be removed by straining the juice after it thaws.

Ground Cherries

Husk. Scald for 2 minutes. Pack in 40 percent syrup. Leave head space. Seal and freeze.

Guavas

Select ripe, tender fruit. Wash, peel and cut in half.

Syrup pack: Pack in container. Cover with cold 30 percent syrup. Leave head space. Seal and freeze.

Mangos

Select firm, ripe mangos that yield to gentle pressure. Wash, peel and slice.

Syrup pack: Pack slices in containers. Cover with 30 percent syrup. Leave head space. Seal and freeze.

Unsweetened tray pack: Arrange slices on a flat pan and freeze. When frozen, remove and store in sealed containers.

Puree: Press mango slices through a sieve, blender chop or chop in a food processor. Pack into containers with or without sugar. Leave head space. Seal and freeze.

Melons *(cantaloupe, crenshaw, honeydew, Persian, watermelon)*

Syrup pack: Select firm-fleshed, well-colored melons. Cut in half, remove seeds and peel. Cut melons into slices, cubes or balls. Pack into containers and cover with cold 30 percent syrup. Leave head space. Seal and freeze.

Unsweetened pack: Select and prepare as for syrup pack. Place in freezer bag. Seal and freeze. Serve before completely thawed.

Nectarines

Halves, quarters or slices _ Choose fully ripe, well-colored, firm nectarines. Overripe fruit may take on a disagreeable flavor in frozen storage.

Sort, wash and pit the fruit. Peel if desired. Cut in halves, quarters or slices.

Cut fruit directly into cold 40 percent syrup, starting with ½ cup for each pint container. For a better product, add ½ teaspoon crystalline ascorbic acid to each quart of syrup. Press fruit down and add syrup to cover, leaving head space. Seal and freeze.

Puree _ Prepare same as peach puree below.

Peaches

Halves and slices - Peaches in halves and slices have better quality when packed in sugar, but a pectin syrup pack will serve if sweetening is not desired.

Select firm, ripe peaches with no green color in the skins. Sort, wash, pit and peel. For a better product, peel peaches without a boiling-water dip. Slice if desired.

Syrup pack: Use 40 percent syrup. For a better quality product, add ½ teaspoon crystalline ascorbic acid for each quart of syrup.

Put peaches directly into cold syrup in container, starting with ½ cup syrup to a pint container. Press fruit down and add syrup to cover, leaving head space. Seal and freeze.

Sugar pack: To each quart (1a pounds) of prepared fruit, add b cup sugar and mix well. To retard darkening, sprinkle ascorbic acid dissolved in water over the peaches before adding sugar. Use ¼ teaspoon crystalline ascorbic acid in 3 tablespoons cold water for each quart of fruit. Pack into containers, leaving head space. Seal and freeze.

Pectin syrup pack: Pack peaches into containers and cover with cold pectin syrup *(see page 2)*. Leave head space. Seal and freeze.

Puree: To loosen skins, dip peaches in boiling water ½ to 1 minute. The riper the fruit, the less scalding needed. Cool in cold water, remove skins and pit.

To puree, press through a sieve, or heat pitted peaches 4 minutes in just enough water to prevent scorching and then press through a sieve.

With each quart (2 pounds) of pureed peaches, mix 1 cup sugar. For better quality, add c teaspoon crystalline ascorbic acid to each quart of fruit.

Pack into containers, leaving head space. Seal and freeze.

Pears

Halves or quarters _ Select pears that are ripened and firm but not hard. Wash fruit in cold water. Peel, cut in halves or quarters and remove cores.

Heat pears in boiling water or 40 percent syrup for 1 to 2 minutes, depending on size of pieces. Drain and cool. Pack pears into containers and cover with cold 40 percent syrup. For a better product, add ¾ teaspoon crystalline ascorbic acid to a quart of cold syrup. Leave head space. Seal and freeze.

Persimmons

Select orange-colored, soft, ripe persimmons. Sort, wash, peel and cut into sections. Press fruit through a sieve to make a puree. For a better product, to each quart of puree add c teaspoon ascorbic acid. Puree made from native varieties needs no sugar. Puree made from cultivated varieties may be packed with or without sugar.

Puree: Pack unsweetened puree into containers. Leave head space. Seal and freeze. Or mix 1 cup sugar with each quart (2 pounds) puree and pack into containers. Leave head space. Seal and freeze.

Pineapples

Select firm, ripe pineapples with full flavor and aroma. Pare and remove core and eyes. Slice, dice, crush or cut the pineapple into wedges or sticks.

Unsweetened pack: Pack fruit tightly into containers without sugar. Leave head space. Seal and freeze.

Syrup pack: Pack fruit tightly into containers. Cover with 30 percent syrup made with pineapple juice, if available, or with water. Leave head space. Seal and freeze.

Dry pack: Pack fruit tightly into containers without sugar. Leave head space. Seal and freeze.

Plums and Prunes

Whole, halves or quarters _ Choose firm tree-ripened fruit of deep color. Sort and wash. Leave whole or cut in halves or quarters. Pack in one of the following ways:

Unsweetened pack: Pack whole fruit into containers, leaving head space. Seal and freeze.

To serve uncooked, dip frozen fruit in cold water for 5 to 10 seconds, remove skins and cover with 40 percent syrup to thaw.

Syrup pack: Pack cut fruit into containers. Cover fruit with cold 40 percent or 50 percent syrup, depending on tartness of fruit. For improved quality, add ½ teaspoon crystalline ascorbic acid to a quart of syrup. Leave head space. Seal and freeze.

Plum sauce: Boil well-ripened clingstone plums without water until soft, then remove pits and skins. Continue cooking the pulp and juice until it thickens. Add one part sugar (with spices, if desired) to four parts plums. Cool and package, leaving head space. Seal and freeze.

Pomegranates

Select fully ripe pomegranates. Wash and cut in half. Place cut side down and rap the shell with a blunt instrument, such as a hammer handle. This will break section walls and open juice sacs.

Syrup pack: Pack juice and pulp into containers. Cover with a cold 30 percent syrup, leaving head space. Seal and freeze.

Raspberries

Whole _ Select fully ripe, juicy berries. Sort, wash carefully in cold water and drain thoroughly.

Sugar pack: To 1 quart (1a pounds) berries, add ¾ cup sugar and mix carefully to avoid crushing. Put into containers, leaving head space. Seal and freeze.

Syrup pack: Put berries into containers and cover with cold 40 percent syrup, leaving head space. Seal and freeze.

Unsweetened pack: Put berries into containers, leaving head space. Seal and freeze.

Crushed or puree: Prepare as for whole raspberries, then crush or press through a sieve for puree. To 1 quart (2 pounds) crushed berries or puree, add ¾ to 1 cup sugar, depending on sweetness of fruit. Mix until sugar is dissolved. Put into containers, leaving head space. Seal and freeze.

Rhubarb

Stalks or pieces _ Choose firm, tender, well-colored stalks with good flavor and few fibers. Wash, trim and cut into 1- or 2-inch pieces or in lengths to fit the package. Heating rhubarb in boiling water for 1 minute and cooling promptly in cold water helps retain color and flavor.

Unsweetened pack: Tray pack or pack either raw or preheated rhubarb tightly into containers without sugar. Leave head space. Seal and freeze.

Pie pack: Use directions given for apples.

Syrup pack: Pack either raw or preheated rhubarb tightly into containers, cover with cold 40 percent syrup. Leave head space. Seal and freeze.

Sugar pack: Mix either raw or preheated rhubarb with ½ cup sugar per quart of prepared fruit. Pack, leave head space. Seal and freeze.

Strawberries

Whole _ Choose firm, ripe, red berries preferably with a slightly tart flavor. Large berries are better sliced or crushed. Sort berries, wash them in cold water, drain well and remove hulls.

Syrup pack: Put berries into containers and cover with cold 50 percent syrup, leaving head space. Seal and freeze.

Sugar pack: Add ¾ cup sugar to 1 quart (1a pounds) strawberries. Stir until most of the sugar is dissolved or let stand for 15 minutes. Put into containers, leaving head space. Seal and freeze.

Unsweetened pack: Tray pack or pack into containers, leaving head space. For better color, cover with water containing ascorbic acid for each quart of water. Seal and freeze.

Sliced or crushed _ Prepare for packing as for whole strawberries; then slice or crush partially or completely. To 1 quart (1a pounds) berries, add ¾ cup sugar; mix thoroughly. Pack into containers, leaving head space. Seal and freeze.

Puree _ Prepare strawberries as for freezing whole. Then press berries through a sieve. To 1 quart (2 pounds) puree, add 2/3 cup sugar and mix well. Put into containers, leaving head space. Seal and freeze.

6

Canning Meat

Poultry, red meats, game and seafoods are low acid foods and must be processed in a pressure canner to assure their safety. Use the processing time and pressure that is specified for each type of product.

General Tips for Quality Products

- Can only good quality poultry, red meat, game and seafood.
- Chill home-produced meat soon after slaughter to 40 degrees Fahrenheit or lower
- to prevent spoilage.
- Keep all work areas sanitary and meat clean.
- If meat must be held for longer than a few days before canning, freeze it.
- Keep frozen until ready to can it.
- Trim meat of gristle, bruised spots and fat before canning. Too much fat left on
- meat can lead to sealing failures.
- Have dial gauges on pressure canners checked annually.
- All pressure canners need to be vented for 10 minutes.

GENERAL PROCEDURES

Jars and Lids

Use Mason-type canning jars no larger than the size specified in the directions for the specific food being canned. Use two-piece self-sealing lids. Buy only the quantity of lids that will be used in a year and follow the manufacturer's directions for preparing the lids.

Mayonnaise-type jars are not recommended for use with foods to be processed in a pressure canner because of excessive jar breakage.

Filling Jars

After filling jars with food, release air bubbles by inserting a flat plastic (not metal) spatula between the food and the jar. Slowly turn the jar and move the spatula up and down to allow air bubbles to escape.

Salt may be added if desired. When canning meat and seafoods, salt seasons the food but is not necessary to ensure safety.

Adjust the headspace and then clean the jar rim (sealing surface) with a dampened paper towel. Place the lid, gasket down, onto the cleaned jar-sealing surface. Uncleaned jar sealing surfaces may cause seal failures.

Then fit the metal screw band over the flat lid. Follow the manufacturer's guidelines enclosed with or on the box for tightening the jar lids properly.

Using Pressure Canners

Follow these steps for successful pressure canning:

1. Put 2 to 3 inches of hot water in the canner. Place filled jars on the rack, using a jar lifter. Fasten canner lid securely.
2. Leave weight off vent port or open petcock. Heat at the highest setting until steam flows from the petcock or vent port.
3. Maintain high heat setting, exhaust steam 10 minutes, and then place weight on vent port or close petcock. The canner will pressurize during the next three to five minutes.
4. Start timing the process when the pressure reading on the dial gauge indicates that the recommended pressure has been reached, or when the weighted gauge begins to jiggle or rock.

5. Regulate heat under the canner to maintain a steady pressure at or slightly above the correct gauge pressure. Quick and large pressure variations during processing may cause unnecessary liquid losses from jars. Weighted gauges on Mirro canners should jiggle about two or three times per minute. On Presto canners, they should rock slowly throughout the process.
6. When the timed process is completed, turn off the heat, remove the canner from heat if possible, and let the canner depressurize. Do not force-cool the canner. Forced cooling may result in food spoilage. Cooling the canner with cold running water or opening the vent port before the canner is fully depressurized will cause loss of liquid from jars and seal failures. Force-cooling may also warp the canner lid of older model canners, causing steam leaks. Depressurization of older models should be timed. Standard-sized heavy-walled canners require about 30 minutes when loaded with pints and 45 minutes with quarts. Newer thin-wailed canners cool more rapidly and are equipped with vent locks. These canners are depressurized when their vent lock piston drops to a normal position .
7. After the canner is depressurized, remove the weight from the vent port or open the petcock. Wait two minutes, unfasten the lid, and remove it carefully. Lift the lid away from you so that the steam does not burn your face.
8. Remove jars with a lifter, and place on towel or cooling rack, if desired.

Do not retighten lids after processing jars.

Cooling Jars

Cool the jars at room temperature for 12 to 24 hours. Jars may be cooled on racks or towels to minimize heat damage to counters. The food level and liquid volume of raw-packed jars will be noticeably lower after cooling.

Air is exhausted during processing and food shrinks. If a jar loses excessive liquid during processing, do not open it to add more liquid. Check for seals, wash jars, label and store.

Reprocessing unsealed Jars

If a lid fails to seal on a jar, remove the lid and check the jar-sealing surface for tiny nicks.

If necessary, change the jar and add a new, properly prepared lid; and reprocess within 24 hours using the same processing time.

Headspace in unsealed jars may be adjusted to 1-1/2 inches, and jars could be frozen instead of reprocessed. Foods in single unsealed jars could be stored in the refrigerator and consumed within several days.

Adjust for altitude

As altitudes increase air becomes thinner, and this affects both pressures and boiling points in home canning. Using the water bath process times for canning food at sea level may result in spoilage if you live at altitudes of 1,000 feet or more.

Water boils at lower temperatures as altitude increases. Lower boiling temperatures are less effective for killing bacteria. Increasing the processing time or canner pressure compensates for lower boiling temperatures. Select the proper processing time and canner pressure for the altitude where you live.

RECIPES

Chicken or Rabbit

(duck, goose, turkey or game birds)

Procedure: Choose freshly killed and dressed, healthy animals. Large chickens are more flavorful than fryers. Dressed chicken should be chilled for 6 to 12 hours before canning. Dressed rabbits should be soaked one hour in water containing one tablespoon of salt per quart and then rinsed. Remove excess fat. Cut the chicken or rabbit into suitable sizes for canning. Can with or without bones.

Hot pack — Boil, steam or bake meat until about two-thirds done. Add one teaspoon salt per quart to the jar, if desired. Fill jars with pieces and hot broth, leaving 1-1/4 inch headspace.

Raw pack — Add one teaspoon salt per quart, if desired. Fill jars loosely with raw meat pieces, leaving 1-1/4 inch headspace. Do not add liquid.

Ground or Chopped Meat

Bear, beef, lamb, pork, sausage, veal, venison

Procedure: Choose fresh, chilled meat. With venison, add one part high-quality pork fat to three or four parts venison before grinding. Use freshly made sausage, seasoned with salt and cayenne pepper (sage may cause a bitter off-flavor). Shape chopped meat into patties or balls or cut cased sausage into 3- to 4-inch links.

Cook until lightly browned. Ground meat may be sauteed without shaping. Remove excess fat. Fill jars with pieces. Add boiling meat broth, tomato juice, or water, leaving 1-inch headspace. Add one teaspoon of salt per quart to the jars, if desired. Adjust lids and process according to Table 1 or 2.

Meat Stock (Broth)

Beef: Saw or crack fresh trimmed beef bones to enhance extraction of flavor. Rinse bones and place in a large stockpot or kettle, cover bones with water, add pot cover, and simmer three to four hours. Remove bones, cool broth, and pick off meat. Skim off fat, add meat removed from bones to broth, and reheat to boiling. Fill jars, leaving 1-inch headspace. Adjust lids and process according to Table 1 or 2.

Chicken or turkey: Place large carcass bones in a large stockpot, add enough water to cover bones, cover pot and simmer 30 to 45 minutes or until meat can be easily stripped from bones.

Remove bones, cool broth, strip meat from bones, remove and discard excess fat, and return meat to broth. Reheat to boiling and fill jars, leaving 1-inch headspace. Adjust lids and process according to Table 1 or 2.

Strips, Cubes Or Chunks Of Meat

Bear, beef, lamb, pork, veal, venison

Procedure: Choose quality chilled meat. Remove excess fat. Soak strong-flavored wild meats for one hour in brine water containing one tablespoon of salt per quart. Rinse. Remove large bones.

Hot pack — Precook meat until rare by roasting, stewing or browning in a small amount of fat. Add one teaspoon of salt per quart to the jar, if desired. Fill jars with pieces and add boiling broth, meat drippings, water or tomato juice (especially with wild game), leaving 1-inch headspace.

Raw pack — Add one teaspoon of salt per quart to the jar, if desired. Fill jars with raw meat pieces, leaving 1-inch headspace. Do not add liquid.

Adjust lids and process according to Table 1 or 2.

Chili Con Carne

3 cups dried pinto or red kidney beans

5-1/2 cups water

5 teaspoons salt (separated)

3 pounds ground beef

1-1/2 cups chopped onions

1 cup chopped peppers of your choice (optional)

1 teaspoon black pepper

3 to 6 tablespoons chili powder

2 quarts crushed or whole tomotoes

Yield: 9 pints

Procedure: Wash beans thoroughly and place them in a 2-quart saucepan. Add cold water to level of 2 to 3 inches above the beans and soak 12 to 18 hours. Drain and discard water. Combine beans with 5-1/2 cups of fresh water and 2 teaspoons salt. Bring to a boil. Reduce heat and simmer 30 minutes. Drain and discard water. Adjust lids and process according to tables 1 or 2.

Soups

Vegetable

Dried bean or pea

Meat

Poultry

Seafoods

Procedure: Select, wash and prepare vegetables, meat and seafoods as described for the specific foods. Cover meat with water and cook until tender. Cool meat and remove bones. Cook vegetables.

For each cup of dried beans or peas, add 3 cups of water, boil 2 minutes, remove from heat, soak 1 hour, and heat to boil. Drain and add meat broth, tomatoes, or water till covered. Boil 5 minutes.

Caution: Do not thicken.

Salt to taste, if desired. Fill jars halfway with solid mixture. Add remaining liquid, leaving 1-inch headspace. Adjust lids and process according to Table 1 or 2.

Fish

Blue, mackerel, salmon, steelhead, trout, and other fatty fish except tuna

Caution: Eviscerate fish within two hours after they are caught. Keep cleaned fish on ice until ready to can.

Note: Glass-like crystals of magnesium ammonium phosphate sometimes form in canned salmon.

There is no way for the home canner to prevent these crystals from forming, but they usually dissolve when heated and are safe to eat.

Procedure: Remove head, tail, fins and scales. Wash and remove all blood. Split fish lengthwise, if desired. Cut cleaned fish into 3-1/2 inch lengths.

Fill pint jars, skin side next to glass, leaving 1-inch headspace. Add one teaspoon of salt per pint, if desired. Do not add liquid. Adjust lids and process according to Table 1 or 2.

Table 1. Recommended process times in a dial-gauge pressure canner.

	Style of Pack	Jar Size	Process Time	Canner Pressure (PSI) at Altitudes of 0-2,000 ft.	2,001-4,000 ft.	4,001-6,000 ft.
Chicken Without bones:						
or	Hot	Pints	75 min	11 lb	12 lb	13 lb
Rabbit	and Raw	Quarts	90 min	11 lb	12 lb	13 lb
	With bones:					
	Hot	Pints	65 min	11 lb	12 lb	13 lb
	and Raw	Quarts	75 min	11 lb	12 lb	13 lb
Ground or	Hot	Pints	75 min	11 lb	12 lb	13 lb
Chopped Meat		Quarts	90 min	11 lb	12 lb	13 lb
Strips,	Hot	Pints	75 min	11 lb	12 lb	13 lb
Cubes or	and					
Chunks	Raw	Quarts	90 min	11 lb	12 lb	13 lb
Meat	Hot	Pints	20 min	11 lb	12 lb	13 lb
Stock, (Broth)		Quarts	25 min	11 lb	12 lb	13 lb
Soups*	Hot	Pints	60 min	11 lb	12 lb	13 lb
		Quarts	75 min	11 lb	12 lb	13 lb
Fish	Raw	Pints	100 min	11 lb	12 lb	13 lb
Chili Con Carne	Hot	Pints	75 min	11 lb	12 lb	13 lb

*Caution: Process 100 minutes if soup contains seafood.

Table 2. Recommended process times in a weighted-gauge pressure canner.

				Canner Pressure (PSI) at Altitudes of	
	Style of Pack	Jar Size	Process Time	0-1,000 ft.	Above 1,000 ft.
Chicken Without bones:					
or	Hot and	Pints	75 min	10 lb	15 lb
Rabbit	Raw	Quarts	90 min	10 lb	15 lb
	With bones:				
	Hot and	Pints	65 min	10 lb	15 lb
	Raw	Quarts	75 min	10 lb	15 lb
Ground or	Hot	Pints	75 min	10 lb	15 lb
Chopped					
Meat		Quarts	90 min	10 lb	15 lb
Strips, Hot	Pints	75 min	10 lb	15 lb	
Cubes or and					
Chunks	Raw	Quarts	90 min	10 lb	15 lb
Meat	Hot	Pints	20 min	10 lb	15 lb
Stock,					
(Broth)		Quarts	25 min	10 lb	15 lb
Soups*	Hot	Pints	60 min	10 lb	15 lb
		Quarts	75 min	10 lb	15 lb
Fish	Raw	Pints	100 min	10 lb	15 lb
Chili Con Carne	Hot	Pints	75 min	10 lb	15 lb

*Caution: Process 100 minutes if soup contains seafood.

7

Making Pickled Products

Pickling is one of the oldest known methods of food preservation. It remains popular today and pickled foods add a special touch to many snacks and meals.

The many varieties of pickled and fermented foods are classified by ingredients and method of preparation. The four general classes are: brined or fermented, fresh-pack or quick-process, fruit and relishes.

Caution: The level of acidity in a pickled product is as important to its safety as it is to taste and texture.

- Do not alter vinegar, food, or water proportions in a recipe or use a vinegar with unknown acidity.
- Use only recipes with tested proportions of ingredients.
- There must be a minimum, uniform level of acid throughout the mixed product to prevent the growth of botulinum bacteria.

INGREDIENTS

Produce

Select fresh, firm fruits or vegetables which are free of spoilage. Use a pickling variety of cucumber because the table or slicing varieties may give a poor quality of pickle.

Plan to pickle fruits or vegetables within 24 hours after the harvest for highest quality. If produce cannot be used immediately, refrigerate it and use as soon as possible.

A bushel of cucumbers weighs 48 pounds and yields 16 to 24 quarts — an average of 2 pounds per quart. Choose the appropriate size. Use cucumbers about 1-1/2 inches long for gherkins and 4 inches for dills. Odd shaped and more mature cucumbers can be used for relishes and bread-and-butter style pickles. Measure or weigh produce carefully. Weighing gives the most accurate measures.

Salt

Use a canning or pickling salt. Noncaking material added to other salts may make the brine cloudy. Do not reduce salt in fermented pickles, because proper fermentation depends on the correct proportions of salt and other ingredients.

Some fresh-pack pickles can be safely prepared with reduced or no salt. Use only tested recipes formulated to produce the proper acidity. Both the texture and flavor of these pickles may be noticeably different than expected. The quick pickle recipes in this circular may be made with reduced sodium salts, such as light or lite salts. Use of salt substitutes is not recommended.

Vinegar

White distilled or cider vinegars of 5 percent acidity (50 grain) are recommended. White vinegar is usually preferred when light color is desirable, as for fruits and cauliflower.

Do not dilute vinegar unless the recipe so specifies. If a less sour pickle is preferred, add sugar rather than decrease vinegar.

Sugar

White granulated and brown sugars are most often used. Brown sugar gives a darker color and distinct flavor. Corn syrup and honey may alter the flavor.

Water

A soft water is recommended for pickle making. Very hard water may have an undesirable effect on the color and flavor of pickled products. However, some hard water might produce a firmer pickle.

Hard water may be softened somewhat by the following method. Boil water for five minutes. Skim off the scum and let the water set for 24 hours. Then ladle off the water without disturbing the sediment in the bottom. Another option is to dilute hard water with soft water. To dilute, mix one part hard water with two parts soft water.

Spices

Use fresh, whole spices for the best flavor in pickles. Powdered spices may cause the product to darken or become cloudy. It is best to tie whole spices loosely in a cheesecloth bag, put the bag in the pickling liquid, then remove the bag before canning. If desired, add individual spices such as a cinnamon stick from the bag to each jar. Spices deteriorate and quickly lose their pungency in heat and humidity. Store opened spices in an airtight container in a cool dark place.

Firming Agents

Alum may be safely used to firm fermented pickles. However, it is unnecessary and is not included in the recipes in this publication. Alum does not improve the firmness of quick-processed pickles. The calcium in lime definitely improves pickle firmness. Food-grade lime may be used as a lime-water solution for soaking fresh cucumbers before pickling them. Excess lime absorbed by the cucumbers must be removed to make safe pickles. To further improve pickle firmness, you may process cucumber pickles for 30 minutes in water at 180 degrees Fahrenheit. This process also prevents spoilage, but the water temperature should not fall below 180 °F. Use a candy or jelly thermometer to check the water temperature.

EQUIPMENT

For Pickling Liquids

For heating pickling liquids use unchipped enamelware, stainless steel, aluminum, or glass pots. DO NOT use copper, brass, iron or galvanized utensils. These metals may react with acids or salts and cause undesirable color and flavors, or even form toxic compounds in the pickle mixture.

For Brining or Fermenting

A 1-gallon container holds 5 pounds of fresh cucumbers, and a 5-gallon container holds 25 pounds. Glass and food-grade plastic containers are excellent substitutes for stone crocks. Other 1- to 3-gallon food grade containers may be used if lined inside with a clean food grade plastic bag. **Do not use garbage bags or trash liners.** A large sealed food-grade plastic bag containing 4-1/2 tablespoons of salt and 3 quarts of water may be used as a weight to hold cucumbers under the surface of brine. A plate and jars of water may also be used. Select a pie or dinner plate just small enough to fit inside the fermentation container. Cover the weight and container top with a heavy clean bath towel to reduce mold growth on the brine surface.

PREPARATION

Wash fruits and vegetables and sort according to size when they are used whole. Cut 1/16 inch off the blossom end of cucumbers.

If especially firm pickles are preferred, mix 1 cup pickling lime and 1/2 cup salt to 1 gallon of water in a 2- to 3-gallon crock or enamelware container. Do not use aluminum. Avoid inhaling lime-water solution while mixing. Soak cucumbers in lime water for 12 to 24 hours. Remove cucumbers from lime solution, rinse, and resoak 1 hour in fresh cold water. Repeat the rinsing and soaking steps in fresh water two more times. Handle carefully, as slices will be brittle. Drain well.

CANNING PROCEDURE

Wash jars. Prepare lids according to manufacturer's instructions. Fill jars uniformly with product. Avoid packing so tight that the brine or syrup cannot surround and cover the food. Remove the air bubbles by running a rubber scraper or nonmetal spatula between the food and the jar. Wipe sealing edge of jars with a clean, damp paper towel. Add lids and tighten screw bands. Process jars in a boiling water canner or use the low temperature pasteurization treatment.

To process in a boiling water canner, fill canner halfway with water and preheat to 180 F for hot packs or 140 F for raw packs. Load sealed jars into the canner rack and lower with handles or load one jar at a time with a jar lifter onto rack in canner. Cover canner and turn heat to high. Add water if needed to a level of

1 inch above jars. When water boils vigorously, lower heat to maintain a gentle boil and process jars for the time given in Table 1.

To process using low-temperature pasteurization treatment, place jars in a canner filled halfway with warm (120 F to 140 F) water. Add hot water to a level 1 inch above jars. Heat the water and maintain 180 F water temperature for 30 minutes. Use a candy or jelly thermometer to be certain that the water temperature is at least 180 F during the entire 30 minutes. Temperatures higher than 185 F may cause unnecessary softening of pickles. This treatment results in a better product texture but must be carefully managed to avoid possible spoilage. **Caution: Use only when recipe indicates.**

After processing is completed, remove jars from canner with a jar lifter and place on a towel or rack. Do not retighten screw bands. Cool jars 12 to 24 hours and remove screw bands. Check lid seals. If the center of the lid is indented, the jar is sealed. Wash, dry, label and store sealed jars in a clean, cool, dark place. If the lid is unsealed, examine and replace jar if defective, use new lid, and reprocess as before. Wash screw bands and store separately. Pickles are best if used within a year but are safe as long as lids remain vacuum sealed.

RECIPES

Quick Fresh Pack Dill Pickles

8 pounds of 3- to 5-inch pickling cucumbers
2 gallons water
1-1/4 cups canning or pickling salt
1-1/2 quarts vinegar (5%)
1/4 cup sugar
2 quarts water
2 tablespoons whole mixed pickling spice
about 3 tablespoons whole mustard seed (tsp per pint jar)
about 14 heads of fresh dill (1-1/2 heads per pint jar)
or 4-1/2 tablespoons dill seed (1-1/2 tsp per pint jar)
Yield: 7 to 9 pints

Procedure: Wash cucumbers. Leave 1/4 inch of cucumber stem ends attached but cut 1/16 inch slice off blossom end. Dissolve 3/4 cup salt in 2 gallons of water. Pour brine water over cucumbers and let stand 12 hours. Drain. Combine vinegar, 1/2 cup salt, sugar and 2 quarts water. Add mixed pickling spices tied in a clean white cloth. Heat to boiling. Fill jars with pickles. Add 2 teaspoons mustard seed and 3 heads fresh dill per quart. Cover with boiling liquid, leaving 1/2 inch headspace. Adjust lids and process jars as described in Table 1 or use the low-temperature pasteurization treatment described under "Canning Procedure."

Pickled Horseradish Sauce

2 cups (3/4 lb) freshly grated horseradish

1 cup white vinegar (5%)

1/2 tsp canning or pickling salt

1/4 tsp powdered ascorbic acid

Yield: About 2 half-pints

Procedure: The pungency of fresh horseradish fades within 1 to 2 months, even when refrigerated. Therefore, make only small quantities at a time. Wash horseradish roots thoroughly and peel off brown outer skin. The peeled roots may be grated in a food processor or cut into small cubes and put through a food grinder. Combine ingredients and fill into sterile jars, leaving 1/4 inch headspace. Seal jars tightly and store in a refrigerator.

Fermented Dill Pickles

Use the following quantities for each gallon capacity of your container.

4 pounds of 4-inch pickling cucumbers

2 tablespoons dill seed or 4 to 5 heads fresh or dry dill

1/2 cup salt

1/4 cup vinegar (5%)

8 cups water and one or more of the following ingredients:

2 cloves garlic (optional)

2 dried red peppers (optional)

2 teaspoons whole mixed pickling spices (optional)

Procedure: Wash cucumbers. Cut 1/16 inch slice off blossom end and discard. Leave 1/4 inch of stem attached. Place half of dill and spices on bottom of a clean, suitable container (see Equipment). Add cucumbers, remaining dill and spices. Dissolve salt in vinegar and water and pour over cucumbers. Add suitable cover and weight. Store where temperature is between 70 F and 75 F for about 3 to 4 weeks while fermenting. Temperatures of 55 to 65 F are acceptable, but the fermentation will take 5 to 6 weeks. Avoid temperatures above 80 F or pickles will become too soft during fermentation. Fermenting pickles cure slowly. Check the container several times a week and promptly remove surface scum or mold. **Caution: If the pickles become soft, slimy, or develop a disagreeable odor, discard them.** Fully fermented pickles may be stored in the original container for about 4 to 6 months, provided they are refrigerated and surface scum and molds are removed regularly. Canning fully fermented pickles is a better way to store them. To can them, pour the brine into a pan, heat slowly to a boil and simmer 5 minutes. Filter brine through paper coffee filters to reduce cloudiness, if desired. Fill jar with pickles and hot brine, leaving 1/2 inch headspace. Adjust lids with process as directed in Table 1, or use the low-temperature pasteurization treatment described under "Canning Procedure."

Reduced Sodium Sliced Dill Pickles

4 pounds pickling (3- to 5-inch) cucumbers

6 cups vinegar (5%)

6 cups sugar

2 tablespoons canning or pickling salt

1-1/2 teaspoons celery seed

1-1/2 teaspoons mustard seed

2 large onions, thinly sliced

8 heads fresh dill

Yield: About 8 pints

Procedure: Wash cucumbers. Cut 1/16 inch slice off blossom end and discard. Cut cucumbers in 1/4 inch slices. Combine vinegar, sugar, salt, celery and mustard seeds in large saucepan. Bring mixture to boiling. Place 2 slices of onion and 1/2 dill head on bottom of each pint jar. Fill jars with cucumber slices, leaving 1/2 inch headspace. Add 1 slice of onion and 1/2 dill head on top. Pour hot pickling solution over cucumbers, leaving 1/4 inch headspace. Adjust lids and process according to Table 1.

Quick Sweet Pickles

May be canned as either strips or slices

8 pounds of 3- to 4-inch pickling cucumbers

1/3 cup canning or pickling salt

4-1/2 cups sugar

3-1/2 cups vinegar (5%)

2 teaspoons celery seed

1 tablespoon whole allspice

2 tablespoons mustard seed

1 cup pickling lime (optional - for use in variation below for making firmer pickles)

Yield: About 7 to 9 pints

Procedure: Wash cucumbers. Cut 1/16 inch off blossom end and discard, but leave 1/4 inch of stem attached. Slice or cut in strips, if desired. Place in bowl and sprinkle with 1/3 cup salt. Cover with 2 inches of crushed or cubed ice. Refrigerate 3 to 4 hours. Add more ice as needed. Drain well.

Combine sugar, vinegar, celery seed, allspice, and mustard seed in 6-quart kettle. Heat to boiling.

Hot pack — Add cucumbers and heat slowly until vinegar solution returns to boil. Stir occasionally to make sure mixture heats evenly. Fill sterile jars, leaving 1/2 inch headspace.

Raw pack — Fill jars, leaving 1/2 inch headspace. Add hot pickling syrup, leaving 1/2 inch headspace.

Adjust lids and process according to Table 1, or use the low-temperature pasteurization treatment described under "Canning Procedure."

Variation for firmer pickles: Wash cucumbers. Cut 1/16 inch off blossom end and discard, but leave 1/4 inch of stem attached. Slice or strip cucumbers. Mix 1 cup pickling lime and 1/2 cup salt to 1 gallon water in a 2-to 3-gallon crock or enamel-ware container. **Caution: Avoid inhaling lime dust while mixing the lime-water solution.** Soak cucumber slices or strips in lime water solution for 12 to 24 hours, stirring occasionally. Remove from lime solution and rinse and resoak 1 hour in fresh cold water. Repeat the rinsing and resoaking two more times. Handle carefully because slices or strips will be brittle. Drain well.

Storage: After processing and cooling, jars should be stored 4 to 5 weeks to develop ideal flavor.

Variation: Add 2 slices of raw whole onion to each jar before filling with cucumbers.

Sweet Gherkin Pickles

7 pounds cucumbers (1-1/2 inch or less)

1/2 cup canning or pickling salt

8 cups sugar

6 cups vinegar (5%)

3/4 teaspoon turmeric

2 teaspoons celery seeds

2 teaspoons whole mixed pickling spice

2 cinnamon sticks

1/2 teaspoon fennel (optional)

2 teaspoons vanilla (optional)

Yield: 6 to 7 pints

Procedure: Wash cucumbers. Cut 1/16 inch slice off blossom end and discard, but leave 1/4 inch of stem attached. Place cucumbers in large container and cover with boiling water. Six to 8 hours later, and on the second day, drain and cover with 6 quarts of fresh boiling water containing 1/4 cup salt. On the third day, drain and prick cucumbers with a table fork. Combine and bring to boil 3 cups vinegar, 3 cups sugar, turmeric, and spices. Pour over cucumbers. Six to 8 hours later, drain and save the pickling syrup. Add another 2 cups each of sugar and vinegar and reheat to boil. Pour over pickles. On the fourth day, drain and save syrup. Add another 2 cups sugar and 1 cup vinegar. Heat to boiling and pour over pickles. Drain and save pickling syrup 6 to 8 hours later. Add 1 cup sugar and 2 teaspoons vanilla and heat to boiling. Fill sterile pint jars with pickles and cover with hot syrup, leaving 1/2 inch headspace. Adjust lids and process according to Table 1, or use the low-temperature pasteurization treatment described under "Canning Procedure."

Reduced-Sodium Sliced Sweet Pickles

4 pounds (3- to 4-inch) pickling cucumbers

Brining solution:

1 quart distilled white vinegar (5%)

1 tablespoon canning or pickling salt

1 tablespoon mustard seed

1/2 cup sugar

Canning syrup:

1-2/3 cups distilled white vinegar (5%)

3 cups sugar

1 tablespoon whole allspice

2-1/4 teaspoons celery seed

Yield: About 4 to 5 pints

Procedure: Wash cucumbers and cut 1/16 inch off blossom end and discard. Cut cucumbers into 1/4 inch slices. Combine all ingredients for canning syrup in a saucepan and bring to boiling. Keep syrup hot until used. In a large kettle, mix the ingredients for the brining solution. Add the cut cucumbers, cover, and simmer until the cucumbers change color from bright to dull green (about 5 to 7 minutes). Drain the cucumber slices. Fill jars, and cover with hot canning syrup leaving 1/2 inch headspace. Adjust lids and process according to Table 1.

Bread and Butter Pickles

6 pounds of 4- to 5-inch pickling cucumbers

8 cups thinly sliced onions (about 3 pounds)

1/2 cup canning or pickling salt

4 cups vinegar (5%)

4-1/2 cups sugar

2 tablespoons mustard seed

1-1/2 tablespoons celery seed

1 tablespoon ground turmeric

1 cup pickling lime (optional - for use in variation below for making firmer pickles)

Yield: About 8 pints

Procedure: Wash cucumbers. Cut 1/16 inch off blossom end and discard. Cut into 3/16 inch slices. Combine cucumbers and onions in a large bowl. Add salt. Cover with 2 inches crushed or cubed ice. Refrigerate 3 to 4 hours, adding more ice as needed.

Combine remaining ingredients in a large pot. Boil 10 minutes. Drain and add cucumbers and onions and slowly reheat to boiling. Fill pint jars with slices and cooking syrup, leaving 1/2 inch headspace. Adjust lids and process according to Table 1 or use low-temperature pasteurization treatment described under "Canning Procedure."

Variation for firmer pickles: Wash cucumbers. Cut 1/16 inch off blossom end and discard. Cut into 3/16 inch slices. Mix 1 cup pickling lime and 1/2 cup salt to 1 gallon water in a 2- to 3-gallon crock or enamelware container. Avoid inhaling lime dust while mixing the lime-water solution. Soak cucumber slices in lime water for 12 to 24 hours, stirring occasionally. Remove from lime solution, rinse, and resoak 1 hour in fresh cold water. Repeat the rinsing and soaking steps two more times. Handle carefully, as slices will be brittle. Drain well. Continue as above.

Storage: After processing and cooling, jars should be stored four to five weeks to develop ideal flavor.

Pickle Relish

3 quarts chopped cucumbers

3 cups each of chopped sweet green and red peppers

1 cup chopped onions

3/4 cup canning or pickling salt

4 cups ice

8 cups water

2 cups sugar

4 teaspoons each of mustard seed, turmeric, whose allspice and whole cloves

6 cups white vinegar (5%)

Yield: About 9 pints

Procedure: Add cucumbers, peppers, onions, salt and ice to water and let stand 4 hours. Drain and re-cover vegetables with fresh ice water for another hour. Drain again. Combine spices in a spice or cheesecloth bag. Add spices to sugar and vinegar. Heat to boiling and pour mixture over vegetables. Cover and refrigerate 24 hours. Heat mixture to boiling and fill hot into clean jars, leaving 1/2 inch headspace. Adjust lids and process according to Table 1.

Pickled Corn Relish

10 cups fresh whole kernel corn (16 to 20 medium size ears), or six 10-ounce packages of frozen corn

2-1/2 cups diced sweet red peppers

2-1/2 cups diced sweet green peppers

2-1/2 cups chopped celery

1-1/4 cups diced onions

1-3/4 cups sugar

5 cups vinegar (5%)

2-1/2 tablespoons canning or pickling salt

2-1/2 teaspoons celery seed

2-1/2 tablespoons dry mustard

1-1/4 teaspoons turmeric

Yield: About 9 pints

Procedure: Boil ears of corn 5 minutes. Dip in cold water. Cut whole kernels from cob or use six 10-ounce frozen packages of corn. Combine peppers, celery, onions, sugar, vinegar, salt and celery seed in a saucepan. Bring to boil and simmer 5 minutes, stirring occasionally. Mix mustard and turmeric in 1/2 cup of the simmered mixture. Add this mixture and corn to the hot mixture. Simmer another 5 minutes. If desired, thicken mixture with flour paste (1/4 cup flour blended in 1/4 cup water) and stir frequently.

Fill jars with hot mixture, leaving 1/2 inch headspace. Adjust lids and process according to Table 1.

Pickled Pepper-Onion Relish

6 cups finely chopped onions

3 cups finely chopped sweet red peppers

3 cups finely chopped green peppers

1-1/2 cups sugar

6 cups vinegar (5%), preferably white distilled

2 tablespoons canning or pickling salt

Yield: 9 half-pints

Procedure: Wash and chop vegetables. Combine all ingredients and boil gently until mixture thickens and volume is reduced by one-half (about 30 minutes). Fill sterile jars with hot relish, leaving 1/2 inch headspace, and seal tightly. Store in refrigerator and use within one month.

Caution: If extended storage is desired, this product must be processed according to Table 1.

Pickled Hot Peppers

Hungarian, banana, chile, jalapeno

4 pounds hot long red, green or yellow peppers

3 pounds sweet red and green peppers, mixed

5 cups vinegar (5%)

1 cup water

4 teaspoons canning or pickling salt

2 tablespoons sugar

2 cloves garlic

Yield: About 9 pints

Caution: Wear rubber gloves when handling hot peppers or wash hands thoroughly with soap and water before touching your face.

Procedure: Small peppers may be left whole. Large peppers may be quartered. Wash, slash two to four slits in each pepper, and blanch in boiling water or blister in order to peel tough-skinned hot peppers.

Peppers may be blistered using one of the following methods: **Oven or broiler method:** Place peppers in a hot oven (400 F) or broiler for 6 to 8 minutes or until skins blister. **Range-top method:** Cover hot burner, either gas or electric, with heavy wire mesh. Place peppers on burner for several minutes until skins blister.

Place peppers in pan and cover with a damp cloth. This will make peeling the peppers easier. After several minutes of cooling, peel each pepper.

Flatten small peppers. Fill jars, leaving 1/2 inch headspace. Combine and heat other ingredients to boiling and simmer 10 minutes. Remove garlic. Add hot pickling solution over peppers, leaving 1/2 inch headspace. Adjust lids and process according to Table 1.

Pickled Mixed Vegetables

4 pounds of 4- to 5-inch pickling cucumbers, washed, and cut into 1- inch slices (cut off 1/16 inch from blossom end and discard)

2 pounds peeled and quartered small onions

4 cups cut celery (1-inch pieces)

2 cups peeled and cut carrots (1/2 inch pieces)

2 cups cut sweet red peppers (1/2 inch pieces)

2 cups cauliflower flowerets

5 cups white vinegar (5%)

1/4 cup prepared mustard

1/2 cup canning or pickling salt

3-1/2 cups sugar

3 tablespoons celery seed

2 tablespoons mustard seed

1/2 teaspoon whole cloves

1/2 teaspoon ground turmeric

Yield: About 10 pints

Procedure: Combine vegetables, cover with 2 inches of cubed or crushed ice, and refrigerate 3 to 4 hours. In 8-quart kettle, combine vinegar and mustard and mix well. Add salt, sugar, celery seed, mustard seed, cloves, turmeric. Bring to a boil. Drain vegetables and add to hot pickling solution. Cover and slowly bring to boil. Drain vegetables but save pickling solution. Fill vegetables in sterile pint jars, or clean quarts, leaving 1/2 inch headspace. Add pickling solution, leaving 1/2 inch headspace. Adjust lids and process according to Table 1.

Pickled Dilled Beans

4 pounds fresh tender green or yellow beans (5 to 6 inches long)

8 to 16 heads fresh dill

8 cloves garlic (optional)

1/2 cup canning or pickling salt

4 cups white vinegar (5%)

4 cups water

1 teaspoon hot red pepper flakes (optional)

Yield: About 8 pints

Procedure: Wash and trim ends from beans and cut to 4-inch lengths. In each sterile pint jar, place 1 to 2 dill heads and, if desired, 1 clove of garlic. Place whole beans upright in jars, leaving 1/2 inch headspace. Trim beans to ensure proper fit, if necessary. Combine salt, vinegar, water, and pepper flakes (if desired). Bring to a boil. Add hot solution to beans, leaving 1/2 headspace. Adjust lids and process according to Table 1.

Pickled Beets

7 pounds of 2- to 2-1/2 inch diameter beets

4 cups vinegar (5%)

1-1/2 teaspoons canning or pickling salt

2 cups sugar

2 cups water

2 cinnamon sticks

12 whole cloves

4 to 6 onions (2- to 2-1/2 inch diameter), if desired

Yield: About 8 pints

Procedure: Trim off beet tops, leaving 1 inch of stem and roots to prevent bleeding of color. Wash thoroughly. Sort for size. Cover similar sizes together with boiling water and cook until tender (about 25 to 30 minutes). **Caution: Drain and discard liquid.** Cool beets. Trim off roots and stems and slip off skins. Slice into 1/4 inch slices. Peel and thinly slice onions. Combine vinegar, salt, sugar, and fresh water. Put spices in cheesecloth bag and add to vinegar mixture. Bring to a boil. Add beets and onions. Simmer 5 minutes. Remove spice bag. Fill jars with beets and onions, leaving 1/2-inch headspace. Add hot vinegar solution, allowing 1/2-inch headspace. Adjust lids and process according to Table 1.

Variation: Pickled whole baby beets. Follow above directions but use beets that are 1- to 1-1/2 inches in diameter. Pack whole; do not slice. Onions may be omitted.

Pickled Three Bean Salad

1-1/2 cups cut and blanched green or yellow beans (prepared as below)

1-1/2 cups canned, drained, red kidney beans

1 cup canned, drained garbanzo beans

1/2 cup peeled and thinly sliced onion (about 1 medium onion)

1/2 cup trimmed and thinly sliced celery (1-1/2 medium stalks)

1/2 cup sliced green peppers (1/2 medium pepper)

1/2 cup white vinegar (5%)

1/4 cup bottled lemon juice

3/4 cup sugar

1/4 cup oil

1/2 teaspoon canning or pickling salt

1-1/4 cups water

Yield: About 5 to 6 half-pints

Procedure: Wash and snap off ends of fresh beans. Cut or snap into 1- to 2-inch pieces. Blanch 3 minutes and cool immediately. Rinse kidney beans with tap water and drain again. Prepare and measure all other vegetables. Combine vinegar, lemon juice, sugar and water and bring to a boil. Remove from heat. Add oil and salt and mix well. Add beans, onions, celery and green pepper to solution and bring to a simmer. Marinate 12 to 14 hours in refrigerator, then heat entire mixture to a boil. Fill clean jars with solids. Add hot liquid, leaving 1/2 inch headspace. Adjust lids and process according to Table 1.

Marinated Peppers

Bell, Hungarian, banana, or jalapeno

4 lbs firm peppers*

1 cup bottled lemon juice

2 cups white vinegar (5%)

1 tbsp oregano leaves

1 cup olive or salad oil

1/2 cup chopped onions

2 cloves garlic, quartered (optional)

2 tbsp prepared horseradish (optional)

***Note:** It is possible to adjust the intensity of pickled jalapeno peppers by using all hot jalapeno peppers (hot style), or blending with sweet and mild peppers (medium or mild style).

For hot style: Use 4 lbs jalapeno peppers.

For medium style: Use 2 lbs jalapeno peppers and 2 lb sweet and mild peppers.

For mild style: Use 1 lb jalapeno peppers and 3 lbs sweet and mild peppers.

Yield: About 9 half-pints

Procedure: Select your favorite pepper. **Caution: If you select hot peppers, wear rubber or plastic gloves while handling them or wash hands thoroughly with soap and water before touching your face.** Peppers may be left whole. Large peppers may be quartered. Wash, slash two to four slits in each pepper, and blanch in boiling water or blister in order to peel tough-skinned hot peppers.

Peppers may be blistered using one of the following methods: **Oven or broiler method:** Place peppers in a hot oven (400 F) or broiler for 6-8 minutes or until skins blister.

Range-top method: Cover hot burner, either gas or electric, with heavy wire mesh. Place peppers on burner for several minutes until skins blister.

Allow peppers to cool. Place in pan and cover with a damp cloth. This will make peeling the peppers easier. After several minutes of cooling, peel each pepper.

Flatten whole peppers. Mix all remaining ingredients in a saucepan and heat to boiling. Place 1/4 garlic clove (optional) and 1/4 teaspoon salt in each half pint or 1/2 teaspoon per pint. Fill jars with peppers, add hot, well-mixed oil/pickling solution over peppers, leaving 1/2-inch headspace. Adjust lids and process according to Table 1.

Piccalilli

6 cups chopped green tomatoes

1-1/2 cups chopped sweet red peppers

1-1/2 cups chopped green peppers

2-1/4 cups chopped onions

7-1/2 cups chopped cabbage

1/2 cup canning or pickling salt

3 tbsp whole mixed pickling spice

4-1/2 cups vinegar (5%)

3 cups brown sugar

Yield: 9 half-pints

Procedure: Wash, chop, and combine vegetables with 1/2 cup salt. Cover with hot water and let stand 12 hours. Drain and press in a clean white cloth to remove all possible liquid. Tie spices loosely in a spice bag and add to combined vinegar and brown sugar, and heat to a boil in a saucepan. Add vegetables and boil gently 30 minutes or until the volume of the mixture is reduced by one-half. Remove spice bag. Fill hot sterile jars with hot mixture, leaving 1/2-inch headspace. Adjust lids and process according to Table 1.

Marinated Whole Mushrooms

7 lbs small whole mushrooms

1/2 cup bottled lemon juice

2 cups olive or salad oil

2-1/2 cups white vinegar (5%)

1 tbsp oregano leaves

1 tbsp dried basil leaves

1 tbsp canning or pickling salt

1/2 cup finely chopped onions

1/4 cup diced pimento

2 cloves garlic, cut in quarters

25 black peppercorns

Yield: About 9 half-pints

Procedure: Select very fresh unopened mushrooms with caps less than 1-1/4 inch in diameter. Wash. Cut stems, leaving 1/4 inch attached to cap. Add lemon juice and water to cover. Bring to boil. Simmer 5 minutes. Drain mushrooms. Mix olive oil, vinegar, oregano, basil, and salt in a saucepan. Stir in onions and pimento and heat to boiling. Place 1/4 garlic clove and 2-3 peppercorns in a half-pint jar. Fill jars with mushrooms and hot, well-mixed oil/vinegar solution, leaving 1/2-inch headspace. Adjust lids and process according to Table 1.

Table 1. Recommended Processing Times in a Boiling Water Canner.

			Process Time at Altitudes of	
Pickles	Style of Pack	Jar Size	0-1000 ft.	1001-6000 ft.
			— minutes —	
1. Quick fresh pack dills	Raw	Pints	10	15
		Quarts	15	20
2. Fermented dills	Raw	Pints	10	15
		Quarts	15	20

3. Reduced sodium dills	Raw	Pints	15	20
4. Quick sweet	Hot	Pints or Quarts	5	10
	Raw	Pints	10	15
		Quarts	15	20
5. Sweet gherkin	Raw	Pints	5	10
6. Reduced sodium sliced sweet	Hot	Pints	10	15
7. Bread-and-butter	Hot	Pints or Quarts	10	15
8. Pickle relish	Hot	Half-pints or Pints	10	15
9. Pepper-onion relish	Hot	Half-pints or Pints	5	10
10. Corn relish	Hot	Half-pints or Pints	15	20
11. Hot peppers	Raw	Half-pints or Pints	10	15
12. Mixed vegetables	Hot	Pints	5	10
		Quarts	10	15
13. Dilled beans	Raw	Pints	5	10
14. Three-bean salad	Hot	Half-pints or Pints	15	20
15. Pickled beets	Hot	Pints or Quarts	30 *	
16. Marinated peppers	Raw	Half-pints	15	20
		Pints	15 **	
17. Marinated mushrooms	Hot	Half-pints	20 **	
18. Piccalilli	Hot	Half-pints or Pints	5	10

* 1001-3000 ft. — 35 minutes

3001-6000 ft. — 40 minutes

** 1001-3000 ft. — 25 minutes

3001-6000 ft. — 30 minutes

ADJUST FOR ALTITUDE

As altitudes increase air becomes thinner, and this affects both pressures and boiling points in home canning. Using the water bath process times for canning food at sea level may result in spoilage if you live at altitudes of 1,000 feet or more. Water boils at lower temperatures as altitude increases. Lower boiling temperatures are less effective for killing bacteria. Increasing the processing time or canner pressure compensates for lower boiling temperatures. Select the proper processing time and canner pressure for the altitude where you live.

8

Preserving Fruit Pie Fillings

General

The following fruit fillings are excellent and safe products. Each canned quart makes one 8-inch to 9-inch pie. Fillings may be used as toppings on dessert or pastries. Clear Jel is a starch modified to produce excellent sauce consistency even after fillings are canned and baked. Other available household starches break down, causing a runny sauce consistency when used in pie fillings.

Because the variety of fruit may alter the flavor of the fruit pie, you should first make a single quart, make a pie with it, and serve. Then adjust the sugar and spices in the recipe to suit your personal preferences. The amount of lemon juice should not be altered, because it aids in controlling the safety and storage stability of the fillings.

When using frozen cherries and blueberries, select unsweetened fruit. If sugar has been added, rinse it off while fruit is frozen. Collect, measure, and use juice from thawing fruit to partially replace the water specified in the recipe and only ½ cup Clear Jel per quart, or 1½ cups for 7 quarts.

Apple Pie Filling

	Quantities of ingredients needed for	
Ingredient	1 quart	7 quarts
Fresh sliced apples (blanched)	3 1/2 cups	6 quarts
Granulated sugar	3/4 cups + 2 tbsp.	5 1/2 cups
Clear Jel	1/4 cup	1 1/2 cups

Cinnamon	1/2 tsp.	1 tbsp.
Cold water	1/2 cup	2 1/2 cups
Apple juice	3/4 cup	5 cups
Bottled lemon juice	2 tbsp.	3/4 cup
Nutmeg (optional)	1/8 tsp.	1 tsp.
Yellow food coloring (optional)	1 drop	7 drops

Quality. Use firm, crisp apples. Stayman, Golden Delicious, Rome, and other varieties of similar quality are suitable. If apples lack tartness, use an additional ½ cup of lemon juice for each 6 quarts of slices.

Procedure: Wash, peel and core apples. Prepare half-inch wide slices and place in water containing 1 teaspoon of ascorbic acid crystals or six-500 milligram vitamin C tablets in 1 gallon of water to prevent browning.

For fresh fruit, place 6 cups at a time in 1 gallon of boiling water. Boil each batch 1 minute after the water returns to a boil. Drain but keep heated fruit in a covered bowl or pot. Combine sugar, Clear Jel and cinnamon in a large kettle with water and apple juice. If desired, food coloring and nutmeg may be added. Stir and cook on medium-high heat until mixture thickens and begins to bubble. Add lemon juice and boil 1 minute, stirring constantly. Fold in drained apple slices immediately and fill jars with mixture without delay, leaving 1 inch headspace. Adjust lids and process immediately.

Blueberry Pie Filling

	Quantities of ingredients needed for	
Ingredient	1 quart	7 quarts
Fresh blueberries	3 1/2 cups	6 quarts
Granulated sugar	3/4 cup + 2 tbsp.	6 cups
Clear Jel	1/4 cup + 1 tbsp.	2 1/2 cups
Cold water	1 cup	7 cups
Bottled lemon juice	3 1/2 tsp.	1/2 cup
Blue food coloring (optional)	3 drops	20 drops
Red food coloring (optional)	1 drop	7 drops

Quality: Select sweet, very ripe but firm, deep blue fruit.

Procedure: Wash and drain fresh blueberries. For fresh fruit, place 6 cups at a time in 1 gallon of boiling water. Boil each batch 1 minute after the water returns to a boil. Drain, but keep heated fruit in a covered bowl or pot. Combine sugar and Clear Jel in a large kettle. Stir. Add water and, if desired, food coloring. Cook on medium high heat until mixture thickens and begins to bubble. Add lemon juice and boil 1 minute, stirring constantly. Fold in drained berries immediately and fill jars with mixture without delay, leaving 1 inch headspace. Adjust lids and process immediately.

Cherry Pie Filling

	Quantities of ingredients needed for	
Ingredient	1 quart	7 quarts
Fresh sour cherries	3 1/3 cups	6 quarts
Granulated sugar	1 cup	7 cups
Clear Jel	1/4 cup + 1 tbsp.	1 3/4 cups
Cold water	1 1/3 cups	9 1/3 cups
Bottled lemon juice	1 tbsp. + 1 tsp.	1/2 cup
Cinnamon (optional)	1/8 tsp.	1 tsp.
Almond extract (optional)	1/4 tsp.	2 tsp.
Red food coloring (optional)	6 drops	1/4 tsp.

Quality: Select very ripe, firm, tart cherries.

Procedure: Rinse and pit fresh cherries, and hold in cold water. To prevent stem end browning, hold pitted cherries in water containing 1 teaspoon of ascorbic acid crystals or six-500 milligram vitamin C tablets in 1 gallon of water.

For fresh fruit, place 6 cups at a time in 1 gallon of boiling water. Boil each batch 1 minute after the water returns to a boil. Drain but keep heated fruit in a covered bowl or pot. Combine sugar and Clear Jel in a large saucepan and add water. If desired, add cinnamon, almond extract and food coloring. Stir mixture and cook over medium high heat until mixture thickens and begins to bubble. Add lemon juice and boil 1 minute, stirring constantly. Fold in drained cherries immediately and fill jars with mixture without delay, leaving 1 inch headspace. Adjust lids and process immediately.

Peach pie filling

	Quantities of ingredients needed for	
Ingredient	1 quart	7 quarts
Fresh sliced peaches	3 1/2 cups	6 quarts
Granulated sugar	1 cup	7 cups
Clear Jel	1/4 cup + 1 tbsp.	2cups+3 tbsp.
Cold water	3/4 cup	5 1/4 cups
Bottled lemon juice	1/4 cup	1 3/4 cups
Cinnamon (optional)	1/8 tsp.	1 tsp.
Almond extract (optional)	1/8 tsp.	1 tsp.

Quality. Select ripe but firm peaches. Red Haven, Redskin, Sun High, and other varieties of similar quality are suitable.

Procedure. Peel peaches. To loosen skins, submerge peaches in boiling water for approximately 30 to 60 seconds and then place in cold water for 20 seconds. Slip off skins and prepare slices ½-inch thick. Place slices in water containing 1 teaspoon of ascorbic acid crystals or six 500-milligram vitamin C tablets in 1 gallon of water to prevent browning. For fresh fruit, place 6 cups at a time in 1 gallon of boiling water. Boil each batch 1 minute after the water returns to a boil. Drain but keep heated fruit in a covered bowl or pot. Combine water, sugar, Clear Jel and, if desired, cinnamon and/or almond extract in a large kettle. Stir mixture and cook over medium high heat until mixture thickens and begins to bubble. Add lemon juice and boil 1 minute, stirring constantly. Fold in drained peach slices and continue to heat mixture for 3 minutes. Fill jars without delay, leaving 1 inch headspace. Adjust lids and process immediately.

PROCEDURE FOR CANNING ALL FILLINGS

Wash jars. Prepare lids according to manufacturer's instructions. Fill fruit mixtures into jars, leaving 1 inch headspace. Wipe sealing surface of jars with a clean, damp paper towel. Add lids, tighten screw bands, and process.

To process in a boiling water canner, preheat canner half filled with water to 180 degrees Fahrenheit. Load sealed jars into the canner rack and lower with handles, or load one jar at a time with a jar lifter onto rack in canner. Add water if needed to a level of 1 inch above jars and cover. When water boils vigorously, lower heat to maintain a gentle boil and process for recommended time.

Process times

Recommended process times for fruit pie filling in a boiling water canner.

		Process time at altitude of		
Fruit filling	**Jar size**	0-1000 **feet**	1001-3000 **feet**	3001-6000 **feet**
		- - - - - - minutes - - - - - - -		
Apple	Pints	25	30	35
Blueberry or	30	35	40	
Cherry quarts	30	35	40	
Peach	30	35	40	

After processing is completed, remove jars from canner with a jar lifter and place them on a towel or rack. *Do not retighten screw bands.* Air-cool jars 12 to 24 hours. Remove screw bands and check lid seals. A jar is sealed if the center of its lid is indented or concave. Wash, dry, label, and store sealed jars in a clean, cool, dark place. If a jar is unsealed, examine and replace it if defective, use a new lid, and reprocess as before. Wash screw bands and store separately. Fillings are best if used within 1 year and safe as long as lids remain vacuum sealed.

The information given herein is for educational purposes only. Reference to commercial products or trade names is made with the understanding that no discrimination is intended and no endorsement by Cooperative Extension Service is implied.

9

Care and Handling of Fish

Fish are fun to catch and nutritious to eat. They are high in protein, rich in vitamins and minerals, and low in saturated fat. Fish oils are high in polyunsaturated fats that may function in lowering blood cholesterol.

A 3½-ounce portion of fish (before cooking) provides about half of the daily adult protein requirement and has, depending on the species of fish, only 100 to 150 calories.

Proper handling of fish from the time you catch them until you get them to the table will help maintain optimum eating quality. Keep the following fish handling tips in mind.

Care on the Water

- **Keep fish alive as long as possible. Fish flesh is very perishable.**
  - o A metal link basket or live box is best. A stringer can damage the flesh and increase chances of bacterial contamination.
  - o If the water is warm, place the fish on ice or keep them in cool water.
  - o Don't toss fish into the bottom of the boat where they will dry out or where their flesh may become bruised and susceptible to contamination.
  - o Keep fish out of sunlight and direct heat.
- **During winter fishing trips, keep fish covered to prevent them from freezing and drying out.**
  - o For optimal eating quality, fish should not be frozen by throwing them out onto the ice. Put fish in an ice

chest or styrofoam cooler to prevent freezing and dehydration. Clean them prior to freezing.

- **Check fish for signs of disease or parasites.**
  - o A healthy fish should have firm flesh with no signs of discoloration/browning, a mild fresh smell, bright clear eyes and red gills.
  - o A diseased fish may have sunken eyes or "pop-eyes," discolored skin, loose scales, open wounds or gills that are white and slimy or bloody.
  - o In some cases, the fish is edible if the diseased area is removed. Fish should be thoroughly cooked.
  - o After removing the usable flesh, do not throw the remains back in the water. Dispose of them properly.
  - o Decide on the fate of the fish immediately. If you do not want them, release them right away instead of waiting to decide at the end of the day, when they may have a reduced chance for survival.
  - o Check with your local game and fish representative if you find abnormal growths in the flesh.
- **Fish in safe waters.**
  - o Some waters may be contaminated by pesticides or other substances. For information on the safety of fishing waters, contact your local health department.
  - o Contaminants are concentrated in the fatty parts of the fish. To reduce your risk of consuming contaminants, remove the skin and fat deposits when you clean fish, or use fillets instead of whole fish. Choose a cooking method that removes additional fat, such as baking, broiling or charbroiling.

Care in Cleaning and Storage

- **Clean and cool fish as soon as possible. Time and heat can rob freshness and flavor.**
  - o Fish spoil rapidly due to their strong digestive juices. If fish are not cleaned promptly, off flavors may develop.

- o You will need a sharp knife, a clean towel or paper towels (to wipe the fish after rinsing), plastic bags and crushed ice in an ice chest.
- o Use a clean fillet knife to clean the fish. Bleed the fish. Cut the throat as you would any game animal, and remove the gills and entrails. Wipe the surface of the fish with a clean cloth or paper towel, put the fish in a plastic bag, and put on ice.
- o If making fillets, rinse the fish in clean cold water to remove blood, bacteria and enzymes.

- **Don't cross-contaminate. Clean the knife after each use.**
  - o When you clean fish at home, wash your hands, the knife and the cutting board with warm soapy water after each use.
- **Store cleaned, fresh fish in the refrigerator at 40 F or lower in a covered container and use within two days.**
  - o Fish should be kept moist but not wet.
- **Cleaned fish may be frozen whole or as fillets.**
  - o Traditionally, fish have been frozen whole, as they come from the water. This practice is **not recommended,** because deterioration may occur, and poor eating quality may result.
  - o Improperly wrapped frozen fish may become dehydrated — that is, suffer "freezer burn"— due to contact with air. This condition negatively affects taste and texture.
  - o Divide fish into family-size servings and use a plastic cling-type wrap as an inner covering and moisture/vapor-proof freezer wrap as an outer covering. Bread bags, waxed paper and cellophane wraps are poor freezer wraps.
  - o Remember to press air from the package to help prevent off-flavors or odors characteristic of rancidity.
  - o If freezer space is available, smaller fish may be placed in water in plastic containers, in clean wax- or plastic-lined milk containers, and then frozen.
  - o Label each package with the contents and date.

- o The temperature of the freezer should be 0 F or lower. When freezing large amounts of food, scatter the packages throughout the freezer so the food freezes quickly.

Care in Preparation and Preservation

- **Prepare fish properly. Cook fish until it flakes with a fork.**
  - o Don't cross-contaminate. Keep raw fish and cooked fish separate.
  - o Thaw fillets in the refrigerator, in the microwave or under cold running water. Food defrosted in the microwave should be cooked immediately. Other thawed fish should be used within one to two days.
  - o Undercooking fish can be risky, while overcooking can result in an unpalatable product.
  - o Fish is generally low in fat and very tender. Moist heat cooking methods are unnecessary. Methods that develop flavor, such as broiling, baking or frying, are preferred.
- **Fish may be safely preserved by proper smoking procedures.**
  - o After cleaning the fish, cut it into uniform pieces. Do not allow fish to stand unrefrigerated for more than two hours.
  - o Salt is a preservative. Fish **must** be salted in the proper brine solution for an appropriate length of time. Generally, soaking the fish in a strong brine (1 cup salt/7 cups water) for 1 hour is adequate.
  - o After salting, the fish **must** be heated to an internal temperature of 160 F and held at this temperature for at least 30 minutes during the smoking cycle.
  - o Store smoked fish in the refrigerator if it is to be used within two weeks.
  - o For long-term storage, smoked fish should be frozen. It also may be preserved by following current pressure canning recommendations.

CARE AND HANDLING OF DEER AND ELK

Concern has grown in recent years about a disease affecting deer and elk called Chronic Wasting Disease (CWD), which belongs to a family of diseases known as Transmissible Spongiform Encephalopathies (TSEs). CWD symptoms include weight loss, stumbling, tremors, lack of coordination, blank facial expressions, excessive salivation, loss of appetite, excessive thirst and urination, listlessness, teeth grinding, abnormal head posture, and drooping ears.

Hunters should be vigilant about identifying deer or elk displaying CWD symptoms and report suspected cases to wildlife officials immediately. Many states have specific CWD guidelines for hunters. Hunters need to know not only the CWD regulations of the states in which they hunt, but also those of the states in which they may pass through during interstate hunting trips.

To date, there is no evidence that CWD has been transmitted or can be transmitted to humans under natural conditions. However, neither is there strong evidence that such transmissions **could not** occur. Research thus far indicates that the abnormal proteins responsible for causing CWD accumulate only in the brain, eyes, spinal cord, lymph nodes, tonsils, pancreas, and spleen—but not in muscle tissue.

Therefore, hunters should take a few simple precautions when handling and transporting deer or elk carcasses:

- Do not shoot, handle or consume any wild animal that appears sick.
- Wear rubber gloves when field dressing and processing animals.
- Request commercial processors handle animals individually so meat from other animals won't become commingled.
- Minimize handling brain or spinal tissues and fluids.
- Bone out carcasses or at least avoid consuming brain, spinal cord, eyes, spleen and lymph nodes of harvested animals.
- Do not consume the meat from any animal that tests positive for CWD.

A 3½-ounce portion (before cooking) of game meat provides about half of the daily adult protein requirement and 130 to 150 calories. Game meats are usually slightly lower in total fat but higher in polyunsaturated fats than grain-fed beef.

Care in the Field

Be prepared for the hunt.

- Remember to bring a sharp hunting knife, a small hatchet, a whetstone or steel, about 12 feet of light rope or nylon cord, plastic bags and clean cloths or paper towels. Other essentials include proper clothing, binoculars, a canteen of fresh water, a compass, a map and matches.
- In warm weather you may want to bring a can of ground pepper and some cheesecloth. The carcass may be sprinkled with pepper and covered with cheesecloth to repel flies.

Abide by game regulations for hunting, transporting and storing game.

Bleed, field dress and cool the carcass promptly. Improper temperature is meat's worst enemy.

- The surface of the carcass may be contaminated with bacteria that can spoil the meat unless the growth is stopped by chilling.
- Clean your hunting knife often with clean water and a cloth to prevent contamination of the meat.
- Usually it is not necessary to bleed the animal, because the bullet or arrow has caused enough damage to the animal to bleed it sufficiently. However, if the animal is shot in the head it will need to be bled. If the animal is a trophy buck that you plan to mount, do not sever its throat, because this will cause problems during mounting.
- Cool the animal quickly. Cool the carcass by propping the chest open with a clean stick and allowing air to circulate. Filling the cavity with bags of ice will also enhance cooling.
- To aid cooling in warm weather, the deer may be skinned if you have provisions to keep the carcass clean. Use ground pepper and cheesecloth to protect the skinned carcass from contamination by flies.

- In cool weather (28° to 35° F), wrap the carcass or quarters in a sheet and hang in a ventilated shed.
- Do not allow the carcass to freeze. Freezing may toughen the meat.

Keep the carcass clean.

- Remove all foreign particles and loose hair. Remove bloodshot areas.
- Wipe out excess blood in gutted cavity with a paper towel or clean cloth and clean water. Use as little water as possible, because damp meat spoils faster than dry meat.
- Do not use grass or snow to wipe out the carcass, because this may contaminate the carcass.

Field Dressing (Wear rubber gloves during field dressing.)

1. Place the animal on its back with the front end elevated and spread the hind legs. Support carcass in position by placing rocks or sticks on each side.
2. Cut along the midline of the belly from the breastbone to the anus. Avoid cutting into the paunch and intestines by using the handle of the knife and the heel of your hand to crowd the guts away. Cut around the anus, loosening the bung so it will come out with the guts.
3. Cut the diaphragm (the thin sheet of muscle and connective tissue between the chest and the abdomen) free from the rib cage by cutting through the white tissue near the rib cage.
4. Reach forward to cut the windpipe, gullet and blood vessels at the base of the throat.
5. Pull the lungs, heart and guts out of the animal.

Care in Transport and Processing

Keep the carcass cool during transport.

- Do not tie a deer carcass across the hood of the car or put it in the trunk when it is still warm.

The game may be processed commercially or at home.

- Be sure to keep the carcass cool until it reaches the locker plant. Keep the carcass out of direct sunlight and allow for adequate air circulation.

- If you choose to process your own game, don't cross-contaminate during processing. Wash your knife, hands and cutting board often with warm, soapy water. Wear rubber gloves.
- Aging meat is the practice of holding carcasses or cuts of meat at temperatures of 34° to 37° F for 10 to 14 days to allow the enzymes in the meat to break down some of the complex proteins in the carcass. Aged meat is often more tender and flavorful.
- Aging is not recommended for carcasses with little or no fat covering. They may dry out during aging.
- Leave the hide on and maintain the proper temperature when aging a carcass. If you do not have the proper cooler space, spoilage or dehydration may result.
- Aging the carcass two to three days is sufficient.
- If you intend to grind the meat into sausage, aging is unnecessary.

Care in the Kitchen

For immediate use, store the meat in the refrigerator and use within two or three days.

- Keep raw meat and cooked meat separate to prevent cross-contamination.

Freeze game properly. Prevent "freezer burn" by using the right packaging materials.

- Divide meat into meal-size quantities.
- Use moisture/vapor-proof wrap such as heavily waxed freezer wrap, laminated freezer wrap, heavy duty aluminum foil or freezer-weight polyethylene bags.
- Press air out of the packages prior to sealing.
- Label packages with contents and date.
- Avoid overloading the freezer. Freeze only the amount that will become solidly frozen within 24 hours.
- Game will keep nine to 12 months in the freezer if properly wrapped.

Do not can meat unless you have a pressure canner.

- Low acid foods, such as meat and most mixtures of foods, should never be canned using the water-bath method.
- Pressure and adequate time are necessary to produce safe canned meat. For the latest canning information, contact your county NDSU extension office.

Thaw frozen meat in the refrigerator or microwave oven. Cook game meats thoroughly.

- Foods thawed in the microwave oven should be cooked immediately. Refrigerator-thawed meat should be used within one to two days.
- Game meats should be cooked to an internal temperature of at least 165° F to reduce risk of foodborne illness.
- Big game animals usually exercise more than domestic animals, so game meats may be drier and less tender. Moist heat methods such as braising (simmering in a small amount of liquid in a covered pot) may result in a better product. Chops and steaks may be pan fried or broiled.
- The distinctive flavor of game meats is mainly due to the fat they contain. To reduce the gamey flavor, trim the fat from the meat. You may wish to add other sources of fat to maintain the juiciness of the meat.
- Spices or marinades may be used to mask the gamey flavor. Meat should always be marinated in the refrigerator.

10

Freezing and Food Safety

Foods in the freezer — are they safe? Every year, thousands of callers to the USDA Meat and Poultry Hotline aren't sure about the safety of items stored in their own home freezers. The confusion seems to be based on the fact that few people understand how freezing protects food. Here is some information on how to freeze food safely and how long to keep it.

WHAT CAN YOU FREEZE?

You can freeze almost any food. Some exceptions are canned food or eggs in shells. However, once the food (such as a ham) is out of the can, you may freeze it. Being able to freeze food and being pleased with the quality after defrosting are two different things. Some foods simply don't freeze well. Examples are mayonnaise, cream sauce and lettuce. Raw meat and poultry maintain their quality longer than their cooked counterparts because moisture is lost during cooking.

Is Frozen Food Safe?

Food stored constantly at 0 °F will always be safe. Only the quality suffers with lengthy freezer storage. Freezing keeps food safe by slowing the movement of molecules, causing microbes to enter a dormant stage. Freezing preserves food for extended periods because it prevents the growth of microorganisms that cause both food spoilage and foodborne illness.

Does Freezing Destroy Bacteria & Parasites?

Freezing to 0 °F inactivates any microbes — bacteria, yeasts and molds - - present in food. Once thawed, however, these microbes can again become active, multiplying under the right conditions to levels that can lead to foodborne illness. Since they will then grow at about the same rate as microorganisms on fresh food, you must handle thawed items as you would any perishable food.

Trichina and other parasites can be destroyed by sub-zero freezing temperatures. However, very strict government-supervised conditions must be met. It is not recommended to rely on home freezing to destroy trichina. Thorough cooking will destroy all parasites.

Freshness & Quality

Freshness and quality at the time of freezing affect the condition of frozen foods. If frozen at peak quality, foods emerge tasting better than foods frozen near the end of their useful life. So freeze items you won't use quickly sooner rather than later. Store all foods at 0° F or lower to retain vitamin content, color, flavor and texture.

Nutrient Retention

The freezing process itself does not destroy nutrients. In meat and poultry products, there is little change in nutrient value during freezer storage.

Enzymes

Enzyme activity can lead to the deterioration of food quality. Enzymes present in animals, vegetables and fruit promote chemical reactions, such as ripening. Freezing only slows the enzyme activity that takes place in foods. It does not halt these reactions which continue after harvesting.

Enzyme activity does not harm frozen meats or fish and is neutralized by the acids in frozen fruits. But most vegetables that freeze well are low acid and require a brief, partial cooking to prevent deterioration.

This is called "blanching." For successful freezing, blanch or partially cook vegetables in boiling water or in a microwave oven. Then rapidly chill the vegetables prior to freezing and storage. Consult a cookbook for timing.

Packaging

Proper packaging helps maintain quality and prevent "freezer burn." **It is safe to freeze meat or poultry directly in its supermarket wrapping** but this type of wrap is permeable to air. Unless you will be using the food in a month or two, overwrap these packages as you would any food for long-term storage using airtight heavy-duty foil, (freezer) plastic wrap or freezer paper, or place the package inside a (freezer) plastic bag. Use these materials or airtight freezer containers to repackage family packs into smaller amounts. It is not necessary to rinse meat and poultry before freezing. Freeze unopened vacuum packages as is. If you notice that a package has accidentally been torn or has opened while food is in the freezer, the food is still safe to use; merely overwrap or rewrap it.

Freezer Burn

Freezer burn does not make food unsafe, merely dry in spots. It appears as grayish-brown leathery spots and is caused by air reaching the surface of the food. Cut freezer-burned portions away either before or after cooking the food. Heavily freezer-burned foods may have to be discarded for quality reasons.

Color Changes

Color changes can occur in frozen foods. The bright red color of meat as purchased usually turns dark or pale brown depending on its variety. This may be due to lack of oxygen, freezer burn or abnormally long storage.

Freezing doesn't usually cause color changes in poultry. However, the bones and the meat near them can become dark. Bone darkening results when pigment seeps through the porous bones of young poultry into the surrounding tissues when the poultry meat is frozen and thawed. The dulling of color in frozen vegetables and cooked foods is usually the result of excessive drying due to improper packaging or over-lengthy storage.

Freeze Rapidly

Freeze food as fast as possible to maintain its quality. Rapid freezing prevents undesirable large ice crystals from forming throughout the product because the molecules don't have time to take their positions in the characteristic six-sided snowflake. Slow freezing creates large, disruptive ice crystals. During thawing, they damage the cells and dissolve emulsions. This causes meat to "drip"--lose juiciness. Emulsions such as mayonnaise or cream will separate and appear curdled.

Ideally, a food 2-inches thick should freeze completely in about 2 hours. If your home freezer has a "quick-freeze" shelf, use it. Never stack packages to be frozen. Instead, spread them out in one layer on various shelves, stacking them only after frozen solid.

Refrigerator - Freezers

If a refrigerator freezing compartment can't maintain zero degrees or if the door is opened frequently, use it for short-term food storage. Eat those foods as soon as possible for best quality. Use a free-standing freezer set at 0° F or below for long-term storage of frozen foods. Keep a thermometer in your freezing compartment or freezer to check the temperature. This is important if you experience power-out or mechanical problems.

Length of Time

Because freezing keeps food safe almost indefinitely, recommended storage times are for quality only. Refer to the freezer storage chart at the end of this document, which lists optimum freezing times for best quality.

If a food is not listed on the chart, you may determine its quality after defrosting. First check the odor. Some foods will develop a rancid or off odor when frozen too long and should be discarded. Some may not look picture perfect or be of high enough quality to serve alone but may be edible; use them to make soups or stews. Cook raw food and if you like the taste and texture, use it.

Safe Defrosting

Never defrost foods in a garage, basement, car, dishwasher or plastic garbage bag; out on the kitchen counter, outdoors or on the porch. These methods can leave your foods unsafe to eat.

There are three safe ways to defrost food: in the refrigerator, in cold water, or in the microwave. It's best to plan ahead for slow, safe thawing in the refrigerator. Small items may defrost overnight; most foods require a day or two. And large items like turkeys may take longer, approximately one day for each 5 pounds of weight.

For faster defrosting, place food in a leak proof plastic bag and immerse it in cold water. (If the bag leaks, bacteria from the air or surrounding environment could be introduced into the food. Tissues can also absorb water like a sponge, resulting in a watery product.) Check the water frequently to be sure it stays cold. Change the water every 30 minutes. After thawing, cook immediately.

When microwave-defrosting food, plan to cook it immediately after thawing because some areas of the food may become warm and begin to cook during microwaving.

Refreezing

Once food is thawed in the refrigerator, it is safe to refreeze it without cooking, although there may be a loss of quality due to the moisture lost through defrosting. After cooking raw foods which were previously frozen, it is safe to freeze the cooked foods. If previously cooked foods are thawed in the refrigerator, you may refreeze the unused portion.

If you purchase previously frozen meat, poultry or fish at a retail store, you can refreeze if it has been handled properly.

Cooking Frozen Foods

Raw or cooked meat, poultry or casseroles can be cooked or reheated from the frozen state. However, it will take approximately one and a half times the usual cooking time for food which has been thawed. Remember to discard any wrapping or absorbent paper from meat or poultry.

When cooking whole poultry, remove the giblet pack from the cavity as soon as you can loosen it. Cook the giblets separately. Read the label on USDA-inspected frozen meat and poultry products. Some, such as pre-stuffed whole birds, **MUST** be cooked from the frozen state to ensure a safely cooked product. The inspection mark on the packaging tells you the product was prepared in a USDA or State-inspected plant under controlled conditions. Follow the package directions for thawing, reheating, and storing.

Power Outage in Freezer

If there is a power outage, the freezer fails, or if the freezer door has been left ajar by mistake, the food may still be safe to use. As long as a freezer with its door ajar is continuing to cool, the foods should stay safe overnight. If a repairman is on the way or it appears the power will be on soon, just don't open the freezer door.'

A freezer full of food will usually keep about 2 days if the door is kept shut; a half-full freezer will last about a day. The freezing compartment in a refrigerator may not keep foods frozen as long. If the freezer is not full, quickly group packages together so they will retain the cold more effectively. Separate meat and poultry items from other foods so if they begin to thaw, their juices won't drip onto other foods.

When the power is off, you may want to put dry ice, block ice, or bags of ice in the freezer or transfer foods to a friend's freezer until power is restored. Use an appliance thermometer to monitor the temperature.

When it is freezing outside and there is snow on the ground, it seems like a good place to keep food until the power comes on; however, frozen food can thaw if it is exposed to the sun's rays even when the temperature is very cold. Refrigerated food may become too warm and foodborne bacteria could grow. The outside temperature could vary hour by hour and the temperature outside will not protect refrigerated and frozen food. Additionally, perishable items could be exposed to unsanitary conditions or to animals. Animals may harbor bacteria or disease; never consume food that has come in contact with an animal.

To determine the safety of foods when the power goes on, check their condition and temperature. If food is partly frozen, still has ice crystals, or is as cold as if it were in a refrigerator (40 °F), it is safe to refreeze or use. It's not necessary to cook raw foods before refreezing. **Discard foods that have been warmer than 40 °F for more than 2 hours. Discard any foods that have been**

contaminated by raw meat juices. Dispose of soft or melted ice cream for quality's sake.

Frozen Cans

Accidentally frozen cans, such as those left in a car or basement in sub-zero temperatures, can present health problems. If the cans are merely swollen — and you are sure the swelling was caused by freezing — the cans may still be usable. Let the can thaw in the refrigerator before opening. If the product doesn't look and/ or smell normal, throw it out. DO NOT TASTE IT! If the seams have rusted or burst, throw the cans out immediately, wrapping the burst can in plastic and disposing the food where no one, including animals can get it.

Frozen Eggs

Shell eggs should not be frozen. If an egg accidentally freezes and the shell cracked during freezing, discard the egg. Keep an uncracked egg frozen until needed; then thaw in the refrigerator. It can be hard cooked successfully but other uses may be limited. That's because freezing causes the yolk to become thick and syrupy so it will not flow like an unfrozen yolk or blend very well with the egg white or other ingredients.

Freezer Storage Chart (0 °F)

Note: Freezer storage is for quality only. Frozen foods remain safe indefinitely.

Item	Months
Bacon and Sausage	1 to 2
Casseroles	2 to 3
Egg whites or egg substitutes	12
Frozen Dinners and Entrees	3 to 4
Gravy, meat or poultry	2 to 3
Ham, Hotdogs and Lunchmeats	1 to 2
Meat, uncooked roasts	4 to 12
Meat, uncooked steaks or chops	4 to 12
Meat, uncooked ground	3 to 4

Meat, cooked	2 to 3
Poultry, uncooked whole	12
Poultry, uncooked parts	9
Poultry, uncooked giblets	3 to 4
Poultry, cooked	4
Soups and Stews	2 to 3
Wild game, uncooked	8 to 12

Molds On Food: Are They Dangerous?

Some molds cause allergic reactions and respiratory problems. And a few molds, in the right conditions, produce "mycotoxins," poisonous substances that can make people sick. When you see mold on food, is it safe to cut off the moldy part and use the rest? To find the answer to that question, delve beneath the surface of food to where molds take root.

What Are Molds?

Molds are microscopic fungi that live on plant or animal matter. No one knows how many species of fungi exist, but estimates range from tens of thousands to perhaps 300,000 or more. Most are filamentous (threadlike) organisms and the production of spores is characteristic of fungi in general. These spores can be transported by air, water, or insects. Unlike bacteria that are one-celled, molds are made of many cells and can sometimes be seen with the naked eye. Under a microscope, they look like skinny mushrooms. In many molds, the body consists of:

- Root threads that invade the food it lives on,
- A stalk rising above the food, and
- Spores that form at the ends of the stalks.

The spores give mold the color you see. When airborne, the spores spread the mold from place to place like dandelion seeds blowing across a meadow.

Molds have branches and roots that are like very thin threads. The roots may be difficult to see when the mold is growing on food and may be very deep in the food. Foods that are moldy may also have invisible bacteria growing along with the mold.

Are Some Molds Dangerous?

Yes, some molds cause allergic reactions and respiratory problems. And a few molds, in the right conditions, produce "mycotoxins," poisonous substances that can make you sick.

Are Molds Only on the Surface of Food?

No, you only see part of the mold on the surface of food — gray fur on forgotten bologna, fuzzy green dots on bread, white dust on Cheddar, coin-size velvety circles on fruits, and furry growth on the surface of jellies. When a food shows heavy mold growth, "root" threads have invaded it deeply. In dangerous molds, poisonous substances are often contained in and around these threads. In some cases, toxins may have spread throughout the food.

Where Are Molds Found?

Molds are found in virtually every environment and can be detected, both indoors and outdoors, year round. Mold growth is encouraged by warm and humid conditions. Outdoors, they can be found in shady, damp areas or places where leaves or other vegetation are decomposing. Indoors, they can be found where humidity levels are high.

Molds form spores which, when dry, float through the air and find suitable conditions where they can start the growth cycle again.

What Are Some Common Foodborne Molds?

Molds most often found on meat and poultry are *Alternaria, Aspergillus, Botrytis, Cladosporium, Fusarium, Geotrichum, Monilia, Manoscus, Mortierella, Mucor, Neurospora, Oidium, Oosproa, Penicillium, Rhizopus* and *Thamnidium*. These molds can also be found on many other foods.

What Are Mycotoxins?

Mycotoxins are poisonous substances produced by certain molds found primarily in grain and nut crops, but are also known to be on celery, grape juice, apples, and other produce. There are many of them and scientists are continually discovering new ones. The Food and Agriculture Organization (FAO) of the United Nations estimates that 25% of the world's food crops are affected by mycotoxins, of which the most notorious are aflatoxins.

What is Aflatoxin?

Aflatoxin is a cancer-causing poison produced by certain fungi in or on foods and feeds, especially in field corn and peanuts. They are probably the best known and most intensively researched mycotoxins in the world. Aflatoxins have been associated with various diseases, such as aflatoxicosis in livestock, domestic animals, and humans throughout the world. Many countries try to limit exposure to aflatoxin by regulating and monitoring its presence on commodities intended for use as food and feed. The prevention of aflatoxin is one of the most challenging toxicology issues of present time.

How Does the U.S. Government Control Aflatoxins?

Aflatoxins are considered unavoidable contaminants of food and feed, even where good manufacturing practices have been followed. The U.S. Food and Drug Administration and the USDA monitor peanuts and field corn for aflatoxin and can remove any food or feed with unacceptable levels of it.

Is Mushroom Poisoning Caused by Molds?

No, it is due to the toxin produced by the fungi, which are in the same family as molds. Mushroom poisoning is caused by the consumption of raw or cooked mushrooms, which are higher-species of fungi. The term "toadstool" (from the German "Todesstuhl" — death's stool) is commonly given to poisonous mushrooms, but there is no general rule of thumb for distinguishing edible mushrooms from poisonous toadstools. The toxins that cause mushroom poisoning are produced naturally by the fungi. Most mushrooms that cause human poisoning cannot be made safe by cooking, canning, freezing, or any other processing. The only way to avoid poisoning is not to eat poisonous mushrooms.

Are Any Food Molds Beneficial?

Yes, molds are used to make certain kinds of cheeses and can be on the surface of cheese or be developed internally. Blue veined cheese such as Roquefort, blue, Gorgonzola, and Stilton are created by the introduction of *P. roqueforti* or *Penicillium roqueforti* spores. Cheeses such as Brie and Camembert have white surface molds. Other cheeses have both an internal and a surface mold. The molds used to manufacture these cheeses are safe to eat.

Why Can Mold Grow in the Refrigerator?

While most molds prefer warmer temperatures, they can grow at refrigerator temperatures, too. Molds also tolerate salt and sugar better than most other food invaders. Therefore, molds can grow in refrigerated jams and jelly and on cured, salty meats — ham, bacon, salami, and bologna.

How Can You Minimize Mold Growth?

Cleanliness is vital in controlling mold. Mold spores from affected food can build up in your refrigerator, dishcloths, and other cleaning utensils.

- Clean the inside of the refrigerator every few months with 1 tablespoon of baking soda dissolved in a quart of water. Rinse with clear water and dry. Scrub visible mold (usually black) on rubber casings using 3 teaspoons of bleach in a quart of water.
- Keep dishcloths, towels, sponges, and mops clean and fresh. A musty smell means they're spreading mold around. Discard items you can't clean or launder.
- Keep the humidity level in the house below 40%.

Don't Buy Moldy Foods

Examine food well before you buy it. Check food in glass jars, look at the stem areas on fresh produce, and avoid bruised produce. Notify the store manager about mold on foods!

Fresh meat and poultry are usually mold free, but cured and cooked meats may not be. Examine them carefully. Exceptions: Some salamis — San Francisco, Italian, and Eastern European types — have a characteristic thin, white mold coating which is safe to consume; however, they shouldn't show any other mold. Dry-cured country hams normally have surface mold that must be scrubbed off before cooking.

Must Homemade Shelf-Stable Preserves be Water-Bath Processed?

Yes, molds can thrive in high-acid foods like jams, jellies, pickles, fruit, and tomatoes. But these microscopic fungi are easily destroyed by heat processing high-acid foods at a temperature of 212 °F in a boiling water canner for the recommended length of time. For more information about processing home-canned foods, go to the National Center for Home Food Preservation at: www.uga.edu/nchfp/.

How Can You Protect Food from Mold?

- When serving food, keep it covered to prevent exposure to mold spores in the air. Use plastic wrap to cover foods you want to stay moist — fresh or cut fruits and vegetables, and green and mixed salads.
- Empty opened cans of perishable foods into clean storage containers and refrigerate them promptly.
- Don't leave any perishables out of the refrigerator more than 2 hours.
- Use leftovers within 3 to 4 days so mold doesn't have a chance to grow.

How Should You Handle Food with Mold on It?

Buying small amounts and using food quickly can help prevent mold growth. But when you see moldy food:

- Don't sniff the moldy item. This can cause respiratory trouble.
- If food is covered with mold, discard it. Put it into a small paper bag or wrap it in plastic and dispose in a covered trash can that children and animals can't get into.
- Clean the refrigerator or pantry at the spot where the food was stored.
- Check nearby items the moldy food might have touched. Mold spreads quickly in fruits and vegetables.
- See the attached chart "Moldy Food: When to Use, When to Discard."

Beef...from Farm to Table

Since 1910, the first year that statistics were compiled, Americans have been eating an average of 60 pounds of beef yearly. About 36 million cattle were inspected in 1997 alone by USDA's Food Safety and Inspection Service. This translates into 64 pounds of beef per person in 1997. In calls to the Hotline, beef is the third food category (behind turkey and chicken) callers most ask about. The following information answers many of their questions.

What is Beef?

The domestication of cattle for food dates to about 6500 B.C. in the Middle East. Cattle were not native to America, but brought to the New World on ships by European colonists. Americans weren't big eaters of fresh beef until about 1870, due to the enormous growth of the cattle industry in the West. The introduction of cattle cars and refrigerated cars on the railroad facilitated distribution of the beef.

"Beef" is meat from full-grown cattle about 2 years old. A live steer weighs about 1,000 pounds and yields about 450 pounds of edible meat. There are at least 50 breeds of beef cattle, but fewer than 10 make up most cattle produced. Some major breeds are Angus, Hereford, Charolais, and Brahman.

"Baby beef" and "calf" are 2 interchangeable terms used to describe young cattle weighing about 700 pounds that have been raised mainly on milk and grass. The meat cuts from baby beef are smaller; the meat is light red and contains less fat than beef. The fat may have a yellow tint due to the vitamin A in grass.

"Veal" is meat from a calf which weighs about 150 pounds. Those that are mainly milk-fed usually are less than 3 months old. The difference between "veal" and "calf" is based on the color of their meat, which is determined almost entirely by diet. Veal is pale pink and contains more cholesterol than beef.

NOTE: This information is about whole muscle beef and variety beef. See "Focus on Ground Beef" for information about hamburger and ground beef.

How are Cattle Raised?

All cattle start out eating grass; three-fourths of them are "finished" (grown to maturity) in feedlots where they are fed specially formulated feed based on corn or other grains.

Can Hormones & Antibiotics Be Used in Cattle Raising?

Antibiotics may be given to prevent or treat disease in cattle. A "withdrawal" period is required from the time antibiotics are administered until it is legal to slaughter the animal. This is so residues can exit the animal's system. FSIS randomly samples cattle at slaughter and tests for residues. Data from this Monitoring Plan have shown a very low percentage of residue violations. Not all antibiotics are approved for use in all classes of cattle. However, if there is a demonstrated therapeutic need, a veterinarian may prescribe an antibiotic that is approved in other classes for an animal in a non-approved class. In this case, no detectable residues of this drug may be present in the edible tissues of the animal at slaughter.

Hormones may be used to promote efficient growth. Estradiol, progesterone, and testosterone (three natural hormones), and zeranol and trenbolone acetate (two synthetic hormones) may be used as an implant on the animal's ear. The hormone is time released, and is effective for 90 to 120 days. In addition, melengesterol acetate, which can be used to suppress estrus, or improve weight gain and feed efficiency, is approved for use as a feed additive. Not all combinations of hormones are approved for use in all classes of cattle. Hormones are approved for specific classes of animals only, and cannot be used in non-approved classes.

How is Beef Inspected?

Inspection is mandatory; grading is voluntary, and a plant pays to have its meat graded. USDA-graded beef sold at the retail level is Prime, Choice, and Select. Lower grades (Standard, Commercial, Utility, Cutter, and Canner) are mainly ground or used in processed meat products. Retail stores may use other terms which must be different from USDA grades. USDA Prime beef (about two percent of graded beef) has more fat marbling, so it is the most tender and flavorful. However, it is higher in fat content. Most of the graded beef sold in supermarkets is USDA Choice or USDA Select. The protein, vitamin, and mineral content of beef are similar regardless of the grade.

How Is Ungraded Beef Different?

All beef is inspected for wholesomeness. The overall quality of ungraded beef may be higher or lower than most government grades found in retail markets.

What is Marbling?

Marbling is white flecks of fat within the meat muscle. The greater amount of marbling in beef, the higher the grade because marbling makes beef more tender, flavorful, and juicy.

Retail Cuts of Fresh Beef

There are four basic major (primal) cuts into which beef is separated: chuck, loin, rib, and round. It is recommended that packages of fresh beef purchased in the supermarket be labeled with the primal cut as well as the product, such as "chuck roast" or "round steak."

This helps consumers know what type of heat is best for cooking the product. Generally, chuck and round are less tender and require moist heat such as braising; loin and rib can be cooked by dry heat methods such as broiling or grilling.

Unfortunately, names for various cuts can vary regionally in stores, causing confusion over the choice of cooking method. For example, a boneless top loin steak is variously called: strip steak, Kansas City Steak, N.Y. strip steak, hotel cut strip steak, ambassador steak, or club sirloin steak.

How Much Beef Is Consumed?

Figures from the USDA's Economic Research Service show average annual per capita beef consumption for the following selected periods:

Nutrition Labeling

Nutrition claims such as "lean" and "extra lean" are sometimes seen on beef products. Here are their definitions:

"Lean" - 100 grams of beef with less than 10 grams of fat, 4.5 grams or less of saturated fat, and less than 95 milligrams of cholesterol.

"Extra Lean" - 100 grams of beef with less than 5 grams of fat, less than 2 grams of saturated fat, and less than 95 milligrams of cholesterol.

What Does "Natural" Mean?

All fresh meat qualifies as "natural." Products labeled "natural" cannot contain any artificial flavor or flavoring, coloring ingredient, chemical preservative, or any other artificial or synthetic ingredient; and the product and its ingredients are not more than minimally processed (ground, for example). All products claiming to be natural should be accompanied by a brief statement which explains what is meant by the term "natural."

Some companies promote their beef as "natural" because they claim their cattle weren't exposed to antibiotics or hormones and were totally raised on a range instead of being "finished" in a feedlot..

How Much Beef is Consumed?			
Year	**Weight**	**Year**	**Weight**
1910-15	51 pounds	1960-65	69 pounds
1920-25	46 pounds	1970-75	85 pounds
1930-35	41 pounds	1980-85	78 pounds
1940-45	45 pounds	1990-95	67 pounds
1950-55	55 pounds	1995-97	64 pounds

How & Why is Some Beef Aged?

Beef is aged to develop additional tenderness and flavor. It is done commercially under controlled temperatures and humidity. Since aging can take from 10 days to 6 weeks, USDA does not recommend aging beef in a home refrigerator.

Why is Beef Called a "Red" Meat?

Oxygen is delivered to muscles by the red cells in the blood. One of the proteins in meat, myoglobin, holds the oxygen in the muscle. The amount of myoglobin in animal muscles determines the color of meat. Beef is called a "red" meat because it contains more myoglobin than chicken or fish. Other "red" meats are veal, lamb, and pork.

Color of Beef

Beef muscle meat not exposed to oxygen (in vacuum packaging, for example) is a burgundy or purplish color. After exposure to the air for 15 minutes or so, the myoglobin receives oxygen and the meat turns bright, cherry red.

After beef has been refrigerated about 5 days, it may turn brown due to chemical changes in the myoglobin. Beef that has turned brown during extended storage may be spoiled, have an off-odor, and be tacky to the touch.

Iridescent Color of Roast Beef

Sliced cooked beef or lunch meat can have an iridescent color. Meat contains iron, fat, and many other compounds. When light hits a slice of meat, it splits into colors like a rainbow. There are also various pigments in meat compounds which can give it an iridescent or greenish cast when exposed to heat and processing. Iridescent beef isn't spoiled necessarily. Spoiled cooked beef would probably also be slimy or sticky and have an off-odor.

Additives

Additives are not allowed on fresh beef. If beef is processed, additives such as MSG, salt, or sodium erythorbate must be listed on the label.

Dating of Beef Products

Product dating is not required by Federal regulations. However, many stores and processors may voluntarily date packages of raw beef or processed beef products. If a calendar date is shown, there must be a phrase explaining the meaning of the date.

Use or freeze products with a "Sell-By" date within 3 to 5 days of purchase

If the manufacturer has determined a "Use-By" date, observe it. This is a quality assurance date after which peak quality begins to lessen but the product may still be used. It's always best to buy a product before its date expires. It's not important if a date expires after freezing beef because all foods stay safe while properly frozen.

What Foodborne Organisms are Associated with Beef?

Escherichia coli can colonize in the intestines of animals, which could contaminate muscle meat at slaughter. *E. coli* O157:H7 is a rare strain that produces large quantities of a potent toxin that forms in and causes severe damage to the lining of the intestine. The disease produced by it is called Hemorrhagic Colitis and is characterized by bloody diarrhea. *E. coli* O157:H7 is easily destroyed by thorough cooking.

Salmonella may be found in the intestinal tracts of livestock, poultry, dogs, cats, and other warm-blooded animals. There are about 2,000 *Salmonella* bacterial species. Freezing doesn't kill this microorganism, but it is destroyed by thorough cooking. *Salmonella* must be eaten to cause illness. They cannot enter the body through a skin cut. Cross-contamination can occur if raw meat or its juices contact cooked food or foods that will be eaten raw, such as salad.

Staphylococcus aureus can be carried on human hands, nasal passages, or throats. Most foodborne illness outbreaks are a result of contamination from food handlers and production of a heat-stable toxin in the food. Sanitary food handling and proper cooking and refrigerating should prevent staphylococcal foodborne illness.

Listeria monocytogenes is destroyed by cooking, but a cooked product can be recontaminated by poor handling practices and poor sanitation. FSIS has a zero tolerance for *Listeria monocytogenes* in cooked and ready-to-eat products such as beef franks or lunchmeat. Observe handling information such as "Keep Refrigerated" and "Use-By" dates on labels.

Rinsing Beef

It isn't necessary to wash raw beef before cooking it. Any bacteria which might be present on the surface would be destroyed by cooking.

How to Handle Beef Safely

- **Raw Beef:** Select beef just before checking out at the register. Put packages of raw beef in disposable plastic bags, if available, to contain any leakage which could cross-contaminate cooked foods or produce. Beef, a perishable product, is kept cold during store distribution to retard the growth of bacteria.

Take beef home immediately and refrigerate it at 40 °F; use within 3 to 5 days (1 or 2 days for variety meats such as liver, kidneys, tripe, sweetbreads, or tongue) or freeze (0 °F). If kept frozen continuously, it will be safe indefinitely. It is safe to freeze beef in its original packaging or repackage it. However, for long-term freezing, overwrap the porous store plastic with aluminum foil, freezer paper, or freezer-weight plastic wrap or bags to prevent "freezer burn," which appears as grayish-brown leathery spots and is caused by air reaching the surface of food. Cut freezer-burned portions away either before or after cooking the beef. Heavily freezer-burned products may have to be discarded for quality reasons. For best quality, use steaks and roasts within 9 to 12 months.

- **Ready-Prepared Beef:** For fully-cooked, take-out beef dishes such as Chinese food, barbecued ribs, or fast food hamburgers, be sure they are hot at pickup. Use cooked beef within 2 hours (1 hour if the air temperature is above 90 °F) or refrigerate it at 40 °F in shallow, covered containers. Eat within 3 to 4 days, either cold or reheated to 165 °F (hot and steaming). It is safe to freeze ready-prepared beef dishes. For best quality, use within 4 months.

Safe Defrosting

There are three safe ways to defrost beef: in the refrigerator, in cold water, and in the microwave. Never defrost on the counter or in other locations.

- **Refrigerator:**. It's best to plan ahead for slow, safe thawing in the refrigerator. Ground beef, stew meat, and steaks may defrost within a day. Bone-in parts and whole roasts may take 2 days or longer. Once the raw beef defrosts, it will be safe in the refrigerator for 3 to 5 days before cooking. During this time, if you decide not to use the beef, you can safely refreeze it without cooking it first.
- **Cold Water:**. To defrost beef in cold water, do not remove packaging. Be sure the package is airtight or put it into a leakproof bag. Submerge the beef in cold water, changing the water every 30 minutes so that it continues to thaw. Small packages of beef may defrost in an hour or less; a 3- to 4-pound roast may take 2 to 3 hours.
- **Microwave:**. When microwave defrosting beef, plan to cook it immediately after thawing because some areas of the food may become warm and begin to cook during microwaving. Holding partially-cooked food is not recommended because any bacteria present wouldn't have been destroyed.

Foods defrosted in the microwave or by the cold water method should be cooked before refreezing because they may have been held at temperatures above 40 °F.

It is safe to cook frozen beef in the oven, on the stove, or grill without defrosting it first; the cooking time may be about 50% longer. Do not cook frozen beef in a slow cooker.

Marinating

Marinate beef in the refrigerator up to 5 days. Boil used marinade before brushing on cooked beef. Discard any uncooked leftover marinade.

Partial Cooking

Never brown or partially cook beef to refrigerate and finish cooking later because any bacteria present wouldn't have been destroyed. It is safe to partially pre-cook or microwave beef immediately before transferring it to the hot grill to finish cooking.

Liquid in Package

Many people think the red liquid in packaged fresh beef is blood. However, blood is removed from beef during slaughter and only a small amount remains within the muscle tissue. Since beef is about 3/4 water, this natural moisture combined with protein is the source of the liquid in the package.

Safe Cooking

For safety, the USDA recommends cooking hamburgers and ground beef mixtures such as meat loaf to 160 °F on a meat thermometer. However, whole muscle meats such as steaks and roasts may be cooked to 145 °F (medium rare), 160 °F (medium), 170 °F (well done). For approximate cooking times for use in meal planning, see the following chart compiled from various resources.

Times are based on beef at refrigerator temperature (40 °F). Remember that appliances and outdoor grills can vary in heat. Use a meat thermometer to check for safe cooking and doneness of beef.

Microwave Directions:

- When microwaving unequal size pieces of beef, arrange in dish or on rack so thick parts are toward the outside of dish and thin parts are in the center; cook on medium-high or medium power.
- Place a roast in an oven cooking bag or in a covered pot.
- Refer to the manufacturer's directions that accompany the microwave oven for suggested cooking times.

- Use a meat thermometer to test for doneness in several places to be sure temperatures listed above have been reached.

Storage Times

Since product dates aren't a guide for safe use of a product, how long can the consumer store the food and still use it at top quality? Follow these tips:

- Purchase the product before the date expires.
- Follow handling recommendations on product.
- Keep beef in its package until using.
- It is safe to freeze beef in its original packaging. If freezing longer than 2 months, overwrap these packages with airtight heavy-duty foil, plastic wrap, or freezer paper or place the package inside a plastic bag.
- For storage times, consult the following chart.

Home Storage of Beef Products

If product has a "Use-By" Date, follow that date. If product has a "Sell-By" Date or no date, cook or freeze the product by the times on the following chart.

HAM AND FOOD SAFETY

Hams: They can be fresh, cook-before-eating, cooked, picnic, and country types. There are so many kinds, and their storage times and cooking times can be quite confusing. This background information serves to carve up the facts and make them easier to understand.

Definition

Hams may be fresh, cured, or cured-and-smoked. Ham is the cured leg of pork. Fresh ham is an uncured leg of pork. Fresh ham will bear the term "fresh" as part of the product name and is an indication that the product is not cured. "Turkey" ham is a ready-to-eat product made from cured thigh meat of turkey. The term "turkey ham" is always followed by the statement "cured turkey thigh meat." The usual color for cured ham is deep rose or pink; fresh ham (which is not cured) has the pale pink or beige color of a fresh pork roast; country hams and prosciutto (which are dry cured) range from pink to a mahogany color.

Hams are either ready to eat or not. Ready-to-eat hams include prosciutto and cooked hams; they can be eaten right out of the package. Fresh hams and hams that are only trichinae treated (which may include heating, freezing, or curing in the plant) must be cooked by the consumer before eating. Hams that must be cooked will bear cooking instructions and safe handling instructions.

Hams that are not ready to eat, but have the appearance of ready-to-eat products, will bear a prominent statement on the principal display panel indicating the product needs cooking, e.g., "cook thoroughly." In addition, the label must bear cooking directions.

Curing Solutions

Curing is the addition of salt, sodium or potassium nitrate (or saltpeter), nitrites, and sometimes sugar, seasonings, phosphates and cure accelerators, e.g., sodium ascorbate, to pork for preservation, color development and flavor enhancement.

Nitrate and nitrite contribute to the characteristic cured flavor and reddish-pink color of cured pork. Nitrite and salt inhibit the growth of *Clostridium botulinum*, a deadly microorganism which can occur in foods under certain situations.

Curing and flavoring solutions are added to pork by injection and by massaging and tumbling the solution into the muscle, both of which produce a more tender product.

Dry Curing

In dry curing, the process used to make country hams and prosciutto, fresh ham is rubbed with a dry-cure mixture of salt and other ingredients. Dry curing produces a salty product. In 1992, FSIS approved a trichinae treatment method that permits substituting up to half of the sodium chloride with potassium chloride to result in lower sodium levels.

Since dry curing draws out moisture, it reduces ham weight by at least 18% — usually 20 to 25%; this results in a more concentrated ham flavor.

Dry-cured hams may be aged more than a year. Six months is the traditional process but may be shortened according to aging temperature.

These uncooked hams are safe stored at room temperature because they contain so little water, bacteria can't multiply in them. Dry-cured ham is not injected with a curing solution or processed by immersion in a curing solution, but it may be smoked. Today, dry cured hams may be marketed as items that need preparation on the part of the consumer to make them safe to eat. So, as with all meat products, it is important to read the label of hams to determine the proper preparation needed.

Wet Curing or Brine Cure

Brine curing is the most popular way of producing hams. It is a wet cure whereby fresh meat is injected with a curing solution before cooking. Brining ingredients can include ingredients such as salt, sugar, sodium nitrite, sodium nitrate, sodium erythorbate, sodium phosphate, potassium chloride, water and flavorings. Smoke flavoring (liquid smoke) may also be injected with brine solution. Cooking *may* occur during this process.

Smoking and Smoke Flavoring

After curing, some hams are smoked. Smoking is a process by which ham is hung in a smokehouse and allowed to absorb smoke from smoldering fires, which gives added flavor and color to meat and slows the development of rancidity. Not all smoked meat is smoked from smoldering fires. A popular process is to heat the ham in a smoke house and generate smoke from atomized smoke flavor.

Foodborne Pathogens

These foodborne pathogens (organisms in food that can cause disease) are associated with ham:

- *Trichinella spiralis* (trichinae) - Parasites are sometimes present in hogs. All hams must be processed according to USDA guidelines to kill trichinae.
- *Staphylococcus aureus* (staph) - Bacteria are destroyed by cooking and processing but can be re-introduced via

mishandling. The bacteria can then produce a toxin which is not destroyed by further cooking. Dry curing of hams may or may not destroy *S. aureus,* but the high salt content on the exterior inhibits these bacteria. When the ham is sliced, the moister interior will permit staphylococcal multiplication. Thus sliced dry-cured hams must be refrigerated.

- *Mold* - Can often be found on country cured ham. Most of these are harmless but some molds can produce mycotoxins. Molds grow on hams during the long curing and drying process because the high salt and low temperatures do not inhibit these robust organisms. DO NOT DISCARD the ham. Wash it with hot water and scrub off the mold with a stiff vegetable brush.

Quantity to Buy

When buying a ham, estimate the size needed according to the number of servings the type of ham should yield:

- 1/4 - 1/3 lb. per serving of boneless ham
- 1/3 - 1/2 lb. of meat per serving of bone-in ham

Cooking or Reheating Hams

Both whole or half, cooked, vacuum-packaged hams packaged in federally inspected plants and canned hams can be eaten cold just as they come from their packaging.

However, if you want to reheat these cooked hams, set the oven no lower than 325 °F and heat to an internal temperature of 140 °F as measured with a food thermometer.

Unpackaged, cooked ham is potentially contaminated with pathogens. For cooked hams that have been repackaged in any other location outside the plant or for leftover cooked ham, heat to 165 °F.

Spiral-cut cooked hams are also safe to eat cold. The unique slicing method, invented in 1957, solves any carving difficulties. These hams are best served cold because heating sliced whole or half hams can dry out the meat and cause the glaze to melt and run off the meat. However, if reheating is desired, hams that were packaged in plants under USDA inspection must be heated to

140 °F as measured with a food thermometer (165 °F for leftover spiral-cut hams or ham that has been repackaged in any other location outside the plant). To reheat a spiral-sliced ham in a conventional oven, cover the entire ham or portion with heavy aluminum foil and heat at 325 °F for about 10 minutes per pound. Individual slices may also be warmed in a skillet or microwave.

Cook-before-eating hams or fresh hams must reach 160 °F to be safely cooked before serving. Cook in an oven set no lower than 325 °F. Hams can also be safely cooked in a microwave oven, other countertop appliances and on the stove. Consult a cookbook for specific methods and timing.

Country hams can be soaked 4 to 12 hours or longer in the refrigerator to reduce the salt content before cooking. Then they can be cooked by boiling or baking. Follow the manufacturer's cooking instructions.

TIMETABLE FOR COOKING HAM

NOTE: Set oven temperature to 325 °F. Both cook-before-eating cured and fresh hams should be cooked to 160 °F. Reheat cooked hams packaged in USDA-inspected plants to 140 °F and all others to 165 °F.

COUNTRY HAM

Whole or Half. (Soak 4 to 12 hours in refrigerator. Cover with water and boil 20 to 25 minutes per pound. Drain, glaze, and brown at 400 °F for 15 minutes.)

Hot Dogs and Food Safety

Whether you call it a frankfurter, hot dog, wiener, or bologna, it's a cooked sausage and a year-round favorite. They can be made from beef, pork, turkey, chicken, or a combination — the label must state which. And there are Federal standards of identity for their content.

Definitions

Frankfurters (a.k.a., hot dogs, wieners, or bologna) are cooked and/or smoked sausages according to the Federal standards of identity. Federal standards of identity describe the requirements for processors to follow in formulating and marketing meat, poultry, and egg products produced in the United States for sale in this country and in foreign commerce. The standard also requires that they be comminuted (reduced to minute particles), semisolid products made from one or more kinds of raw skeletal muscle from livestock (like beef or pork), and may contain poultry meat. Smoking and curing ingredients contribute to flavor, color, and preservation of the product. They are link-shaped and come in all sizes — short, long, thin, and chubby.

The most popular of all categories, the skinless varieties, have been stripped of their casings after cooking. Water or ice, or both, may be used to facilitate chopping or mixing or to dissolve curing ingredients. The finished products may not contain more than 30% fat or no more than 10% water, or a combination of 40% fat and added water. Up to 3.5% non-meat binders and extenders (such as nonfat dry milk, cereal, or dried whole milk) or 2% isolated soy protein may be used, but must be shown in the ingredients statement on the product's label by its common name.

Casings

Some hot dogs have a casing, or a thin skin. If the species of the casing is different than that of the hot dog, the label must say so. For example, if a turkey hot dog has a pork casing, the label must list the pork casing on the ingredients list. If the casing is artificially colored, the label must indicate this as well.

Byproducts, Variety Meats

"Frankfurter, Hot Dog, Wiener, or Bologna With Byproducts" or "With Variety Meats" are made according to the specifications for cooked and/or smoked sausages (see above), except they consist of not less than 15% of one or more kinds of raw skeletal muscle meat with raw meat byproducts. The byproducts (heart, kidney, or liver, for example) must be named with the derived species and be individually named in the ingredients statement.

Species

Beef Franks or Pork Franks are cooked and/or smoked sausage products made according to the specifications above, but with meat from a single species and do not include byproducts.

Turkey Franks or Chicken Franks can contain turkey or chicken and turkey or chicken skin and fat in proportion to a turkey or chicken carcass.

Ingredients Statement

All ingredients in the product must be listed in the ingredients statement in order of predominance, from highest to lowest amounts.

"Meat" Derived By Advanced Meat Bone Separation and Meat Recovery Systems

The definition of "meat" was amended in December 1994 to include any "meat" product that is produced by advanced meat/bone separation machinery. This meat is comparable in appearance, texture, and composition to meat trimmings and similar meat products derived by hand. This machinery separates meat from bone by scraping, shaving, or pressing the meat from the bone without breaking or grinding the bone. Product produced by advanced meat recovery (AMR) machinery can be labeled using terms associated with hand-deboned product (e.g., "pork trimmings" and "ground pork").

The AMR machinery cannot grind, crush, or pulverize bones to remove edible meat tissue, and bones must emerge essentially intact. The meat produced in this manner can contain no more than 150 milligrams (mg) of calcium per 100 grams product (within a tolerance of 30 mg. of calcium). Products that exceed the calcium content limit must be labeled "mechanically separated pork" in the ingredients statement.

Mechanically Separated Meat (MSM)

Mechanically separated meat is a paste-like and batter-like meat product produced by forcing bones, with attached edible meat, under high pressure through a sieve or similar device to separate the bone from the edible meat tissue.

In 1982, a final rule published by FSIS on mechanically separated meat said it was safe and established a standard of identity for the food product. Some restrictions were made on how much can be used and the type of products in which it can be used. These restrictions were based on concerns for limited intake of certain components in MSM, like calcium. **Due to FSIS regulations enacted in 2004 to protect consumers against Bovine Spongiform Encephalopathy, mechanically separated beef is considered inedible and is prohibited for use as human food. It is not permitted in hot dogs or any other processed product.** Mechanically separated pork is permitted and must be labeled as "mechanically separated pork" in the ingredients statement. Hot dogs can contain no more than 20% mechanically separated pork.

Mechanically Separated Poultry (MSP)

Mechanically separated poultry is a paste-like and batter-like poultry product produced by forcing bones, with attached edible tissue, through a sieve or similar device under high pressure to separate bone from the edible tissue. Mechanically separated poultry has been used in poultry products since the late 1960's. In 1995, a final rule on mechanically separated poultry said it was safe and could be used without restrictions. However, it must be labeled as "mechanically separated chicken or turkey" in the product's ingredients statement. The final rule became effective November 4, 1996. Hot dogs can contain any amount of mechanically separated chicken or turkey.

Food Product Dating Terms

The labeling on a package of hot dogs may contain one of several different types of dates. Product dating is voluntary and not required by Federal regulations. If a date is used, it must also state what the date means.

- **"Sell-By"** date tells the store how long to display the product for sale. You should buy the product before the date expires.
- **"Use-By"** date is the last date recommended for use of the product while at peak quality. This date has been determined by the manufacturer of the product.
- **"Best if Used By (or Before)"** date helps consumers by stating a precise date for best flavor or quality.
- **"Expiration Date"** helps stores and consumers by stating the shelf-life or the last day product should be used while it is wholesome.

Safety After Date Expires

Except for "Use-By" dates, product dates don't refer to home storage and use after purchase. If a "Sell-By," "Best if Used By (or Before)," or "Expiration Date" date expires during home storage, a product should be safe and wholesome if handled safely and kept at 40 °F or below.

FOOD SAFETY GUIDELINES

The same general food safety guidelines apply to hot dogs as to all perishable products — "Keep hot food hot and cold food cold." Although all hot dogs are fully cooked, always reheat before eating. Use a food thermometer to make sure hot dogs reach 165 °F or are steamy hot throughout.

Studies have shown a high level of the harmful bacteria *Listeria* in hot dogs. Thus, for added precaution, persons at risk may choose to avoid eating hot dogs and luncheon meats, such as bologna, unless they are reheated until steamy hot.

When you leave the grocery store with hot dogs, head straight home and refrigerate or freeze them immediately. If there is no product date, hot dogs can be safely stored in the unopened package for 2 weeks in the refrigerator; once opened, only 1 week. For maximum quality, freeze hot dogs no longer than 1 or 2 months. And, of course, never leave hot dogs at room temperature for more than 2 hours and no more than 1 hour when the temperature goes above 90 °F.

SAFETY OF FRESH PORK...FROM FARM TO TABLE

Although pork is the number one meat consumed in the world, U.S. consumption dropped during the 1970s, largely because its high fat content caused health-conscious Americans to choose leaner meats. Today's hogs have much less fat due to improved genetics, breeding and feeding. Read on for more information about this red meat.

What is Pork?

Pork is the meat from hogs, or domestic swine. The domestication of "pigs" (immature hogs) for food dates back to about 7000 B.C. in the Middle East. However, evidence shows that

Stone Age man ate wild boar, the hog's ancestor, and the earliest surviving pork recipe is Chinese, at least 2000 years old.

Hogs were brought to Florida by Hernando de Soto in 1525, and soon was America's most popular meat. In the 19th century — as America urbanized and people began living away from the farm, "salt pork" — pork that is prepared with a high level of salt to preserve it — became the staple food. Pork has continued to be an important part of our diet since that time.

Pork is generally produced from young animals (6 to 7 months old) that weigh from 175 to 240 pounds. Much of a hog is cured and made into ham, bacon and sausage. Uncured meat is called "fresh pork."

Can Antibiotics and Hormones Be Used in Pork Raising?

Antibiotics may be given to prevent or treat disease in hogs. A "withdrawal" period is required from the time antibiotics are administered until it is legal to slaughter the animal. This is so residues can exit the animal's system and won't be in the meat.

FSIS randomly samples pork at slaughter and tests for residues. Data from this monitoring program have shown a very low percentage of residue violations.

No hormones are used in the raising of hogs.

How is Pork Inspected?

All pork found in retail stores is either USDA inspected for wholesomeness or inspected by state systems which have standards equal to the federal government. Each animal and its internal organs are inspected for signs of disease. The "Passed and Inspected by USDA" seal insures the pork is wholesome and free from disease.

Is Pork Graded?

Although inspection is mandatory, its grading for quality is voluntary, and a plant pays to have its pork graded. USDA grades for pork reflect only two levels: "Acceptable" grade and "Utility" grade. Pork sold as Acceptable quality pork is the only fresh pork sold in supermarkets. It should have a high proportion of lean meat to fat and bone. Pork graded as Utility is mainly used in processed products and is not available in supermarkets for consumers to purchase.

What to Look For When Buying Pork

When buying pork, look for cuts with a relatively small amount of fat over the outside and with meat that is firm and a grayish pink color. For best flavor and tenderness, meat should have a small amount of marbling.

Retail Cuts of Fresh Pork

There are four basic (primal) cuts into which pork is separated: shoulder, loin, side and leg.

Shoulder

- Shoulder Butt, Roast or Steak
- Blade Steak
- Boneless Blade Boston Roast
- Smoked Arm Picnic
- Smoked Hock
- Ground Pork for Sausage

Side

- Spare Ribs/Back Ribs
- Bacon

Loin

- Boneless Whole Loin (Butterfly Chop)
- Loin Roast
- Tenderloin
- Sirloin Roast
- Country Style Ribs
- Chops

Leg

- Ham/Fresh or Smoked and Cured

How Much Pork is Consumed in America?

Figures from the USDA's Economic Research Service show average annual per capita pork consumption for the following selected periods:

- 1970: 48 pounds
- 1975: 39 pounds
- 1980: 52 pounds

- 1985: 48 pounds
- 1990: 46 pounds
- 1994: 50 pounds

What Does "Natural" Mean?

All fresh meat qualifies as "natural." Products labeled "natural" cannot contain any artificial flavor or flavoring, coloring ingredient, chemical preservative or any other artificial or synthetic ingredient; and the product and its ingredients are not more than minimally processed (ground, for example). All products claiming to be natural should be accompanied by a brief statement which explains what is meant by the term "natural."

Why is Pork a "Red" Meat?

Oxygen is delivered to muscles by the red cells in the blood. One of the proteins in meat, myoglobin, holds the oxygen in the muscle. The amount of myoglobin in animal muscles determines the color of meat. Pork is classified a "red" meat because it contains more myoglobin than chicken or fish. When fresh pork is cooked, it becomes lighter in color, but it is still a red meat. Pork is classed as "livestock" along with veal, lamb and beef. All livestock are considered "red meat."

Dating of Pork

Product dating (i.e. applying "sell by" or "use by" dates) is not required by Federal regulations. However, many stores and processors may voluntarily choose to date packages of raw pork. Use or freeze products with a "sell-by" date within 3 to 5 days of *purchase*. If the manufacturer has determined a "use-by" date, observe it. It's always best to buy a product before its date expires. *It's not important if a date expires after freezing pork because all foods stay safe while properly frozen.*

What Foodborne Organisms Are Associated With Pork?

Pork must be adequately cooked to eliminate disease-causing parasites and bacteria that may be present. Humans may contract trichinosis (caused by the parasite, *Trichinella spiralis*) by eating undercooked pork. Much progress has been made in reducing trichinosis in grain-fed hogs and human cases have greatly declined since 1950. Today's pork can be enjoyed when cooked to an internal temperature of 160 °F. Some other foodborne micro-organisms that can be found in pork, as well as other meats and poultry, are *Escherichia coli*, *Salmonella*, *Staphylococcus aureus* and *Listeria monocytogenes*. They are all destroyed by proper handling and thorough cooking to an internal temperature of 160 °F.

Rinsing Pork

It isn't necessary to wash raw pork before cooking it. Any bacteria which might be present on the surface would be destroyed by cooking.

How to Handle Pork Safely

Raw Pork. Select pork just before checking out at the supermarket register. Put packages of raw pork in disposable plastic bags (if available) to contain any leakage which could cross contaminate cooked foods or produce. Take pork home immediately and refrigerate it at 40 °F; use within 3 to 5 days or freeze (0 °F).

Ready-Prepared Pork. For fully cooked take-out pork dishes such as Chinese food or barbecued ribs, be sure they are hot at pick-up. Use cooked pork within two hours (one hour if air temperature is above 90 °F) or refrigerate it at 40 °F or less in shallow, covered containers. Eat within 3 to 4 days, either cold or reheated to 165 °F (hot and steaming). It is safe to freeze ready prepared pork dishes. For best quality, use within 3 months.

Safe Defrosting

There are three safe ways to defrost pork: in the refrigerator, in cold water (in an airtight or leak-proof bag) and in the microwave. Never defrost on the counter or in other locations. It's best to plan ahead for slow, safe thawing in the refrigerator. After defrosting raw pork by this method, it will be safe in the refrigerator 3 to 5 days before cooking. During this time, if you decide not to use the pork, *you can safely refreeze it without cooking it first*. When microwave-defrosting pork, plan to cook it immediately after thawing because some areas of the food may become warm and begin to cook during microwaving. Holding partially cooked food is not recommended because any bacteria present wouldn't have been destroyed. *Foods defrosted in the microwave or by the cold water method should be cooked before refreezing because they potentially may have been held at temperatures above 40 °F.*

It is safe to cook frozen pork in the oven, on the stove or grill without defrosting it first; the cooking time may be about 50% longer. Use a meat thermometer to check for doneness. Do not cook frozen pork in a slow cooker.

Marinating

Marinate pork in the refrigerator in a covered container up to 5 days. Boil used marinade before brushing on cooked pork. Discard any uncooked leftover marinade.

Irradiation

Irradiation has been approved for use on pork by FDA and USDA/FSIS in low-doses (to control trichina). Treated pork would not be sterile and would still need to be handled safely. *Trichinella* could be alive but would be unable to reproduce. Packages of irradiated pork must be labeled with the irradiation logo as well as the words "Treated with Irradiation" or "Treated by Irradiation" so they would be easily recognizable at the store.

Partial Cooking

Never brown or partially cook pork, then refrigerate and finish cooking later, because any bacteria present wouldn't have been destroyed. It is safe to partially pre-cook or microwave pork *immediately* before transferring it to the hot grill to finish cooking.

Safe Cooking

For safety, the USDA recommends cooking ground pork patties and ground pork mixtures such as meat loaf to 160 °F. Whole muscle meats such as chops and roasts should be cooked to 160 °F. For approximate cooking times for use in meal planning, see the attached chart compiled from various resources. Times are based on pork at refrigerator temperature (40 °F). Remember that appliances and outdoor grills can vary in heat. Use a meat thermometer to check for safe cooking and doneness of pork.

Can Safely Cooked Pork Be Pink?

Cooked muscle meats can be pink even when the meat has

reached a safe internal temperature. If fresh pork has reached 160 °F throughout, even though it may still be pink in the center, it should be safe. The pink color can be due to the cooking method or added ingredients.

Microwave Directions

- When microwaving unequal size pieces of pork, arrange in dish or on rack so thick parts are toward the outside of dish and thin parts are in the center, and cook on medium-high or medium power.
- Place a roast in an oven cooking bag or in a covered pot.
- Refer to the manufacturer's directions that accompany the microwave oven for suggested cooking times.
- Use a meat thermometer to test for doneness in several places to be sure temperatures listed above have been reached.

For storage times, consult the following chart.

Home Storage of Fresh Pork		
Product	**Refrigerator 40 °F**	**Freezer 0 °F**
Fresh pork roast, steaks, chops or ribs	3 - 5 days	4 - 6 months
Fresh pork liver or variety meats	1 - 2 days	3 - 4 months
Home cooked pork; soups, stews or casseroles	3 - 4 days	2 - 3 months
Store-cooked convenience meals	1 - 2 days	2 - 3 months
TV dinners, frozen casseroles	Keep frozen before cooking	3 - 4 months
Canned pork products in pantry	2 - 5 years in pantry; 3 - 4 days after opening	After opening, 2 - 3 months

FRESH PORK: Safe Cooking Chart Internal temperature of safely cooked pork should reach 160 °F when measured with a meat thermometer.

Fresh Pork: Safe Cooking Chart		
Cut	**Thickness or Weight**	**Cooking Time**
ROASTING: Set oven at 350 °F. Roast in a shallow pan, uncovered. Internal temperature: 160°.		
Loin Roast, Bone-in or Boneless	2 to 5 pounds	20-30 minutes per pound
Crown Roast	4 to 6 pounds	20-30 minutes per pound
Leg, (Fresh Ham) Whole, Bone-in	12 to 16 pounds	22-26 minutes per pound
Leg, (Fresh Ham) Half, Bone-in	5 to 8 pounds	35-40 minutes per pound
Boston Butt	3 to 6 pounds	45 minutes per pound
Tenderloin (Roast at 425-450 °F)	½ to 1½ pounds	20 to 30 minutes total
Ribs (Back, Country-style or Spareribs)	2 to 4 pounds	1½ to 2 hours (or until fork tender)
BROILING 4 inches from heat or GRILLING		
Loin Chops, Bone-in or Boneless	¾-inch or 1½ inches	6-8 minutes or 12-16 minutes
Tenderloin	½ to 1½ pounds	15 to 25 minutes
Ribs (indirect heat), all types	2 to 4 pounds	1½ to 2 hours
Ground Pork Patties (direct heat)	½ inch	8 to 10 minutes
IN SKILLET ON STOVE		
Loin Chops or Cutlets	¼-inch or ¾-inch	3-4 minutes or 7-8 minutes
Tenderloin Medallions	¼ to ½-inch	4 to 8 minutes
Ground Pork Patties	½ inch	8 to 10 minutes
BRAISING: Cover and simmer with a liquid.		
Chops, Cutlets, Cubes, Medallions	¼ to 1-inch	10 to 25 minutes
Boston Butt, Boneless	3 to 6 pounds	2 to 2½ hours
Ribs, all types	2 to 4 pounds	1½ to 2 hours
STEWING: Cover pan; simmer, covered with liquid.		
Ribs, all types	2 to 4 pounds	2 to 2½ hours, or until tender
Cubes	1-inch	45 to 60 minutes

NOTE: Cooking times compiled from various resources.

FOCUS ON: CHICKEN

What's for dinner tonight? There's a good chance it's chicken—now the number one species consumed by Americans. Interest in the safe handling and cooking of chicken is reflected in thousands of calls to the USDA Meat and Poultry Hotline, second only to turkey in number of specific inquiries. The following information answers many of the questions these callers have asked about chicken.

History & Definitions

The chicken is a descendant of the Southeast Asian red jungle fowl first domesticated in India around 2000 B.C. Most of the birds raised for meat in America today are from the Cornish (a British breed) and the White Rock (a breed developed in New England). Broiler-fryers, roasters, stewing/baking hens, capons and Rock Cornish hens are all chickens. The following are definitions for these:

- *Broiler-fryer* a young, tender chicken about 7 weeks old which weighs 2 1/2 to 4 1/2 pounds when eviscerated. Cook by any method.
- *Rock Cornish Game Hen* - a small broiler-fryer weighing between 1 and 2 pounds. Usually stuffed and roasted whole.
- *Roaster* - an older chicken about 3 to 5 months old which weighs 5 to 7 pounds. It yields more meat per pound than a broiler-fryer. Usually roasted whole.
- *Capon* - Male chickens about 16 weeks to 8 months old which are surgically unsexed. They weigh about 4 to 7 pounds and have generous quantities of tender, light meat. Usually roasted.
- *Stewing/Baking Hen* - a mature laying hen 10 months to 1 1/2 years old. Since the meat is less tender than young chickens, it's best used in moist cooking such as stewing.
- *Cock or rooster* - a mature male chicken with coarse skin and tough, dark meat. Requires long, moist cooking.

Chicken Inspection

All chickens found in retail stores are either inspected by USDA or by state systems which have standards equivalent to the

Federal government. Each chicken and its internal organs are inspected for signs of disease. The "Inspected for wholesomeness by the U.S. Department of Agriculture" seal insures the chicken is free from visible signs of disease.

Chicken Grading

Inspection is mandatory but grading is voluntary. Chickens are graded according to USDA Agricultural Marketing Service regulations and standards for meatiness, appearance and freedom from defects. Grade A chickens have plump, meaty bodies and clean skin, free of bruises, broken bones, feathers, cuts and discoloration.

Fresh or Frozen

The term *fresh* on a poultry label refers to any raw poultry product that has never been below 26 °F. Raw poultry held at 0 °F or below must be labeled *frozen* or *previously frozen*. No specific labeling is required on raw poultry stored at temperatures between 0-25 °F.

Dating of Chicken Products

Product dating is not required by Federal regulations, but many stores and processors voluntarily date packages of chicken or chicken products. If a calendar date is shown, immediately adjacent to the date there must be a phrase explaining the meaning of that date such as *sell by* or *use before*. The use-by date is for quality assurance; after the date, peak quality begins to lessen but the product may still be used. It's always best to buy a product before the date expires. If a use-by date expires while the chicken is frozen, the food can still be used.

Hormones & Antibiotics

No hormones are used in the raising of chickens.

Antibiotics may be given to prevent disease and increase feed efficiency. A "withdrawal" period is required from the time antibiotics are administered before the bird can be slaughtered. This ensures that no residues are present in the bird's system. FSIS randomly samples poultry at slaughter and tests for residues. Data from this monitoring program have shown a very low percentage of residue violations.

Additives

Additives are not allowed on fresh chicken. If chicken is processed, however, additives such as MSG, salt, or sodium erythorbate may be added but must be listed on the label.

Foodborne Organisms Associated with Chicken

As on any perishable meat, fish or poultry, bacteria can be found on raw or undercooked chicken. They multiply rapidly at temperatures between 40 °F and 140 °F (out of refrigeration and before thorough cooking occurs). Freezing doesn't kill bacteria but they are destroyed by thorough cooking.

USDA's Food Safety and Inspection Service has a zero tolerance for bacteria in cooked and ready-to-eat products such as chicken franks or lunch meat that can be eaten without further cooking.

Most foodborne illness outbreaks are a result of contamination from food handlers. Sanitary food handling and proper cooking and refrigeration should prevent foodborne illnesses. Bacteria must be consumed on food to cause illness. They cannot enter the body through a skin cut. However, raw poultry must be handled carefully to prevent cross-contamination. This can occur if raw poultry or its juices contact cooked food or foods that will be eaten raw such as salad. An example of this is chopping tomatoes on an unwashed cutting board just after cutting raw chicken on it.

Following are some bacteria associated with chicken:

- *Salmonella* Enteritidis may be found in the intestinal tracts of livestock, poultry, dogs, cats and other warm-blooded animals. This strain is only one of about 2,000 kinds of *Salmonella* bacteria; it is often associated with poultry and shell eggs.
- *Staphylococcus aureus* can be carried on human hands, in nasal passages, or in throats. The bacteria are found in foods made by hand and improperly refrigerated, such as chicken salad.
- *Campylobacter jejuni* is one of the most common causes of diarrheal illness in humans. Preventing cross-contamination and using proper cooking methods reduces infection by this bacterium.

- *Listeria monocytogenes* was recognized as causing human foodborne illness in 1981. It is destroyed by cooking, but a cooked product can be contaminated by poor personal hygiene. Observe "keep refrigerated" and "use-by" dates on labels.

Rinsing or Soaking Chicken

It is not necessary to wash raw chicken. Any bacteria which might be present are destroyed by cooking.

Liquid in Package

Many people think the pink liquid in packaged fresh chicken is blood, but it is mostly water which was absorbed by the chicken during the chilling process. Blood is removed from poultry during slaughter and only a small amount remains in the muscle tissue. An improperly bled chicken would have cherry red skin and is condemned at the plant.

How to Handle Chicken Safely

- **Fresh Chicken:** Chicken is kept cold during distribution to retail stores to prevent the growth of bacteria and to increase its shelf life. Chicken should feel cold to the touch when purchased. Select fresh chicken just before checking out at the register. Put packages of chicken in disposable plastic bags (if available) to contain any leakage which could cross-contaminate cooked foods or produce. Make the grocery your last stop before going home.

At home, immediately place chicken in a refrigerator that maintains 40 °F, and use within 1 or 2 days, or freeze at 0 °F. If kept frozen continuously, it will be safe indefinitely.

Chicken may be frozen in its original packaging or repackaged. If freezing longer than two months, over wrap the porous store plastic packages with airtight heavy-duty foil, plastic wrap or freezer paper, or place the package inside a freezer bag. Use these materials or airtight freezer containers to repackage family packs into smaller amounts or freeze the chicken from opened packages.

Proper wrapping prevents "freezer burn," which appears as grayish-brown leathery spots and is caused by air reaching the surface of food. Cut freezer-burned portions away either before or after cooking the chicken. Heavily freezer-burned products may have to be discarded because they might be too dry or tasteless.

- **Ready-Prepared Chicken:** When purchasing fully cooked rotisserie or fast food chicken, be sure it is hot at time of purchase. Use it within two hours or cut it into several pieces and refrigerate in shallow, covered containers. Eat within 3 to 4 days, either cold or reheated to 165 °F (hot and steaming). It is safe to freeze ready-prepared chicken. For best quality, flavor and texture, use within 4 months.

Safe Defrosting

FSIS recommends three ways to defrost chicken: in the refrigerator, in cold water and in the microwave. Never defrost chicken on the counter or in other locations. It's best to plan ahead for slow, safe thawing in the refrigerator. Boneless chicken breasts will usually defrost overnight. Bone-in parts and whole chickens may take 1 to 2 days or longer. Once the raw chicken defrosts, it can be kept in the refrigerator an additional day or two before cooking. During this time, if chicken defrosted in the refrigerator is not used, it can safely be refrozen without cooking first.

Chicken may be defrosted in cold water in its airtight packaging or in a leak proof bag. Submerge the bird or cut-up parts in cold water, changing the water every 30 minutes to be sure it stays cold. A whole (3 to 4-pound) broiler fryer or package of parts should defrost in 2 to 3 hours. A 1-pound package of boneless breasts will defrost in an hour or less.

Chicken defrosted in the microwave should be cooked immediately after thawing because some areas of the food may become warm and begin to cook during microwaving. Holding partially cooked food is not recommended because any bacteria present wouldn't have been destroyed. Foods defrosted in the microwave or by the cold water method should be cooked before refreezing. Do not cook frozen chicken in the microwave or in a slow cooker. However, chicken can be cooked from the frozen state in the oven or on the stove. The cooking time may be about 50% longer.

Stuffed Chicken

The Hotline does not recommend buying retail-stuffed fresh whole chicken because of the highly perishable nature of a previously stuffed item. Consumers should not pre-stuff whole chicken to cook at a later time. Chicken can be stuffed immediately before cooking. Some USDA-inspected frozen stuffed whole poultry MUST be cooked from the frozen state to ensure a safely cooked product. Follow preparation directions on the label.

Marinating

Chicken may be marinated in the refrigerator up to 2 days. Boil used marinade before brushing on cooked chicken. Discard any uncooked leftover marinade.

Safe Cooking

FSIS recommends cooking whole chicken to a safe minimum internal temperature of 165 °F as measured using a food thermometer. Check the internal temperature in the innermost part of the thigh and wing and the thickest part of the breast. For reasons of personal preference, consumers may choose to cook poultry to higher temperatures.

For approximate cooking times to use in meal planning, see the following chart compiled from various resources.

Microwave Directions:

- Microwave on medium-high (70 percent power): whole chicken, 9 to 10 minutes per pound; bone-in parts and Cornish hens, 8 to 9 minutes per pound; boneless breasts halves, 6 to 8 minutes per pound.
- When microwaving parts, arrange in dish or on rack so thick parts are toward the outside of dish and thin or bony parts are in the center.
- Place whole chicken in an oven cooking bag or in a covered pot.
- For boneless breast halves, place in a dish with 1/4 cup water; cover with plastic wrap.
- Allow 10 minutes standing time for bone-in chicken; 5 minutes for boneless breast.

- The USDA recommends cooking whole poultry to a safe minimum internal temperature of 165 °F as measured using a food thermometer. Check the internal temperature in the innermost part of the thigh and wing and the thickest part of the breast. When cooking pieces, the breast, drumsticks, thighs, and wings should be cooked until they reach a safe minimum internal temperature of 165 °F. For reasons of personal preference, consumers may choose to cook poultry to higher temperatures.

Partial Cooking

Never brown or partially cook chicken to refrigerate and finish cooking later because any bacteria present wouldn't have been destroyed. It is safe to partially pre-cook or microwave chicken immediately before transferring it to the hot grill to finish cooking.

Color of Skin

Chicken skin color varies from cream-colored to yellow. Skin color is a result of the type of feed eaten by the chicken, not a measure of nutritional value, flavor, tenderness or fat content. Color preferences vary in different sections of the country, so growers use the type of feed which produces the desired color.

Dark Bones

Darkening around bones occurs primarily in young broiler-fryers. Since their bones have not calcified completely, pigment from the bone marrow can seep through the porous bones. Freezing can also contribute to this seepage. When the chicken is cooked, the pigment turns dark. It's perfectly safe to eat chicken meat that turns dark during cooking.

Pink Meat

The color of cooked chicken is not a sign of its safety. Only by using a food thermometer can one accurately determine that chicken has reached a safe minimum internal temperature of 165 °F throughout. The pink color in safely cooked chicken may be due to the hemoglobin in tissues which can form a heat-stable color. Smoking or grilling may also cause this reaction, which occurs more in young birds.

Color of Giblets

Giblet color can vary, especially in the liver, from mahogany to yellow. The type of feed, the chicken's metabolism and its breed can account for the variation in color. If the liver is green, do not eat it. This is due to bile retention. However, the chicken meat should be safe to eat.

Fatty Deposits

Chickens may seem to have more fatty deposits or contain a larger "fat pad" than in the past. This is because broiler fryer chickens have been bred to grow very rapidly to supply the demand for more chicken.

Feed that is not converted into muscle tissue (meat) is metabolized into fat.

However, the fat is not "marbled" into the meat as is beef or other red meat, and can be easily removed. Geneticists are researching ways to eliminate the excess fat.

Trisodium Phosphate

Food-grade trisodium phosphate (TSP) has been approved by FSIS for use in poultry slaughter as an antimicrobial agent. When immersed in and/or sprayed in a dilute solution on chickens, it can significantly reduce bacteria levels. TSP is "generally recognized as safe" (GRAS) by the FDA, and has been safely used for years, particularly in processed cheese.

Irradiation of Poultry

In 1992, the USDA approved a rule to permit irradiation of raw, fresh or frozen packaged poultry to control certain common bacteria on raw poultry that can cause illness when poultry is undercooked or otherwise mishandled. Irradiation at 1.5 to 3.0 kilo Gray, the smallest, most practical "dose," would eliminate more than 99 percent of Salmonellae organisms on the treated poultry.

Packages of irradiated chicken are easily recognizable at the store because they must carry the international radura symbol along with the statement, "treated with irradiation" or "treated by irradiation."

Storage Times

Since product dates aren't a guide for safe use of a product, how long can the consumer store the food and still use it at top quality? Follow these tips:

- Purchase the product before the date expires.
- Follow handling recommendations on product.
- Keep chicken in its package until using.
- Freeze chicken in its original packaging, overwrap or re-wrap it according to directions in the above section, "How to Handle Chicken Safely".

Handling and Preserving Duck or Goose

The White Pekin duck, native to China, is a relative newcomer to America. In 1873, a Yankee Clipper ship crossed the Pacific with fewer than a dozen of them, marking the beginning of America's domestic duck industry. The domestic goose, bred in ancient Egypt, China and India, arrived from a different direction — across the Atlantic from Europe, where they're immensely popular. Following is background information on these two poultry species.

What are Duck and Goose?

- Broiler Duckling or Fryer Duckling - a young duck (usually under 8 weeks of age) of either sex that is tender meated and has a soft bill and a soft windpipe; ducklings classified as broiler-fryers weigh from 3 to 6 ½ pounds.
- Roaster Duckling - a young duck (usually under 16 weeks of age) of either sex that is tender-meated and has a bill that is not completely hardened and a windpipe that is easily dented; they usually weigh from 4 to 7 ½ pounds.
- Mature Duck or Old Duck - a duck (usually over 6 months of age) of either sex with toughened flesh and a hardened bill; these ducks are usually too old to lay eggs and their meat is used in processed products.
- Young Goose or Gosling - may be of either sex and is tender meated. A gosling weighs about 8 pounds; a young goose weighs 12 to 14 pounds.

- Mature Goose or Old Goose - may be of either sex and has toughened flesh. A mature goose is usually a spent breeder and its meat is used in processed products.
- Gander - a male goose.

How are Ducks and Geese Raised?

Almost all ducks are raised indoors to protect from predators and to manage their manure, which is collected and used elsewhere selectively as fertilizer. Most ducks are now raised in Wisconsin and Indiana since land on Long Island, NY, where most ducks were formerly raised, has become increasingly too valuable for farming. Ducks are fed corn and soybeans fortified with vitamins and minerals. Most feed contains no animal by-products.

Geese are raised under cover for the first six weeks of life. Then they are put on the range 14 to 20 weeks where they eat available grass and some grain. California and South Dakota are the main geese-raising states.

Are Duck and Goose USDA Inspected and Graded?

All ducks and geese are federally or state inspected. Grading is voluntary and a plant pays to have its ducks or geese graded. The presence of the USDA Grade shield, usually Grade A, on these products is an indication of quality. USDA Grade A ducklings are the highest quality available. They are plump, meaty and have skin free from cuts, bruises and tears. There are no broken bones, no missing parts and few pin feathers. Grade B and Grade C ducklings are not usually found in supermarkets.

Can Antibiotics and Hormones Be Used in Raising Duck and Goose?

No hormones are allowed in U. S. duck or goose production. The Food and Drug Administration strictly prohibits the use of hormones in these birds.

Very few drugs have been approved for ducks and geese so antibiotics are not routinely given and are not useful for feed efficiency. If a drug is given — usually, through the feed — to cure illness, for example, a "withdrawal" period of days is required from the time it is administered until it is legal to slaughter the bird. This is so residues can exit the bird's system. FSIS randomly samples poultry at slaughter and tests for residues.

How Are Duck and Goose Down Obtained?

When these birds are slaughtered, they are first stunned electrically. After their throats are cut (by hand, for geese) and the birds are bled, they are scalded to facilitate removal of large feathers. To remove fine pinfeathers, the birds are dipped in paraffin wax. Down and feathers, a very valuable by-product of the duck and goose industry, are sorted at another facility.

Additives

Additives are not allowed on fresh duck or goose. If the meat or giblets are processed (such as in paté or smoked breast, for example), any additives such as MSG, salt, or sodium erythorbate, must be listed on the label.

Fatty Deposits

Ducks and geese swim, and they have a fat layer beneath the skin that keeps them buoyant. Before cooking a whole bird, the skin should be pricked all over with a fork to facilitate the fat rendering out. This fat layer must have melted and disappeared for the bird to be done. The fat is not "marbled" into the meat so it can easily be removed from the surface of a raw duck or goose if deboning the meat before cooking.

Retail Cuts of Duck and Goose

- Whole duckling, gosling or goose including giblets and neck.
- Bone-in parts such as whole leg, breast quarter and breast.
- Boneless breast, skin-on or skinless.
- Giblets (liver, heart and gizzard) sold with whole birds but much liver exported to France.
- Tongues and feet (delicacy mostly exported to Hong Kong but some used by Asian Americans).
- Processed products such as smoked cooked breast, sausage and hot dogs.

Some cuts may be used mainly for food service and restaurants.

How Much Duck and Goose Are Consumed?

Today Americans consume about .34 (1/3) pound of duck per person yearly, down from .44 pound in 1986. Consumption of goose is less.

Quantity to Buy

When buying whole duck or goose, allow about 1 to 1 ½ pounds of raw weight per person. Raw boneless meat yields about 3 servings per pound after cooking. Estimate 3 to 4-ounces per person for fully cooked products.

Are Duck and Goose "Red" or "White" Meat?

Duck and goose are poultry and considered "white" meat. Because they are birds of flight, however, the breast meat is darker than chicken and turkey breast. This is because more oxygen is needed by muscles doing work, and the oxygen is delivered to those muscles by the red cells in the blood. One of the proteins in meat, myoglobin, holds the oxygen in the muscle, and gives the meat a darker color. Chickens and turkeys stand a lot but do little if any flying, so their breast meat is white and leg meat, dark. Game birds, however, spend time flying so their breast meat may be as dark as leg meat.

What is the Flavor of Duck and Goose?

Because all the meat on a duck or goose is dark, it has a stronger flavor than chicken breast meat—and even chicken leg meat.

What Does Natural Mean?

All fresh meat qualifies as "natural." Products labeled "natural" cannot contain any artificial flavor or flavoring, coloring ingredient, chemical preservative or any other artificial or synthetic ingredient. All products claiming to be natural should be accompanied by a brief statement which explains what is meant by the term "natural."

What Foodborne Organisms Are Associated With Duck and Goose?

As on any perishable meat, fish or poultry, bacteria can be found on raw or undercooked duck or goose. Bacteria multiply rapidly in the "Danger Zone," at temperatures between 40° and 140 °F (out of refrigeration and before thorough cooking occurs). Freezing may limit growth but does not kill bacteria. They are destroyed by thorough cooking.

Salmonella is often associated with shell eggs and poultry. It may be found in the intestinal tracts of livestock, poultry, dogs, cats and other warm-blooded animals. *Salmonella* Enteritidis is only one of about 2,000 *Salmonella* bacteria. Freezing doesn't kill this microorganism but it is destroyed with thorough cooking.

Salmonella must be eaten to cause illness. Raw poultry must be handled carefully to prevent cross contamination. This can occur if raw duck, goose or their juices contact cooked food or foods that will be eaten raw such as salad. Salmonellosis is a foodborne illness characterized by stomach pain, diarrhea and nausea.

Irradiation

Irradiation has not been approved for duck or goose.

How to Handle Duck and Goose Safely

FRESH DUCK OR GOOSE

Because the demand is not as high as for other poultry such as chicken or turkey, ducks and geese are usually kept in the frozen food cases at supermarkets. At holiday times, fresh duck and goose may be available. Select them just before checking out at the register. Put each duck or goose in a disposable plastic bag (if available) to contain any leakage which could cross contaminate cooked foods or produce. Make the grocery your last stop before going home. At home, refrigerate a duck or goose immediately (40° F) and use within 1 or 2 days, or freeze (0° F) in its original packaging. If kept frozen continuously, it will be safe indefinitely.

READY PREPARED DUCK OR GOOSE

If picking up a cooked duck, or other fully cooked product, be sure it is hot when you pick it up. Use it within 2 hours or cut it into several pieces and refrigerate in shallow, covered containers. Eat either cold or reheated to 165° F. It is safe to freeze ready prepared duck or goose. For recommended storage times, see the chart below.

Marinating

Marinate duck or goose in the refrigerator up to 2 days. Boil used marinade before brushing it on the cooked poultry. Discard any uncooked leftover marinade.

Storage Times for Duck and Goose

Product	Refrigerator 40 °F	Freezer 0 °F
Fresh Duck or Goose	1 to 2 days	6 months
Fresh Giblets (liver, etc.)	1 to 2 days	6 months
Cooked Duck or Goose; gumbo, stews or casseroles	3 to 4 days	2 to 3 months
Leftover takeout or restaurant food	3 to 4 days	2 to 3 months
Smoked duck breast or franks: Vacuum sealed	2 weeks (or 1 week after "use-by date")	1 to 2 months
Smoked duck breast or franks: After opening	7 days	1 to 2 months
Frozen commercial dinners or entrees	Keep frozen before cooking	3 to 4 months
Canned duck or goose products in pantry (paté, soup, etc.)	2 to 5 years in pantry; 3 to 4 days after opening	After opening, 2 to 3 months

Safe Thawing

There are three safe ways to thaw a frozen duck or goose: in the refrigerator, in cold water and in the microwave. Never defrost on the counter or in other locations.

In the refrigerator, whole birds may take 1 to 2 days or longer; parts, about 1 day. Once the raw poultry defrosts, it will be safe in the refrigerator an additional 1 or 2 days before cooking. During this time, if you decide not to use the product, you can safely refreeze it without cooking it first.

To thaw a duck or goose in cold water, do not remove the packaging. Be sure the packaging is airtight or put it in a leakproof bag. Submerge the bird in cold water, changing the water every 30 minutes. A whole (3 to 4-pound) duck or package of parts should defrost in 2 to 3 hours; a goose, which is larger, may take 4 to 6 hours.

When microwave-defrosting a duck or goose, plan to cook it immediately after thawing because some areas of the food may become warm and begin to cook. Holding partially cooked food is not recommended because any bacteria present may not have been destroyed. Foods defrosted in the microwave or by the cold water method should be cooked before refrigerating or refreezing.

Partial Cooking

Never brown or partially cook duck or goose to refrigerate and finish cooking later because any bacteria present may not have been destroyed. It is safe to partially pre-cook or microwave poultry immediately before transferring it to the hot grill to finish cooking.

Can Safely Cooked Duck and Goose Be Pink?

Cooked muscle meats can be pink even when the meat has reached a safe minimum internal temperature. If fresh duck or goose has reached a safe minimum internal temperature of 165 °F as measured with a food thermometer, even though it may still be pink in the center, it should be safe. The pink color can be due to the cooking method or added ingredients. For reasons of personal preference, consumers may choose to cook poultry to higher temperatures.

Safe Cooking

USDA recommends cooking whole duck or goose to a safe minimum internal temperature of 165 °F as measured using a food thermometer. Check the internal temperature in the innermost part of the thigh and wing and the thickest part of the breast. When cooking pieces, the breast, drumsticks, thighs, and wings should be cooked until they reach a safe minimum internal temperature of 165 °F. For approximate cooking times for use in meal planning, see the following chart compiled from various resources and use a food thermometer.

Approximate Duck and Goose Cooking Times				
Type of Duck or Goose	Roast 350°F	Grill Direct heat	Smoke Indirect heat*	Braise
Whole duckling, 4 to 6 lbs Do not stuff.	30 to 35 min/lb	Not preferred	2-½ hours	Not preferred
Duckling breast or parts	2 hrs.	30 to 40 min	2 hours	60 to 75 minutes
Whole young goose, 8 to 12 lbs	2-½ to 3 hours+	Not suitable	2 to 2-½ hrs	Not preferred
Young goose, cut up	2 hours	35 to 40 min.	2 hours	2 hours

NOTE: Prick skin of whole duck or goose before roasting or smoking so fat can render.

+ Unstuffed. If stuffed, add 15 to 30 minutes additional time.

* Indirect method using drip pan.

Microwave Directions:

- Place duck or goose in an oven cooking bag (or in a covered dish). Microwave on high 6 to 7 minutes per pound. Crisp in 500 °F conventional oven 10 to 20 minutes.
- When microwaving parts, arrange in dish or on rack so thick parts are toward the outside of dish and thin or bony parts are in the center.
- Allow 10 minutes standing time for bone-in goose or duck; 5 minutes for boneless breast.

- USDA recommends cooking whole duck or goose to 165 °F. All poultry is safely cooked when the food thermometer reaches a safe minimum internal temperature of 165 °F in the innermost part of the thigh and wing and the thickest part of the breast. When cooking pieces, the breast, drumsticks, thighs, and wings should be cooked until they reach a safe minimum internal temperature of 165 °F.

POULTRY: BASTING, BRINING, AND MARINATING

People are always on the lookout for new and interesting ways to prepare old standards like chicken and turkey. Several methods have become popular in recent years, which involve the use of a liquid to change or improve the flavor, taste, tenderness, or texture of poultry. Various liquids can be added to poultry by many different methods such as injection, marinating, brining, or basting. Consumers can purchase raw poultry products that have already been marinated, basted, or brined.

Marinating

The verb "marinate" means to steep food in a marinade. A marinade is a savory acidic sauce in which a food is soaked to enrich its flavor or to tenderize it.

According to *Woman's Day Encyclopedia of Cookery*, "Marinades began as simple brines for preserving fish. The word marinade stems from the same root as the word maritime. In modern usage, a marinade consists of a cooking oil, an acid (vinegar, lemon juice, wine), and spices. As the food stands in the mixture, the acid and the oil impart the savory flavors of the spices to the food. The acid also has a tenderizing action."

The acid in marinades causes poultry tissue to break down. This has a tenderizing effect. The breaking down of the tissue also causes the poultry to hold more liquid, making it juicier. Too much vinegar or hot sauce in a marinade can have the opposite effect, causing the meat to be stringy and tough.

Brining

The verb "brine" means to treat with or steep in brine. Brine is a strong solution of water and salt. A sweetener such as sugar, molasses, honey, or corn syrup may be added to the solution for flavor and to improve browning. The salt has two effects on poultry, reports Dr. Alan Sams, a professor of poultry science at Texas A & M University. "It dissolves protein in muscle, and the salt and protein reduce moisture loss during cooking. This makes the meat juicer, more tender, and improves the flavor. The low levels of salt enhance the other natural flavors of poultry."

Basting

The verb "baste" means to moisten meat or other food while cooking. Melted butter or other fat, meat drippings, or liquid such as a stock is spooned or brushed on food as it cooks to moisten it. A bulb baster can also be used to drizzle the liquid over the food. Basting adds flavor and color, and prevents poultry from drying out.

Consumers can purchase raw poultry products that have already been marinated, basted, or brined. These products have been injected or marinated with a solution containing butter or other edible fat, broth, stock, or water, plus spices, flavor enhancers, colorings, or other approved substances. If you see terms such as "basted," "self basted," "marinated," or "for flavoring" on a raw poultry label, a solution has been added during processing — up to 3% by weight for bone-in poultry and up to 8% by weight for boneless poultry.

Safe Preparation

Marinating. Whole poultry or poultry parts may be marinated by completely immersing the poultry in the marinade. To help infuse the marinade into the poultry, you may use a fork to make random holes in the meat. A needle-like injector may also be used.

Poultry can be refrigerated for up to 2 days in a marinade. For easy cleanup, use food-grade plastic bags for marinating and discard the bags after marinating. Food-grade plastic, stainless steel, or glass containers may also be used to marinate food. Cover poultry while marinating in the refrigerator. Don't use marinade from raw poultry as a sauce unless it is boiled first to destroy bacteria. If stuffing poultry, marinate the poultry first. Cook immediately after stuffing.

Brining. To prepare a brine solution for poultry, add ¾ cup salt to 1 gallon of water, or 3 tablespoons of salt per quart of water. For best flavor, use sodium chloride–table salt. Add sweetener if desired. Place brining solution in food-grade plastic, stainless steel, or glass containers. Totally submerge poultry in solution and store covered in the refrigerator. For best results, refrigerate at least overnight. Poultry may be left in the refrigerator up to 2 days after thawed or purchased fresh. Remove poultry from brine. Discard brine after use. If stuffing poultry, brine the poultry first. Cook immediately after stuffing.

Basting. If basting poultry, remember that each time the oven door is opened, the oven temperature is lowered and additional cooking time may be needed. Always use clean utensils to avoid cross-contamination.

General Poultry Preparation Information

Safe Cooking. Set oven temperature no lower than 325 °F. Whole poultry and parts are safe cooked to a safe minimum internal temperature of 165 °F as measured with a food thermometer. Check the internal temperature in the innermost part of the thigh and wing and the thickest part of the breast. For reasons of personal preference, consumers may choose to cook poultry to higher temperatures.

For optimum safety, do not stuff whole poultry. If stuffing whole poultry, the center of the stuffing must reach a safe minimum internal temperature of 165 °F.

Storing Leftovers. Remove any stuffing and cut whole or large pieces of poultry into small pieces. Refrigerate leftovers in shallow containers within 2 hours of cooking. Use leftover poultry and stuffing within 3 to 4 days, or freeze these foods. Reheat all leftovers thoroughly to a temperature of 165 °F.

GIBLETS AND FOOD SAFETY

Giblets (pronounced JIBB-letz; also GIBB-letz) are the heart, liver and gizzard of poultry. The word comes from Middle English "gibelet," which in turn came from "gibier" — Old French for "game." The English altered the word to "giberet," and it formerly meant "a game stew." Today many cooks use giblets to make gravy; others broil or fry them to make appetizers or main dishes. Here is some background information about poultry giblets.

What Are Giblets?

Giblets are defined as the heart, liver, and gizzard of a poultry carcass. Although often packaged with them, the neck of the bird is not a giblet.

The *heart* is the muscular organ that pumps blood through the body of the bird.

The *liver* has numerous functions in digestion and absorption of foods. Its primary function in digestion and absorption is the production of bile. Bile facilitates the solubilization and absorption of dietary fats and the excretion of certain wastes.

The *gizzard* is the mechanical "stomach" of a bird. It is located just after the true or glandular stomach in the gastrointestinal system. Since poultry have no teeth and swallow feed whole, this muscular organ, sometimes called "hen's teeth," mechanically grinds and mixes the bird's feed.

How Are They Inspected?

All poultry found in retail stores is either inspected by USDA or by state systems which have standards equivalent to the federal government. At the time of slaughter each bird and its internal organs are inspected for signs of disease. The "Inspected for Wholesomeness by the U.S. Department of Agriculture" seal ensures that the bird and giblets are free from visible signs of disease.

In a poultry slaughter plant, giblets must be chilled to 40 °F or below within two hours of slaughtering the birds. Each hour, plant employees sample the finished poultry and giblets. The product is checked for conditions not meeting inspection standards, and proper trimming to make sure all inedible portions have been removed.

Proper trimming refers to removal of the heart cap, removal of the gizzard lining, and removal of the gall bladder. USDA inspectors sample the product twice a shift to check for conditions that do not meet inspection standards. Anything that does not meet inspection standards is not used for human consumption.

Are Giblets Graded?

No, inspection is mandatory but grading is voluntary. There are no grading standards for giblets.

How Are Giblets Packaged and Labeled?

In whole ready to cook poultry, giblets are located in a bag in the abdominal cavity. *They will not be from the original bird.* Giblets may also be purchased separately as livers, hearts, or a combination thereof, and labeled accordingly.

Ready to cook whole poultry is required to be packaged with giblets and will not bear a product name qualifier to announce the presence of the giblets as they are expected. If a bird is labeled "with giblets," it is optional labeling.

Whole poultry will contain at least half of each giblet. Parts of the giblets may have broken off during handling or may be missing due to trimming. Some are packed into the body cavity of the bird by hand and some are packed by machine.

USDA allows poultry processors to use labels stating that giblets may be missing — or, "without giblets" (commonly known as "wogs" in the poultry industry). Giblets may be lost or broken or may have been pulled from the processing line for not meeting inspection standards. Birds packed without giblets are required to bear labeling that states the giblets are missing. Likewise, the phrase "giblets may be missing" is a flag to alert the consumer that giblets may not be present.

What Color is Normal for Livers?

Normal poultry livers range in color from tan or yellow to deep mahogany red. A yellow liver indicates a fattier liver. The color variation depends on what the bird ate last and has nothing to do with the *age* or *health* of the bird.

Occasionally a liver may be a shade of *green*. Green livers are condemned at the slaughter plant and are rarely seen by consumers. The green coloring is due to bile leaching out from the gallbladder and into the liver. Bile is a yellow or greenish fluid secreted by the liver and stored in the gallbladder. Its function in the body is to aid in the emulsification and absorption of fats.

Green livers are not harmful if eaten but are removed and condemned in the slaughter plant for aesthetic reasons. Sometimes the gallbladder or a portion of it remains attached to the liver. It looks like a "green pill". In the plant the gallbladders are removed by hand or machine and occasionally one is missed inadvertently. It can be removed in the home and the liver consumed with no problems. *It is safe to eat the meat of poultry regardless of the color of the liver it contains. Remember the giblets are not packaged with the original bird.*

Safe Handling of Giblets

Giblets packaged separately from poultry are kept cold during distribution to retail stores to prevent the growth of bacteria and to increase shelf life. Select fresh giblets just before checking out at the register at the store. They should feel cold to the touch. Place them in a disposable plastic bag (if available) to contain any leakage that could contaminate cooked foods or produce.

At home, immediately place giblets (or poultry containing giblets) in a refrigerator that maintains 40 °F or below, and use within 1 or 2 days; or freeze at 0 °F or below. If kept frozen continuously, they will be safe indefinitely. For best quality, use giblets within 3-4 months of freezing.

Safe Thawing of Giblets

There are three safe ways to thaw giblets and poultry containing them: in the refrigerator, in cold water, or in the microwave oven. Never thaw giblets on the kitchen counter.

REFRIGERATOR THAWING. It is best to plan ahead for slow, safe thawing in the refrigerator. As a rule of thumb, whole poultry with giblets will take about 24 hours for every 5 pounds of weight to thaw in the refrigerator. A 1-pound carton of frozen chicken livers will take about 24 hours. Raw poultry and/or giblets defrosted by this method, may be stored in the refrigerator 1 to 2 days. During this time, if giblets are not used, they can be safely refrozen.

COLD WATER THAWING. Leave the giblets or poultry containing them in the original airtight packaging or place in a leak-proof bag. Submerge the product in cold water and change the water every 30 minutes to make sure it stays cold. A whole 3 to 4 pound fryer with giblets should thaw in 2-3 hours by this method and a whole 15 pound turkey will take 7 to 8 hours, or approximately 30 minutes per pound. A 1-pound carton of chicken livers should thaw in 1 or 2 hours. Once thawed, cook immediately.

MICROWAVE THAWING. Cook giblets and poultry containing them immediately after microwave thawing because some areas of the food may become warm and begin to cook. Holding partially cooked food is not recommended because any bacteria that may have been present may not have been destroyed. Foods thawed in the microwave or by the cold water method should be cooked before refreezing.

Dating of Giblets

Product dating is not required by federal regulations, however many stores and processors voluntarily date packages of giblets and poultry with giblets. If a calendar date is shown, there must be a phrase explaining the meaning of the date. Consumers should use or freeze products with a "sell- by" date within 1 or 2 days of purchase. If the manufacturer has determined a "use-by" date, observe it.

The use-by date is for quality assurance, after the date, peak quality begins to lessen but the product may still be used. It's always best to buy a product before its date expires. If a date expires after the giblets are frozen, they may still be used.

Safe Cooking of Giblets

Traditionally, chicken or turkey giblets are cooked by simmering in water for use in flavoring soups, gravies or poultry stuffing. Once cooked, the liver will become crumbly and the heart and gizzard will soften and become easy to chop. Cooked giblets should have a firm texture. Casseroles containing giblets should be cooked to 165 °F. Stuffing should be cooked to 165 °F. Chicken giblets are commonly fried or broiled. Leftovers should be refrigerated within 2 hours.

Accidental Cooking in Packaging

Some giblets are *paper wrapped* before being inserted into the poultry body cavity. In this case, there would be *no concern* if the giblets are accidentally cooked inside the bird to a safe temperature.

If giblets were packed in a *plastic bag,* and the bag has been altered or melted by the cooking process, do not use the giblets or the poultry because harmful chemicals may have leached into the surrounding meat. If the plastic bag was not altered, the giblets and poultry should be safe to use as long as the meat is fully cooked.

EGG PRODUCTS AND FOOD SAFETY

Of the 76 billion eggs consumed in 2004, more than 30 percent were in the form of egg products (eggs removed from their shells). Liquid, frozen, and dried egg products are widely used by the foodservice industry and as ingredients in other foods, such as prepared mayonnaise and ice cream.

What Are Egg Products?

The term "egg products" refers to eggs that are removed from their shells for processing. The processing of egg products includes breaking eggs, filtering, mixing, stabilizing, blending, pasteurizing, cooling, freezing or drying, and packaging. This is done at United States Department of Agriculture (USDA)-inspected plants.

Egg products include whole eggs, whites, yolks and various blends with or without non-egg ingredients that are processed and pasteurized and may be available in liquid, frozen, and dried forms.

Are Egg Products New?

Egg products are not a new invention. Commercial egg drying began in St. Louis, Missouri, about 1880. The first commercial production of frozen whole eggs began in 1903; separated eggs, in 1912. 1951 saw the first commercial egg breaking machines. No-cholesterol refrigerated or frozen egg substitutes first became available to consumers in 1973. They consist of egg whites, artificial color, and other non-egg additives. Specific questions about egg substitutes should be directed to the manufacturer or to the Food and Drug Administration (FDA).

Who Inspects Egg Products?

Congress passed the Egg Products Inspection Act (EPIA) in 1970. The EPIA provides for the mandatory continuous inspection of the processing of liquid, frozen, and dried egg products. For the next 25 years, the Poultry Division of USDA's Agricultural Marketing Service inspected egg products to ensure they were wholesome, otherwise not adulterated, and properly labeled and packaged to protect the health and welfare of consumers.

In 1995, the Food Safety and Inspection Service (FSIS) became responsible for the inspection of egg products. FSIS inspects all egg products, with the exception of those products exempted under the Act, that are used by food manufacturers, foodservice, institutions, and retail markets. Officially inspected egg products will bear the USDA inspection mark. In 2004, FSIS inspected 3.2 billion pounds of egg products.

The Department of Health and Human Services' FDA is responsible for the inspection of egg substitutes, imitation eggs, and similar products which are exempted from continuous inspection under the EPIA.

Are All Egg Products from the U.S.?

Currently, Canada is the only active exporter of egg products to the United States. The EPIA specifies that egg products may not be imported into the United States except from countries which have an egg products inspection system equivalent to that in this country.

Why Are Egg Products Useful?

Egg products are used widely by the foodservice industry and the commercial food industry. They are scrambled or made into omelets, or used as ingredients in egg dishes or other foods such as mayonnaise or ice cream. Food manufacturers use pasteurized egg products because of their convenience and ease in handling and storing. Because egg products are pasteurized, institutional foodservice operators, such as fast food chains, restaurants, hospitals, and nursing homes, use egg products to ensure a high level of food safety. Some egg products are sold in retail food stores.

How Are Egg Products Made?

Egg products are processed in sanitary facilities under continuous inspection by the USDA. The initial step in making egg products is breaking the eggs and separating the yolks and whites from the shells. Eggs are processed by automated equipment that moves the eggs from flats, washes and sanitizes the shells, breaks eggs and separates the whites and yolks, and/or makes mixtures of them. The liquid egg product is filtered, mixed, and then chilled prior to additional processing.

Why and How Are Egg Products Pasteurized?

The law requires that all egg products distributed for consumption be pasteurized. This means that they must be rapidly heated and held at a minimum required temperature for a specified time. This destroys *Salmonella,* but it does not cook the eggs or affect their color, flavor, nutritional value, or use. Dried whites are pasteurized by heating in the dried form, again for a specified time and at a minimum required temperature.

Since many new and different types of egg products are now being formulated, government and industry are currently evaluating the effectiveness of the pasteurization processes used for these and other products. Additional research will determine if supplemental or different safety measures are warranted to continue to provide safe egg products for foodservice, industry, and consumers.

Are All Egg Products Pasteurized?

Certain commodities are not presently considered egg products and are exempt from this law. These commodities, which are under the jurisdiction of the FDA, include freeze-dried products, imitation egg products, and egg substitutes. Inspected, pasteurized egg products are used to make these commodities, and companies may elect to re-pasteurize these products following formulation and before packaging.

Can Egg Products Be Used As An Ingredient In Uncooked Foods?

Egg products can be used in baking or cooking (scrambled eggs, for example). They are pasteurized but are best used in a cooked product, especially if serving high-risk persons, that is, infants and young children, pregnant women and their unborn babies, older adults and people with weakened immune systems (such as those with HIV/AIDS, cancer, diabetes, kidney disease, and transplant patients). Use a food thermometer to be sure that the internal temperature of the cooked product reaches 160 °F.

Egg products can be substituted in recipes typically made with raw eggs that won't be cooked (for example, Caesar salad, Hollandaise sauce, eggnog, homemade mayonnaise, ice cream, and key lime pie). The USDA does not recommend eating raw shell eggs that are not cooked or undercooked due to the possibility that *Salmonella* bacteria may be present.

Buying Tips for Egg Products

Buy only pasteurized egg products that bear the USDA inspection mark. Make sure containers are tightly sealed. Frozen products should show no signs of thawing. Refrigerated products should be kept at 40 °F or below. Dried egg products should not be caked or hardened.

What is Dried Egg Mix?

USDA Dried Egg Mix is a blend of dried whole eggs, nonfat dry milk, soybean oil, and a small amount of salt. There is very little moisture in it. To reconstitute, blend 2 tablespoons of Dried Egg Mix with ¼ cup water to make the equivalent of one large whole egg.

Dried Egg Mix is packaged in 6-ounce pouches, equivalent to about 6 eggs each. It is distributed by USDA to food banks, Indian reservations, and other needy family outlets, and is also used in disaster feeding (for hurricane and flood victims, for example). Dried egg mix was initially developed for the military during the 1930's. A similar product called All Purpose Egg Mix, containing a greater proportion of eggs, is now being manufactured for USDA. It is reconstituted by mixing one part egg mix with two parts of water (by weight). All Purpose Egg Mix is available to schools as part of the School Lunch Program. It is packaged in 10-pound bags.

Safe Handling and Storage of Egg Products

Safe storage and handling is necessary for all egg products to prevent bacterial contamination. Here are recommendations from USDA:

- For best quality, store frozen egg products up to one year. Check to be sure your freezer is set at 0 °F or lower. After thawing, do not refreeze.

- Thaw frozen egg products in the refrigerator or under cold running water. DO NOT THAW ON THE COUNTER.
- If the container for liquid products bears a "use-by" date, observe it. Follow the storage and handling instructions provided by the manufacturer.
- For liquid products without an expiration date, store unopened containers at 40 °F or below for up to 7 days (not to exceed 3 days after opening). Do not freeze opened cartons of liquid egg products.
- Unopened dried egg products and egg white solids can be stored at room temperature as long as they are kept cool and dry. After opening, store in the refrigerator.
- Reconstituted egg products should be used immediately or refrigerated and used that day.
- USDA Commodity Dried Egg Mix should be stored at less than 50 °F, preferably in the refrigerator (at 40 °F or below). After opening, use within 7 to 10 days. Reconstitute only the amount needed at one time. Use reconstituted egg mix immediately or refrigerate and use within 1 hour.

Nutrition of Egg Products

Eggs are still considered one of nature's most complete foods. With the implementation of the Nutrition Labeling and Education Act in 1994, egg products sold at retail are also required to bear nutrition labeling. The "Nutrition Facts" panel will tell you the nutrient composition of that specific product per serving and its contribution to your overall diet.

Labels on Egg Products

In addition to nutrition information on consumer packages, other labeling information is required for egg products. All egg products must be labeled with:

- the common or usual name and (if the product is comprised of two or more ingredients) the ingredients listed in the order of descending proportions;
- the name and address of the packer or distributor;
- the date of pack which may be shown as a lot number or production code number;

- the net contents;
- the official USDA inspection mark and establishment number.

Shell Eggs from Farm to Table

Eggs are among the most nutritious foods on earth and can be part of a healthy diet. However, they are perishable just like raw meat, poultry, and fish. Unbroken, clean, fresh shell eggs may contain *Salmonella* Enteritidis (SE) bacteria that can cause foodborne illness. While the number of eggs affected is quite small, there have been cases of foodborne illness in the last few years. To be safe, eggs must be safely handled, refrigerated, and cooked.

What is the History of the Egg?

"Eggs existed long before chickens," according to *On Food and Cooking: The Science and Lore of the Kitchen* by Harold McGee. "The first eggs were released, fertilized, and hatched in the ocean. Around 250 million years ago, the earliest fully land-dwelling animals, the reptiles, developed a self-contained egg with a tough, leathery skin that prevented fatal water loss. The eggs of birds, animals that arose some 100 million years later, are a refined version of this reproductive adaptation to life on land. Eggs, then, are millions of years older than birds. *Gallus domesticus*, the chicken more or less as we know it, is only a scant 4 or 5 thousand years old."

How Often Does a Hen Lay an Egg?

The entire time from ovulation to laying is about 25 hours. Then about 30 minutes later, the hen will begin to make another one.

How Does *Salmonella* Infect Eggs?

Bacteria can be on the outside of a shell egg. That's because the egg exits the hen's body through the same passageway as feces is excreted. That's why eggs are washed and sanitized at the processing plant. Bacteria can be inside an uncracked, whole egg. Contamination of eggs may be due to bacteria within the hen's ovary or oviduct before the shell forms around the yolk and white. SE doesn't make the hen sick. It is also possible for eggs to become infected by *Salmonella* Enteritidis fecal contamination through the pores of the shells after they're laid.

What Part Carries Bacteria?

Researchers say that, if present, the SE is usually in the yolk or "yellow." However, they can't rule out the bacteria being in egg whites. So everyone is advised against eating raw or undercooked egg yolks and whites or products containing raw or undercooked eggs.

What Safe Handling Instructions are on Egg Cartons?

All packages of raw, shell eggs not treated to destroy *Salmonella* must carry the following safe handling statement:

SAFE HANDLING INSTRUCTIONS: To prevent illness from bacteria: Keep eggs refrigerated, cook eggs until yolks are firm, and cook foods containing eggs thoroughly.

Who is "At Risk" for Eating Raw or Undercooked Eggs?

Infants, young children, older adults, pregnant women, and people with weakened immune systems are particularly vulnerable to SE infections. A chronic illness weakens the immune system, making the person vulnerable to foodborne illnesses.

No one should eat foods containing raw eggs. This includes "health food" milk shakes made with raw eggs, Caesar salad, Hollandaise sauce, and any other foods like homemade mayonnaise, ice cream, or eggnog made from recipes in which the egg ingredients are not cooked. However, in-shell pasteurized eggs may be used safely without cooking.

Who is Working on Eliminating the *Salmonella* in Eggs?

Federal and state governments, the egg industry, and the scientific community are working together to solve the problem. Involved government agencies include: USDA's Food Safety and Inspection Service (FSIS), Agricultural Research Service (ARS), and the Animal and Plant Health Inspection Service (APHIS); the U.S. Food and Drug Administration (FDA); and State departments of agriculture.

Government agencies have implemented an Egg Safety Action Plan to eliminate *Salmonella* Enteritidis illnesses due to eggs. The Action Plan identifies the systems and practices that must be carried out in order to meet the goal of eliminating SE illnesses associated with the consumption of eggs by 2010.

What Government Agencies are Responsible for the Safety of Shell Eggs?

Many government agencies cooperate to ensure the safety of shell eggs from farm to table.

USDA AGENCIES

Agricultural Marketing Service (AMS)

- AMS administers a voluntary egg-quality grading program for shell eggs paid for by processing plants.
- AMS also is responsible for the Shell Egg Surveillance Program to assure that eggs in the marketplace are as good as or better than U.S. Consumer Grade B quality standards. AMS conducts inspection of handlers and hatcheries four times each year to ensure conformance with these requirements. Eggs exceeding the tolerance for checks or loss must be diverted from the marketplace for further segregation or processing.
- The USDA grade mark on egg cartons means the plant processed the eggs following USDA's sanitation and good manufacturing processes.
- Effective June 19, 2006, AMS announced final rulemaking prohibiting the repackaging of eggs previously shipped for retail sale that were packed under its voluntary grading program.

Animal and Plant Health Inspection Service (APHIS)

- APHIS conducts activities to reduce the risk of disease in flocks of laying hens.
- APHIS administers the voluntary National Poultry Improvement Plan (NPIP), which certifies that poultry breeding stock and hatcheries are free from certain diseases. Participation is necessary for producers that ship interstate or internationally.
- APHIS' National Animal Health Monitoring System is currently conducting a nationwide survey of the egg industry whose purpose is to estimate the national prevalence of SE layer flocks.

Food Safety and Inspection Service (FSIS)

- FSIS is responsible for the import of eggs destined for further processing and for assuring that imported shell eggs destined for the retail market are transported under refrigerated conditions.
- FSIS verifies shell eggs packed for the consumer are labeled "Keep Refrigerated" and transported under refrigeration and ambient temperature of no greater than 45 °F.
- USDA also educates consumers about the safe handling of eggs. FSIS has developed numerous publications on egg safety and uses a variety of networks (such as the USDA Meat and Poultry Hotline, "Ask Karen," and USDA cooperative extension agents) to get this information to consumers.

Agricultural Research Service (ARS)

- USDA also carries out food safety research through ARS and through a program administered by USDA's Cooperative State Research, Education & Extension Service (CSREES). Subjects include studying how *Salmonella* adheres to chicken cells, and developing an oral vaccine against SE.
- In 2005, ARS established the Egg Safety and Research Unit at the Russell Research Center in Athens, GA, to expand egg safety and egg processing research.

National Agricultural Statistics Service (NASS)

- USDA collects processing and distribution information for the economic analysis of the egg products industry through NASS.

OTHER GOVERNMENT AGENCIES

FSIS/FDA Cooperation

- FSIS and the FDA share authority for egg safety and are working together toward solving the problem of SE in eggs.
- FSIS and FDA are working to strengthen the Food Code

and to encourage its adoption by States and local jurisdictions.

State Agriculture Departments

- State agriculture departments monitor for compliance of the official U.S. standards, grades, and weight classes by egg packers who do not use the USDA/AMS shell egg grading service.

State and Local Health Departments

- State and local health departments monitor retail food and foodservice establishments for compliance with state and local health department requirements.

What is Candling?

Candling is the process of using light to help determine the quality of an egg. Automated mass-scanning equipment is used by most egg packers to detect eggs with cracked shells and interior defects. During candling, eggs travel along a conveyor belt and pass over a light source where the defects become visible. Defective eggs are removed. Hand candling—holding a shell egg directly in front of a light source—is done to spot check and determine accuracy in grading. Advanced technology, utilizing computerized integrated cameras and sound wave technology, is also being applied for the segregation of eggs.

How Are Eggs Transported Safely to Stores?

The U.S. Department of Commerce's 1990 Sanitary Food Transportation Act requires that vehicles be dedicated to transporting food only. On August 27, 1999, FSIS made effective a new rule requiring:

- Shell eggs packed for consumers be stored and transported under refrigeration at an ambient (surrounding) air temperature not to exceed 45 °F;
- All packed shell eggs be labeled with a statement that refrigeration is required; and
- Any shell eggs imported into the United States, packed for consumer use, include a certification that they have been stored and transported at an ambient temperature of no greater than 45 °F.

What Is Included Under the Egg Products Inspection Act?

The term "egg products" refers to eggs that have been removed from their shells for processing at facilities called "breaker plants." The safety of these products is the responsibility of FSIS. Basic egg products include whole eggs, whites, yolks, and various blends—with or without non-egg ingredients—that are processed and pasteurized. They may be available in liquid, frozen, and dried forms. Most are not available in supermarkets, but are used in restaurants, hospitals, and other foodservice establishments as well as by bakers, noodle makers, and other food manufacturers.

Egg products are pasteurized. The 1970 Egg Products Inspection Act (EPIA) requires that all egg products distributed for consumption be pasteurized. They are rapidly heated and held at a minimum required temperature for a specified time. This destroys *Salmonella*, but it does not cook the eggs or affect their color, flavor, nutritional value, or use. Dried eggs are pasteurized by heating in the dried form.

While inspected pasteurized egg products are used to make freeze-dried egg products, imitation egg products, and egg substitutes, these products are not covered under the EPIA and are under FDA jurisdiction. No-cholesterol egg substitutes consist of egg whites, artificial color, and other non-egg additives. Direct questions about egg substitutes to the manufacturer or to the FDA. For more information about egg products, read "Egg Products and Food Safety" (http://www.fsis.usda.gov/Fact_Sheets/Egg_Products_and_Food_Safety/index.asp).

Can Shell Eggs Be Pasteurized?

Shell eggs can be pasteurized by a processor if FDA approves the process. Pasteurized shell eggs are now available at some grocery stores. Like all eggs, they must be kept refrigerated. The equipment to pasteurize shell eggs isn't available for home use, and it is not possible to pasteurize shell eggs at home without cooking the contents of the egg.

Are Powdered Egg Whites Pasteurized?

Yes. Egg white powder is dried egg white (pure albumen). It can be reconstituted by mixing the powder with water. The reconstituted powder whips like fresh egg white and, because it is pasteurized, can be used safely without cooking or baking it. The product is usually sold along with supplies for cake baking and decorating.

What Points Should You Consider When Buying Eggs?

Always purchase eggs from a refrigerated case. Choose eggs with clean, uncracked shells. Don't buy out-of-date eggs. Look for the USDA grade shield or mark. Graded eggs must meet standards for quality and size. Choose the size most useful and economical for you.

Is Grading of Eggs Mandatory?

USDA's grading service is voluntary; egg packers who request it, pay for it. The USDA grade shield on the carton means that the eggs were graded for quality and checked for weight (size) under the supervision of a trained USDA grader. Compliance with quality standards, grades, and weights is monitored by USDA. State agencies monitor compliance for egg packers who do not use the USDA grading service. These cartons will bear a term such as "Grade A" on their cartons without the USDA shield.

What Are Egg Grades?

There are three consumer grades for eggs: U.S. Grade AA, A, and B. The grade is determined by the interior quality of the egg and the appearance and condition of the egg shell. Eggs of any quality grade may differ in weight (size).

- *U.S. Grade AA* eggs have whites that are thick and firm; yolks that are high, round, and practically free from defects; and clean, unbroken shells. Grade AA and Grade A eggs are best for frying and poaching where appearance is important.
- *U.S. Grade A eggs* have characteristics of Grade AA eggs except that the whites are "reasonably" firm. This is the quality most often sold in stores.
- *U.S. Grade B* eggs have whites that may be thinner and yolks that may be wider and flatter than eggs of higher grades. The shells must be unbroken, but may show slight stains. This quality is seldom found in retail stores because they are usually used to make liquid, frozen, and dried egg products.

SIZING OF EGGS

Size tells you the minimum required net weight per dozen eggs. It does not refer to the dimensions of an egg or how big it looks. While some eggs in the carton may look slightly larger or smaller than the rest, it is the total weight of the dozen eggs that puts them in one of the following classes:

Size or Weight Class	Minimum net weight per dozen
Jumbo	30 ounces
Extra Large	27 ounces
Large	24 ounces
Medium	21 ounces
Small	18 ounces
Peewee	15 ounces

Dating of Cartons

Many eggs reach stores only a few days after the hen lays them. Egg cartons with the USDA grade shield on them must display the "Pack date" (the day that the eggs were washed, graded, and placed in the carton). The number is a three-digit code that represents the consecutive day of the year (the "Julian Date") starting with January 1 as 001 and ending with December 31 as 365. When a "sell-by" date appears on a carton bearing the USDA grade shield, the code date may not exceed 45 days from the date of pack.

Use of either a "Sell-by" or "Expiration" (EXP) date is not federally required, but may be State required, defined by the egg laws in the State where the eggs are marketed. Some State egg laws do not allow the use of a "Sell-by" date. Always purchase eggs before the "Sell-by" or "EXP" date on the carton.

After the eggs reach home, they may be refrigerated 3 to 5 weeks from the day they are placed in the refrigerator. The "sell-by" date will usually expire during that length of time, but the eggs are perfectly safe to use.

Why Should Eggs Be Refrigerated?

Temperature fluctuation is critical to safety. With the concern about *Salmonella*, eggs gathered from laying hens should be refrigerated as soon as possible. After eggs are refrigerated, they need to stay that way. A cold egg left out at room temperature can sweat, facilitating the growth of bacteria. Refrigerated eggs should not be left out more than 2 hours.

Should You Wash Eggs?

No. It's not necessary for consumers to wash eggs. When the chicken lays the egg, a protective coating is put on the outside by the hen. At the plant, government regulations require that USDA-graded eggs be carefully washed and sanitized using special detergent.

Why Do Hard-Cooked Eggs Spoil Faster than Fresh Eggs?

When shell eggs are hard cooked, the protective coating is washed away, leaving bare the pores in the shell for bacteria to enter and contaminate it. Hard-cooked eggs should be refrigerated within 2 hours of cooking and used within a week.

Safe Storage in Stores

At the store, choose Grade A or AA eggs with clean, uncracked shells. Make sure they've been refrigerated in the store. Any bacteria present in an egg can multiply quickly at room temperature. When purchasing egg products or substitutes, look for containers that are tightly sealed.

Bringing Eggs Home from the Store

Take eggs straight home and store them immediately in the refrigerator set at 40 °F or below. Keep them in their carton and place them in the coldest part of the refrigerator, not in the door.

Is It Safe to Use Eggs That Have Cracks?

Bacteria can enter eggs through cracks in the shell. Never purchase cracked eggs. However, if eggs crack on the way home from the store, break them into a clean container, cover it tightly, keep refrigerated, and use within 2 days. If eggs crack during hard cooking, they are safe.

How Are Eggs Handled Safely?

Proper refrigeration, cooking, and handling should prevent most egg-safety problems. Persons can enjoy eggs and dishes containing eggs if these safe handling guidelines are followed:

- Wash utensils, equipment, and work areas with hot, soapy water before and after contact with eggs.
- Don't keep eggs out of the refrigerator more than 2 hours.
- Raw eggs and other ingredients, combined according to recipe directions, should be cooked immediately or refrigerated and cooked within 24 hours.
- Serve cooked eggs and dishes containing eggs immediately after cooking, or place in shallow containers for quick cooling and refrigerate at once for later use. Use within 3 to 4 days.

Are Easter Eggs Safe?

Sometimes eggs are decorated, used as decorations, and hunted at Easter. Here are some safety tips for Easter eggs.

- *Dyeing eggs:* After hard cooking eggs, dye them and return them to the refrigerator within 2 hours. If eggs are to be eaten, use a food-safe coloring. As with all foods, persons dyeing the eggs should wash their hands before handling the eggs.
- *Decorations:* One Easter bread recipe is decorated with dyed, cooked eggs in the braided bread. After baking, serve within 2 hours or refrigerate and use within 3 to 4 days.
- *Blowing out eggshells:* Because some raw eggs may contain *Salmonella*, you must use caution when blowing out the contents to hollow out the shell for decorating, such as for Ukrainian Easter eggs. Use only eggs that have been kept refrigerated and are uncracked. To destroy bacteria that may be present on the surface of the egg, wash the egg in hot water and then rinse in a solution of 1 teaspoon liquid chlorine bleach per half cup of water. After blowing out the egg, refrigerate the contents and use within 2 to 4 days.
- *Hunting Eggs:* Hard-cooked eggs for an egg hunt must be prepared with care to prevent cracking the shells. If the shells crack, bacteria could contaminate the inside. Eggs should be hidden in places that are protected from dirt, pets, and other sources of bacteria. The total time for

hiding and hunting eggs should not exceed 2 hours. The "found" eggs must be re-refrigerated and eaten within 7 days of cooking.

Does the Color of the Shell Affect the Egg's Nutrients?

No. The breed of the hen determines the color of her eggs.

Araucuna chickens in South America lay eggs that range in color from medium blue to medium green. Nutrition claims that araucuna eggs contain less cholesterol than other eggs haven't been proven.

Are Fertilized Eggs More Nutritious?

No. There is no benefit in eating fertilized eggs. There is no nutritional difference in fertilized eggs and infertile eggs. Most eggs sold today are infertile; roosters are not housed with the laying hens. If the eggs are fertile and cell development is detected during the candling process, they are removed from commerce.

Per Capita Consumption

Egg consumption in America was on a 40-year downward slide until the 1990's. Then eggs became increasingly popular. The following figures are from USDA's Economic Research Service.

Year	Eggs per Person
2004	256
1990	236
1950	389

Is the Appearance of Eggs Related to Food Safety?

Sometimes, but not usually. Variation in egg color is due to many factors.

- *Blood spots* are caused by a rupture of one or more small blood vessels in the yolk at the time of ovulation. It does not indicate the egg is unsafe.
- A *cloudy white* (albumen) is a sign the egg is very fresh. A clear egg white is an indication the egg is aging.
- *Pink or iridescent egg white* (albumen) indicates spoilage due to *Pseudomonas* bacteria. Some of these microorganisms —which produce a greenish, fluorescent, water-soluble pigment—are harmful to humans.

- The *color of yolk* varies in shades of yellow depending upon the diet of the hen. If she eats plenty of yellow-orange plant pigments, such as from marigold petals and yellow corn, the yolk will be a darker yellow than if she eats a colorless diet such as white cornmeal. Artificial color additives are not permitted in eggs.
- A *green* ring on a hard-cooked yolk is a result of overcooking, and is caused by sulfur and iron compounds in the egg reacting on the yolk's surface. The green color can also be caused by a high amount of iron in the cooking water. Scrambled eggs cooked at too high a temperature or held on a steam table too long can also develop a greenish cast. The green color is safe to consume.

How Do Time and Refrigeration Affect Egg Quality?

The egg, as laid at 105 °F, normally has no air cell. As the egg cools, an air cell forms usually in the large end of the egg and develops between the two shell membranes. The air cell is formed as a result of the different rates of contraction between the shell and its contents.

Over time, the white and yolk of an egg lose quality. The yolk absorbs water from the white. Moisture and carbon dioxide in the white evaporate through the pores, allowing more air to penetrate the shell, and the air cell becomes larger. If broken open, the egg's contents would cover a wider area. The white would be thinner, losing some of its thickening and leavening powers. The yolk would be flatter, larger and more easily broken. The chalazae (kah-LAY-zuh), the twisted cord-like strands of egg white that anchor the yolk in the center of the white, would be less prominent and weaker, allowing the yolk to move off center. Refrigeration slows the loss of quality over time.

What Does It Mean When an Egg Floats in Water?

An egg can float in water when its air cell has enlarged sufficiently to keep it buoyant. This means the egg is old, but it may be perfectly safe to use. Crack the egg into a bowl and examine it for an off-odor or unusual appearance before deciding to use or discard it. A spoiled egg will have an unpleasant odor when you break open the shell, either when raw or cooked.

Safe Cooking Methods

Many cooking methods can be used to cook eggs safely including poaching, hard cooking, scrambling, frying and baking. However, eggs must be cooked thoroughly until yolks are firm. Scrambled eggs should not be runny. Casseroles and other dishes containing eggs should be cooked to a safe minimum internal temperature of 160 °F. Use a food thermometer to be sure.

Use Safe Egg Recipes

Egg mixtures are safe if they reach 160 °F, so homemade ice cream and eggnog can be made safely from a cooked egg-milk mixture. Heat it gently and use a food thermometer.

- Dry meringue shells are safe. So are divinity candy and 7-minute frosting, made by combining hot sugar syrup with beaten egg whites. Avoid icing recipes using uncooked eggs or egg whites.
- Meringue-topped pies should be safe if baked at 350 °F for about 15 minutes. Chiffon pies and fruit whips made with raw, beaten egg whites cannot be guaranteed to be safe. Instead, substitute pasteurized dried egg whites, whipped cream, or a whipped topping.
- To make a recipe safe that specifies using eggs that aren't cooked, heat the eggs in a liquid from the recipe over low heat, stirring constantly, until the mixture reaches 160 °F. Then combine it with the other ingredients and complete the recipe.
- To determine doneness in egg dishes such as quiche and casseroles, the center of the mixture should reach 160 °F when measured with a food thermometer.
- Use pasteurized eggs or egg products when preparing recipes that call for using eggs raw or undercooked.

What Makes Hard-Cooked Eggs Hard to Peel?

The fresher the egg, the more difficult it is to peel after hard cooking. That's because the air cell, found at the large end of the shell between the shell membranes, increases in size the longer the raw egg is stored. As the contents of the egg contracts and the air cell enlarges, the shell becomes easier to peel. For this reason, older eggs make better candidates for hard cooking.

Egg Storage Chart		
Product	**Refrigerator**	**Freezer**
Raw eggs in shell	3 to 5 weeks	Do not freeze.
Raw egg whites	2 to 4 days	12 months
Raw egg yolks	2 to 4 days	Yolks do not freeze well.
Raw egg accidentally frozen in shell	Use immediately after thawing.	Keep frozen; then refrigerate to thaw.
Hard-cooked eggs	1 week	Do not freeze.
Egg substitutes, liquid Unopened	10 days	Do not freeze.
Egg substitutes, liquid Opened	3 days	Do not freeze.
Egg substitutes, frozen Unopened	After thawing, 7 days, or refer to "Use-By" date on carton.	12 months
Egg substitutes, frozen Opened	After thawing, 3 days, or refer to "Use-By" date on carton.	Do not freeze.
Casseroles made with eggs	3 to 4 days	After baking, 2 to 3 months.
Eggnog, commercial	3 to 5 days	6 months
Eggnog, homemade	2 to 4 days	Do not freeze.
Pies, pumpkin or pecan	3 to 4 days	After baking, 1 to 2 months.
Pies, custard and chiffon	3 to 4 days	Do not freeze.
Quiche with any kind of filling	3 to 4 days	After baking, 1 to 2 months.

What Are Thousand-Year-Old Eggs?

These Chinese eggs are not really 1,000 years old, but are somewhere between a month and several years old. The egg is not retained in its original state, but rather converted into an entirely different food, probably by bacterial action. They are exempt from inspection and grading. The following are several types of thousand-year-old Chinese eggs.

"Hulidan" results when eggs are individually coated with a mixture of salt and wet clay or ashes for a month. This process darkens and partially solidifies the yolks, and gives the eggs a salty taste.

"Dsaudan" eggs are packed in cooked rice and salt for at least 6 months. During this time, the shell softens, the membranes thicken, and the egg contents coagulate. The flavor is wine-like.

"Pidan," a great delicacy, is made by covering eggs with lime, salt, wood ashes, and a tea infusion for 5 months or more. The egg yolks become greenish gray and the albumen turns into a coffee-brown jelly. Pidan smell ammonia-like and taste like lime.

Do Pickled Eggs Keep a Long Time?

Pickled eggs are hard-cooked eggs marinated in vinegar and pickling spices, spicy cider, or juice from pickles or pickled beets. Studies done at the American Egg Board substantiate that unopened containers of commercially pickled eggs keep for several months on the shelf. After opening, keep refrigerated and use within 7 days. Home-prepared pickled eggs must be kept refrigerated and used within 7 days. Home canning of pickled eggs is not recommended.

11

Barbecue and Food Safety

Cooking outdoors was once only a summer activity shared with family and friends. Now more than half of Americans say they are cooking outdoors year round. So whether the snow is blowing or the sun is shining brightly, it's important to follow food safety guidelines to prevent harmful bacteria from multiplying and causing foodborne illness. Use these simple guidelines for grilling food safely.

FROM THE STORE: HOME FIRST

When shopping, buy cold food like meat and poultry last, right before checkout. Separate raw meat and poultry from other food in your shopping cart.

To guard against cross-contamination — which can happen when raw meat or poultry juices drip on other food — put packages of raw meat and poultry into plastic bags.

Plan to drive directly home from the grocery store. You may want to take a cooler with ice for perishables. Always refrigerate perishable food within 2 hours. Refrigerate within 1 hour when the temperature is above 90 °F.

At home, place meat and poultry in the refrigerator immediately. Freeze poultry and ground meat that won't be used in 1 or 2 days; freeze other meat within 4 to 5 days.

THAW SAFELY

Completely thaw meat and poultry before grilling so it cooks more evenly. Use the refrigerator for slow, safe thawing or thaw sealed packages in cold water. You can microwave defrost if the food will be placed immediately on the grill.

MARINATING

A marinade is a savory, acidic sauce in which a food is soaked to enrich its flavor or to tenderize it. Marinate food in the refrigerator, not on the counter. Poultry and cubed meat or stew meat can be marinated up to 2 days. Beef, veal, pork, and lamb roasts, chops, and steaks may be marinated up to 5 days. If some of the marinade is to be used as a sauce on the cooked food, reserve a portion of the marinade before putting raw meat and poultry in it. However, if the marinade used on raw meat or poultry is to be reused, make sure to let it come to a boil first to destroy any harmful bacteria.

Transporting

When carrying food to another location, keep it cold to minimize bacterial growth. Use an insulated cooler with sufficient ice or ice packs to keep the food at 40 °F or below. Pack food right from the refrigerator into the cooler immediately before leaving home.

Keep Cold Food Cold

Keep meat and poultry refrigerated until ready to use. Only take out the meat and poultry that will immediately be placed on the grill.

When using a cooler, keep it out of the direct sun by placing it in the shade or shelter. Avoid opening the lid too often, which lets cold air out and warm air in. Pack beverages in one cooler and perishables in a separate cooler.

Keep Everything Clean

Be sure there are plenty of clean utensils and platters. To prevent foodborne illness, don't use the same platter and utensils for raw and cooked meat and poultry. Harmful bacteria present in raw meat and poultry and their juices can contaminate safely cooked food.If you're eating away from home, find out if there's a source of clean water. If not, bring water for preparation and cleaning. Or pack clean cloths, and wet towelettes for cleaning surfaces and hands.

Precooking

Precooking food partially in the microwave, oven, or stove is a good way of reducing grilling time. Just make sure that the food goes immediately on the preheated grill to complete cooking.

SAFE MINIMUM INTERNAL TEMPERATURES

Whole poultry: 165 °F

Poultry breasts: 165 °F

Ground poultry: 165 °F

Hamburgers, beef: 160 °F

Beef, veal, and lamb (steaks, roasts and chops):

- Medium rare 145 °F
- Medium 160 °F

All cuts of pork: 160 °F

Cook Thoroughly

Cook food to a safe minimum internal temperature to destroy harmful bacteria. Meat and poultry cooked on a grill often browns very fast on the outside.

Use a food thermometer to be sure the food has reached a safe minimum internal temperature. Beef, veal, and lamb steaks, roasts and chops can be cooked to 145 °F. Hamburgers made of ground beef should reach 160 °F. All cuts of pork should reach 160 °F. All poultry should reach a minimum of 165 °F.

NEVER partially grill meat or poultry and finish cooking later.

Reheating

When reheating fully cooked meats like hot dogs, grill to 165 °F or until steaming hot.

Keep Hot Food Hot

After cooking meat and poultry on the grill, keep it hot until served — at 140 °F or warmer.

Keep cooked meats hot by setting them to the side of the grill rack, not directly over the coals where they could overcook. At home, the cooked meat can be kept hot in an oven set at approximately 200 °F, in a chafing dish or slow cooker, or on a warming tray.

Serving the Food

When taking food off the grill, use a clean platter. Don't put cooked food on the same platter that held raw meat or poultry. Any harmful bacteria present in the raw meat juices could contaminate safely cooked food.

In hot weather (above 90 °F), food should never sit out for more than 1 hour.

Leftovers

Refrigerate any leftovers promptly in shallow containers. Discard any food left out more than 2 hours (1 hour if temperatures are above 90 °F).

Safe Smoking

Smoking is cooking food indirectly in the presence of a fire. It can be done in a covered grill if a pan of water is placed beneath the meat on the grill; and meats can be smoked in a "smoker," which is an outdoor cooker especially designed for smoking foods. Smoking is done much more slowly than grilling, so less tender meats benefit from this method, and a natural smoke flavoring permeates the meat. The temperature in the smoker should be maintained at 250 to 300 °F for safety.

Use a food thermometer to be sure the food has reached a safe internal temperature.

Pit Roasting

Pit roasting is cooking meat in a large, level hole dug in the earth. A hardwood fire is built in the pit, requiring wood equal to about 2½ times the volume of the pit. The hardwood is allowed to burn until the wood reduces and the pit is half filled with burning coals. This can require 4 to 6 hours burning time. Cooking may require 10 to 12 hours or more and is difficult to estimate.

A food thermometer must be used to determine the meat's safety and doneness. There are many variables such as outdoor temperature, the size and thickness of the meat, and how fast the coals are cooking.

Does Grilling Pose a Cancer Risk?

Some studies suggest there may be a cancer risk related to eating food cooked by high-heat cooking techniques as grilling, frying, and broiling. Based on present research findings, eating moderate amounts of grilled meats like fish, meat, and poultry cooked — without charring — to a safe temperature does not pose a problem.

To prevent charring, remove visible fat that can cause a flare-up. Precook meat in the microwave immediately before placing it on the grill to release some of the juices that can drop on coals. Cook food in the center of the grill and move coals to the side to prevent fat and juices from dripping on them. Cut charred portions off the meat.

Food Safety While Hiking, Camping & Boating

Outdoor activities are popular with Americans nationwide. The fresh air and exercise revives the spirit and the mind. Hiking, camping, and boating are good activities for active people and families, and in some parts of the country you can enjoy the outdoors for 2 or 3 seasons. In many cases, these activities last all day and involve preparing at least one meal. If the food is not handled correctly, foodborne illness can be an unwelcome souvenir.

"Keep Hot Foods Hot & Cold Foods Cold"

Whether you are in your kitchen or enjoying the great outdoors, there are some food safety principles that remain constant. The first is "Keep hot foods hot and cold foods cold." Meat and poultry products may contain bacteria that cause foodborne illness. They must be cooked to destroy these bacteria and held at temperatures that are either too hot or too cold for these bacteria to grow.

Most bacteria do not grow rapidly at temperatures below 40 °F or above 140 °F. The temperature range in between is known as the "Danger Zone." Bacteria multiply rapidly at these temperatures and can reach dangerous levels after 2 hours.

If you are traveling with cold foods, bring a cooler with a cold source. If you are cooking, use a hot campfire or portable stove. It is difficult to keep foods hot without a heat source when traveling, so it's best to cook foods before leaving home, cool them, and transport them cold.

"Keep Everything Clean"

The second principle is that bacteria present on raw meat and poultry products can be easily spread to other foods by juices dripping from packages, hands, or utensils. This is called cross-contamination. When transporting raw meat or poultry, double wrap or place the packages in plastic bags to prevent juices from the raw product from dripping on other foods. Always wash your hands before and after handling food, and don't use the same platter and utensils for raw and cooked meat and poultry. Soap and water are essential to cleanliness, so if you are going somewhere that will not have running water, bring it with you. Even disposable wipes will do.

Food Safety While Hiking & Camping

Sometimes you just have to get out and walk around in the solitude and beauty of our country. You may want to hike for just a few hours, or you may want to camp for a few days. One meal and some snacks are all that's needed for a short hike. Planning meals for a longer hike requires more thought. You have to choose foods that are light enough to carry in a backpack and that can be transported safely.

Hot or Cold?

The first principle is to keep foods either hot or cold. Since it is difficult to keep foods hot without a heat source (although the new insulated casserole dishes will keep things hot for an hour or so), it is best to transport chilled foods. Refrigerate or freeze the food overnight. For a cold source, bring frozen gel-packs or freeze some box drinks. The drinks will thaw as you hike and keep your meal cold at the same time. What foods to bring? For a day hike, just about anything will do as long as you can fit it in your backpack and keep it cold — sandwiches, fried chicken, bread and cheese, and even salads — or choose non-perishable foods.

Clean

The second principle is to keep everything clean, so remember to bring disposable wipes if you are taking a day trip. (Water is too heavy to bring enough for cleaning dishes!)

Safe Drinking Water

It is not a good idea to depend on fresh water from a lake or stream for drinking, no matter how clean it appears. Some pathogens thrive in remote mountain lakes or streams and there is no way to know what might have fallen into the water upstream. Bring bottled or tap water for drinking. Always start out with a full water bottle, and replenish your supply from tested public systems when possible. On long trips you can find water in streams, lakes, and springs, but be sure to purify any water from the wild, no matter how clean it appears.

The surest way to make water safe is to boil it. Boiling will kill microorganisms. First, bring water to a rolling boil, and then continue boiling for 1 minute. Before heating, muddy water should be allowed to stand for a while to allow the silt to settle to the bottom. Dip the clear water off the top and boil. At higher elevations, where the boiling point of water is lower, boil for several minutes.

As an alternative to boiling water, you can also use water purification tablets and water filters. The purification tablets — which contain iodine, halazone, or chlorine — kill most waterborne bacteria, viruses, and some (but not all) parasites. Because some parasites — such as *Cryptosporidium parvum*, *Giardia lamblia*, and larger bacteria — are not killed by purification tablets, you must also use a water filter. These water filtering devices must be 1 micron absolute or smaller. Over time purification tablets lose their potency, so keep your supply fresh. Water sanitizing tablets for washing dishes can also be purchased (just don't confuse the two). Water purification tablets, filters, and sanitizing tablets can be purchased at camping supply stores.

What Foods to Bring?

If you are backpacking for more than a day, the food situation gets a little more complicated. You can still bring cold foods for the first day, but you'll have to pack shelf-stable items for the next day. Canned goods are safe, but heavy, so plan your menu carefully. Advances in food technology have produced relatively lightweight staples that don't need refrigeration or careful packaging. For example:

- peanut butter in plastic jars;
- concentrated juice boxes;
- canned tuna, ham, chicken, and beef;.
- dried noodles and soups;
- beef jerky and other dried meats;
- dehydrated foods;
- dried fruits and nuts; and
- powdered milk and fruit drinks.

Powdered mixes for biscuits or pancakes are easy to carry and prepare, as is dried pasta. There are plenty of powdered sauce mixes that can be used over pasta, but check the required ingredient list. Carry items like dried pasta, rice, and baking mixes in plastic bags and take only the amount you'll need.

COOKING AT CAMP

After you have decided on a menu, you need to plan how you will prepare the food. You'll want to take as few pots as possible (they're heavy!). Camping supply stores sell lightweight cooking gear that nest together, but you can also use aluminum foil wrap and pans for cooking.

You'll need to decide in advance how you will cook. Will you bring along a portable stove, or will you build a campfire? Many camping areas prohibit campfires, so check first or assume you will have to take a stove. Make sure to bring any equipment you will need.

If you are bringing a camp stove, practice putting it together and lighting it before you pack. If you build a campfire, carefully extinguish the fire and dispose of the ashes before breaking camp. Likewise, leftover food should be burned, not dumped. Lastly, be sure to pack garbage bags to dispose of any other trash, and carry it out with you.

Use a Food Thermometer

Another important piece of camping equipment is a food thermometer. If you are cooking meat or poultry on a portable stove or over a fire, you'll need a way to determine when it is done and safe to eat. Color is not a reliable indicator of doneness, and it can be especially tricky to tell the color of a food if you are cooking in a wooded area in the evening.

When cooking hamburger patties on a grill or portable stove, use a digital thermometer to measure the temperature. Digital thermometers register the temperature in the very tip of the probe, so the safety of thin foods — such as hamburger patties and boneless chicken breasts — as well as thicker foods can be determined. A dial thermometer determines the temperature of a food by averaging the temperature along the stem and, therefore, should be inserted 2 to 2 ½ inches into the food. If the food is thin, the probe must be inserted sideways into the food.

It is critical to use a food thermometer when cooking hamburgers. Ground beef may be contaminated with *E. coli* O157:H7, a particularly dangerous strain of bacteria. Illnesses have occurred even when ground beef patties were cooked until there was no visible pink. The only way to insure that ground beef patties are safely cooked is to use a food thermometer, and cook the patty until it reaches 160 °F.

Cook all meat and poultry to safe minimum internal temperatures:

- Beef, veal, and lamb steaks, roasts, and chops may be cooked to 145 °F.
- All cuts of pork to 160 °F.
- Ground beef, veal and lamb to 160 °F.
- All poultry should reach 165 °F.

Heat hot dogs and any leftover food to 165 °F. Be sure to clean the thermometer between uses.

Keeping Cold

If you are "car camping" (driving to your site), you don't have quite as many restrictions. First, you will have the luxury of bringing a cooler. What kind of cooler? Foam chests are lightweight, low cost, and have good "cold retention" power. But they are fragile and may not last through numerous outings. Plastic, fiberglass, or steel coolers are more durable and can take a lot of outdoor wear. They also have excellent "cold retention" power, but, once filled, larger models may weigh 30 or 40 pounds.

To keep foods cold, you'll need a cold source. A block of ice keeps longer than ice cubes. Before leaving home, freeze clean, empty milk cartons filled with water to make blocks of ice, or use frozen gel-packs. Fill the cooler with cold or frozen foods. Pack foods in reverse order. First foods packed should be the last foods used. (There is one exception: pack raw meat or poultry below ready-to-eat foods to prevent raw meat or poultry juices from dripping on the other foods.) Take foods in the smallest quantity needed (e.g., a small jar of mayonnaise). At the campsite, insulate the cooler with a blanket, tarp, or poncho. When the camping trip is over, discard all perishable foods if there is no longer ice in the cooler or if the gel-pack is no longer frozen.

Cleanup

Whether taking a hike or camping at an established site, if you will be washing dishes or cookware, there are some rules to follow. Camping supply stores sell biodegradable camping soap in liquid and solid forms. But use it sparingly, and keep it out of rivers, lakes, streams, and springs, as it will pollute. If you use soap to clean your pots, wash the pots at the campsite, not at the water's edge. Dump dirty water on dry ground, well away from fresh water. Some wilderness campers use baking soda to wash their utensils. Pack disposable wipes for hands and quick cleanups.

Food Safety While Boating

Keeping food safe for a day on the boat may not be quite as challenging as for a hike, but when you are out on the water, the direct sunlight can be an even bigger food safety problem. Remember the "Danger Zone"? It is true that bacteria multiply rapidly at warm temperatures, and food can become unsafe if held in the "Danger Zone" for over 2 hours. Above 90 °F, food can become dangerous after only 1 hour. In direct sunlight, temperatures can climb even higher than that. So bring along plenty of ice, and keep the cooler shaded or covered with a blanket.

Keep Your Cooler Cool

A cooler for perishable food is essential. It is important to keep it closed, out of the sun, and covered, if possible, for further insulation. Better yet, bring two coolers: one for drinks and snacks, and another for more perishable food. The drink cooler will be opened and closed a lot, which lets hot air in and causes the ice to melt faster. Pack your coolers with several inches of ice, blocks of ice, or frozen gel-packs. Store food in watertight containers to prevent contact with melting ice water.

Keep Cold Foods Cold

Perishable foods, like luncheon meats, cooked chicken (Yes, that includes fried chicken!), and potato or pasta salads, should be kept in the cooler. Remember the rule: hot foods hot, cold foods cold?

And the 2-hour rule: no food should be in the "Danger Zone" for more than 2 hours? Well, unless you plan to eat that bucket of fried chicken within 2 hours of purchase, it needs to be kept in the cooler. For optimum safety, consider buying it the night before, refrigerating it in a shallow container (not the bucket), and then packing it cold in the cooler.

Of course, some foods don't need to be stored in the cooler: whole fresh fruits and vegetables, nuts, trail mix, canned meat spreads, and peanut butter and jelly. (However, once canned foods are opened, put them in the cooler.)

If you don't have an insulated cooler, try freezing sandwiches for your outing. Use coarse-textured breads that don't get soggy when thawed.

Take the mayonnaise, lettuce, and tomato with you to add at mealtime. In a pinch, a heavy cardboard box lined with plastic bags and packed with frozen gel packs or ice will keep things cold until lunchtime. Freeze water in milk cartons for your cold source.

Seafood

If you are planning to fish, check with your fish and game agency or state health department to see where you can fish safely, then follow these guidelines:

Finfish:

- Scale, gut, and clean fish as soon as they're caught.
- Live fish can be kept on stringers or in live wells, as long as they have enough water and enough room to move and breathe.
- Wrap fish, both whole and cleaned, in water-tight plastic and store on ice.
- Keep 3 to 4 inches of ice on the bottom of the cooler. Alternate layers of fish and ice.
- Store the cooler out of the sun and cover with a blanket.
- Once home, eat fresh fish within 1 to 2 days or freeze them. For top quality, use frozen fish within 3 to 6 months.

Shellfish:

- Crabs, lobsters, and other shellfish must be kept alive until cooked.
- Store in live wells or out of water in a bushel or laundry basket under wet burlap or seaweed.
- Crabs and lobsters are best eaten the day they're caught.
- Live oysters should be cooked within 7 to 10 days.
- Live mussels and clams should be cooked within 4 to 5 days.
- Eating raw shellfish is extremely dangerous. People with liver disorders or weakened immune systems are especially at risk.

Cleanup

Cleanup on the boat is similar to cleanup in the wild. Bring disposable wipes for handwashing, and bag up all your trash to dispose of when you return to shore.

General Rules for Outdoor Food Safety

Plan ahead: decide what you are going to eat and how you are going to cook it; then plan what equipment you will need.

- Pack safely: use a cooler if car-camping or boating, or pack foods in the frozen state with a cold source if hiking or backpacking.

- Keep raw foods separate from other foods.
- Never bring meat or poultry products without a cold source to keep them safe.
- Bring disposable wipes or biodegradable soap for hand- and dishwashing.
- Plan on carrying bottled water for drinking. Otherwise, boil water or use water purification tablets.
- Do not leave trash in the wild or throw it off your boat.
- If using a cooler, leftover food is safe only if the cooler still has ice in it. Otherwise, discard leftover food.
- Whether in the wild or on the high seas, protect yourself and your family by washing your hands before and after handling food.

Holiday or Party Buffets

A popular way to celebrate holidays or any party occasion is to invite friends and family to a buffet. However, this type of food service where foods are left out for long periods leave the door open for uninvited guests — bacteria that cause foodborne illness. Festive times for giving and sharing should not include sharing foodborne illness. Here are some tips from the USDA's Meat and Poultry Hotline to help you have a SAFE holiday party.

Safe Food Handling

Always wash your hands before and after handling food. Keep your kitchen, dishes and utensils clean also. Always serve food on clean plates — not those previously holding raw meat and poultry. Otherwise, bacteria which may have been present in raw meat juices can cross contaminate the food to be served.

Cook Thoroughly

If you are cooking foods ahead of time for your party, be sure to cook foods thoroughly to safe minimum internal temperatures.

- Beef, veal, and lamb steaks, roasts, and chops may be cooked to 145 °F.
- All cuts of pork to 160 °F.
- Ground beef, veal and lamb to 160 °F.

- All poultry should reach a safe minimum internal temperature of 165 °F.

Use Shallow Containers

Divide cooked foods into shallow containers to store in the refrigerator or freezer until serving. This encourages rapid, even cooling. Reheat hot foods to 165 °F. Arrange and serve food on several small platters rather than on one large platter. Keep the rest of the food hot in the oven (set at 200-250 °F) or cold in the refrigerator until serving time. This way foods will be held at a safe temperature for a longer period of time. REPLACE empty platters rather than adding fresh food to a dish that already had food in it. Many people's hands may have been taking food from the dish, which has also been sitting out at room temperature.

The Two-Hour Rule

Foods should not sit at room temperature for more than two hours. Keep track of how long foods have been sitting on the buffet table and discard anything there two hours or more.

Keep Hot Foods HOT And Cold Foods COLD

Hot foods should be held at 140 °F or warmer. On the buffet table you can keep hot foods hot with chafing dishes, slow cookers, and warming trays. Cold foods should be held at 40 °F or colder. Keep foods cold by nesting dishes in bowls of ice. Otherwise, use small serving trays and replace them.

Foodborne Bacteria

Bacteria are everywhere but a few types especially like to crash parties. *Staphylococcus aureus, Clostridium perfringens* and *Listeria monocytogenes* frequent people's hands and steam tables. And unlike microorganisms that cause food to spoil, harmful or pathogenic bacteria cannot be smelled or tasted. Prevention is safe food handling. If illness occurs, however, contact a health professional and describe the symptoms.

Staphylococcus aureus

Staphylococcus ("staph") bacteria are found on our skin, in infected cuts and pimples, and in our noses and throats. They are spread by improper food handling. Prevention includes washing hands and utensils before preparing and handling foods and not letting prepared foods — particularly cooked and cured meats and cheese and meat salads — sit at room temperature more than two hours. Thorough cooking destroys "staph" bacteria but staphylococcal enterotoxin is resistant to heat, refrigeration and freezing.

Clostridium perfringens

"*Perfringens*" is called the "cafeteria germ" because it may be found in foods served in quantity and left for long periods of time on inadequately maintained steam tables or at room temperature. Prevention is to divide large portions of cooked foods such as beef, turkey, gravy, dressing, stews and casseroles into smaller portions for serving and cooling. Keep cooked foods hot or cold, not lukewarm.

Listeria monocytogenes

Because *Listeria* bacteria multiply, although slowly, at refrigeration temperatures, these bacteria can be found in cold foods typically served on buffets. To avoid serving foods containing *Listeria*, follow "keep refrigerated" label directions and carefully observe "sell by" and "use by" dates on processed products, and thoroughly reheat frozen or refrigerated processed meat and poultry products before consumption.

Mail Order Food Safety

Convenience means many things to many people, but anything that helps save time is always high on everyone's list of conveniences. With more Americans working and being more time-crunched than ever, the ultimate time saver and convenience is home delivery of mail order foods.

While the mail order industry enjoys a good safety record, ordering food through the mail may cause concerns about food safety, shelf life, and distribution. It's imperative to develop some mental checklists for how both food and packaging should look when perishable mail order foods arrive. This is especially true for meat, poultry, fish, and other perishable foods such as cheesecake, which must be carefully handled in a timely manner to prevent foodborne illness. The following food safety tips will help the purchaser and recipient determine if their perishable foods have been handled properly:

- Make sure the company sends perishable items, like meat or poultry, cold or frozen and packed with a cold source. It should be packed in foam or heavy corrugated cardboard.
- The food should be delivered as quickly as possible — ideally, **overnight**. Make sure perishable items and the outer package are labeled "Keep Refrigerated" to alert the recipient.
- When you receive a food item marked "Keep Refrigerated," open it immediately and check its temperature. The food should arrive frozen or partially frozen with ice crystals still visible or at least refrigerator cold—below 40 °F as measured with a food thermometer. Even if a product is smoked, cured, vacuum-packed, and/or fully cooked, it still is a perishable product and must be kept cold. If perishable food arrives warm — above 40 °F as measured with a food thermometer — notify the company. **Do not consume the food. Do not even taste suspect food.**
- Tell the recipient if the company has promised a delivery date. Or alert the recipient that "the gift is in the mail" so someone can be there to receive it. Don't have perishable items delivered to an office unless you know it will arrive on a work day and there is refrigerator space available for keeping it cold.

Americans also enjoy cooking foods that are family favorites and mailing these items to family and friends. The same rules that cover the mail order industry also apply to foods prepared and mailed from home. Make sure perishable foods are not held at temperatures between 40 and 140 °F, the "Danger Zone", for longer than 2 hours. Pathogenic bacteria can grow rapidly in the "Danger Zone", but they may not affect the taste, smell, or appearance of a food. In other words, you cannot tell that a food has been mishandled or is unsafe to eat.

For perishable foods prepared at home and mailed, follow these guidelines:

- Ship in a sturdy box.
- Pack with a cold source, i.e., frozen gel packs or dry ice.
- When using dry ice:
  - o Don't touch the dry ice with bare hands.
  - o Don't let it come in direct contact with food.
  - o Warn the recipient of its use by writing "Contains Dry Ice" on the outside of the box.

"MINIATURE DEEP-FREEZE" PACKAGING

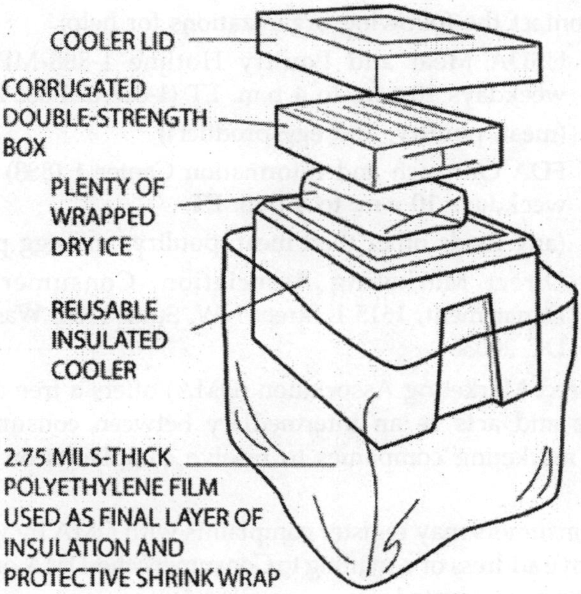

- Wrap box in two layers of brown paper.
- Use permanent markers to label outside of the box. Use recommended packing tape.
- Label outside clearly; make sure address is complete and correct.
- Write "Keep Refrigerated" on outside of the box.
- Alert recipient of its expected arrival.
- Do not send to business addresses or where there will not be adequate refrigerator storage.

- Do not send packages at the end of the week. Send them at the beginning of the week so they do not sit in the post office or mailing facility over the weekend.
- Whenever possible, send foods that do not require refrigeration, e.g., hard salami, hard cheese, country ham.

Use the handy chart, compiled by the USDA Meat and Poultry Hotline and FDA Outreach and Information Center, to plan your purchase, send a home-prepared item, and store popular mail order foods.

If mail order foods arrive in a questionable condition, you may contact the following organizations for help:

- USDA Meat and Poultry Hotline 1-888-MPHotline, weekdays 10 a.m. to 4 p.m. ET (1-888-674-6854)
  (meat, poultry, and egg products)
- FDA Outreach and Information Center 1 (888) 723-3366 weekdays 10 a.m. to 4 p.m. ET
  (any foods other than meat, poultry, and egg products)
- Direct Marketing Association, Consumer Affairs Department, 1615 L Street NW, Suite 1100, Washington, DC 20036

Direct Marketing Association (DMA) offers a free consumer service and acts as an intermediary between consumers and direct marketing companies to resolve complaints on a timely basis.

Consumers may register complaints with DMA by writing to the above address or e-mailing to Consumer@the-DMA.org; phone calls are not accepted.

Consumers requesting assistance through DMA should include the complete name and address of the company involved in the complaint, photocopies (not originals) of any canceled checks, order forms, other relevant documents, and a letter summarizing the facts of the complaint.

DMA will refer the letter to the company on the consumer's behalf and ask that the company resolve the matter. The majority of DMA complaints are resolved successfully within a 30-day period.

Cooking Safely in the Microwave Oven

Microwave ovens can play an important role at mealtime, but special care must be taken when cooking or reheating meat, poultry, fish, and eggs to make sure they are prepared safely. Microwave ovens can cook unevenly and leave "cold spots," where harmful bacteria can survive. For this reason, it is important to use the following safe microwaving tips to prevent foodborne illness.

Microwave Oven Cooking

- Arrange food items evenly in a covered dish and add some liquid if needed. Cover the dish with a lid or plastic wrap; loosen or vent the lid or wrap to let steam escape. The moist heat that is created will help destroy harmful bacteria and ensure uniform cooking. Cooking bags also provide safe, even cooking.
- Do not cook large cuts of meat on high power (100%). Large cuts of meat should be cooked on medium power (50%) for longer periods. This allows heat to reach the center without overcooking outer areas.
- Stir or rotate food midway through the microwaving time to eliminate cold spots where harmful bacteria can survive, and for more even cooking.
- When partially cooking food in the microwave oven to finish cooking on the grill or in a conventional oven, it is important to transfer the microwaved food to the other heat source immediately. Never partially cook food and store it for later use.
- Use a food thermometer or the oven's temperature probe to verify the food has reached a safe minimum internal temperature. Cooking times may vary because ovens vary in power and efficiency. Always allow standing time, which completes the cooking, before checking the internal temperature with a food thermometer.
- Cook foods to the following safe minimum internal temperatures:
  - o Beef, veal, and lamb steaks, roasts, and chops may be cooked to 145 °F.

- o All cuts of pork to 160 °F.
- o Ground beef, veal and lamb to 160 °F.
- o Egg dishes, casseroles to 160 °F.
- o Leftovers to 165 °F.
- o Stuffed poultry is not recommended. Cook stuffing separately to 165 °F.
- o All poultry should reach a safe minimum internal temperature of 165 °F.

- Cooking whole, stuffed poultry in a microwave oven is not recommended. The stuffing might not reach the temperature needed to destroy harmful bacteria.

Microwave Defrosting

- Remove food from packaging before defrosting. Do not use foam trays and plastic wraps because they are not heat stable at high temperatures. Melting or warping may cause harmful chemicals to migrate into food.
- Cook meat, poultry, egg casseroles, and fish immediately after defrosting in the microwave oven because some areas of the frozen food may begin to cook during the defrosting time. Do not hold partially cooked food to use later.
- Cover foods with a lid or a microwave-safe plastic wrap to hold in moisture and provide safe, even heating.
- Heat ready-to-eat foods such as hot dogs, luncheon meats, fully cooked ham, and leftovers until steaming hot.
- After reheating foods in the microwave oven, allow standing time. Then, use a clean food thermometer to check that food has reached 165 °F.

Containers & Wraps

- Only use cookware that is specially manufactured for use in the microwave oven. Glass, ceramic containers, and all plastics should be labeled for microwave oven use.
- Plastic storage containers such as margarine tubs, take-out containers, whipped topping bowls, and other one-time use containers should not be used in microwave ovens.

These containers can warp or melt, possibly causing harmful chemicals to migrate into the food.

- Microwave plastic wraps, wax paper, cooking bags, parchment paper, and white microwave-safe paper towels should be safe to use. Do not let plastic wrap touch foods during microwaving.
- Never use thin plastic storage bags, brown paper or plastic grocery bags, newspapers, or aluminum foil in the microwave oven.

12

Food Safety in the Kitchen

"Food safety." You hear a lot about it...and you know a lot about it.

But as with any comprehensive topic, there may be simple steps that are second nature that you've practiced forever — like hand washing — and then there may be current or updated information that is less familiar, or that may have changed since the last time you looked.

That's what *Kitchen Companion: Your Safe Food Handbook* is all about. This food safety handbook contains all the basic information you need to know about food safety...some old, some new...and all in one place.

Between the information-rich chapters and the easy index in the back, *Kitchen Companion* will likely answer all of your food safety questions. But if not...don't miss the food safety contact information on page 44. The USDA's Food Safety and Inspection Service is always there to help.

So read on...and *Be Food Safe*.

A SPECIAL NOTE TO THOSE MOST "AT RISK"

Some people are at higher risk for developing foodborne illness. These include pregnant women and their unborn babies, newborns, young children, older adults, and people with weakened immune systems.

If you — or someone you care for — are in one of these at-risk groups, it's important to pay extra attention to handling food safely. For more on those most at risk, visit www.fsis.usda.gov.

About USDA's Food Safety and Inspection Service (FSIS)

FSIS is the public health agency within the U.S. Department of Agriculture that is responsible for ensuring that the Nation's commercial supply of meat, poultry, and processed egg products is safe, wholesome, and correctly labeled and packaged.

FSIS focuses on inspecting and protecting the U.S. food supply...and educating consumers about safe food handling and reducing the risks of foodborne illness. Visit FSIS online at www.fsis.usda.gov.

FOODBORNE BACTERIA

There are two kinds of foodborne bacteria: one that spoils your food and one that makes you sick. It's good to be familiar with both...but it's critical that you follow safe food handling practices to keep the second one at bay.

Foodborne Illness Often called "food poisoning," foodborne illness comes from a food you eat. It's caused by ingesting pathogenic bacteria.

Spoilage Bacteria

Spoilage bacteria are bacteria that cause food to go bad - in other words, to "spoil." With spoilage bacteria, the food looks or smells funny or bad, so you know to throw it out. These bacteria can grow at lower temperatures — even in the refrigerator. But while they can make food unappealing and inedible...they do *not* usually cause illness.

Pathogenic Bacteria

These are the ones you need to watch out for — in fact, it's pathogenic bacteria that the food safety precautions throughout this handbook are intended to prevent. You can't see, smell, or taste these pathogens — and this makes them difficult to detect. What's more, they cause a variety of foodborne illnesses — and can make you really, really sick.

Pathogenic Bacteria: The Cause of Foodborne Illness

Pathogenic bacteria cause illness — and they can get in food in a number of ways. Sometimes these bacteria occur naturally and are destroyed by cooking food to safe temperatures. Pathogenic bacteria can also end up contaminating food when proper guidelines for cleaning hands, surfaces, and utensils and for avoiding cross-contamination are not followed.

- Different bacteria are present in different foods...and some are more common in certain situations. For example, *Salmonella* is most often found in poultry or eggs, whereas *E. coli* is more typically found in or on meats and vegetables. Meanwhile, *Staphylococcus aureus* and *Clostridium perfringens* frequent people's hands — and even buffet lines.
- Throughout this *Handbook*, you'll find effective strategies for preventing illness from pathogenic bacteria. Food safety is extremely important and should be practiced with every meal you eat or prepare. The Major Pathogens chart gives greater detail regarding the most common foodborne bacteria...where they are found...and what they can do if ingested.

About Mold on Food

The signs and symptoms of foodborne illness range from upset stomach, diarrhea, fever, vomiting, abdominal cramps, and dehydration to more severe illness — even death. If you become ill and believe your illness is due to a food product:

- **Seek treatment as necessary.** Contact your doctor — especially if symptoms persist or become severe (bloody diarrhea, excessive nausea and vomiting, or high fever). For victims in an at-risk group (pregnant women and their unborn babies, newborns, young children, older adults, and people with weakened immune systems), seek medical care immediately.
- **Call your local health department** if the suspect food was served at a large gathering, at a restaurant or other food service facility, or if it is a commercial product.

Foodborne Illness in the United States The food supply in the United States is safe. However, when certain disease-causing bacteria or pathogens contaminate food, they can cause foodborne illness.

According to the U.S. Centers for Disease Control and Prevention, approximately 76 million persons get sick, 325,000 are hospitalized, and 5,000 people die from foodborne illness and infection each year. Many of these are very young, very old, or have weakened immune systems and may not be able to fight infection normally.

Since foodborne illness can be serious — or even fatal — it is important for you to know and practice safe food handling behaviors to help reduce your risk of accidentally getting sick from contaminated food.

Major Pathogens That Cause Foodborne Illness (Bacteria, Parasites, Viruses)

Major Pathogens That Cause Foodborne Illness (Bacteria, Parasites, Viruses)

Pathogen

Methods of Transmission

Symptoms and Potential Impact

Campylobacter jejuni

- Contaminated water
- Raw milk
- Raw or undercooked meat, poultry, or shellfish
- Fever, headache, and muscle pain followed by diarrhea (sometimes bloody), abdominal pain, and nausea that appear 2 to 5 days after eating; may last 7 to 10 days.
- May spread to bloodstream and cause a serious life-threatening infection.

Clostridium perfringens

- Called the "cafeteria germ" because many outbreaks result from food left for long periods on steam tables or at room temperature.
- Meats, meat products, and gravy
- Intense abdominal cramps and diarrhea begin 8 to 22 hours after eating; usually lasts 24 hours. In the elderly, symptoms may last 1 to 2 weeks.
- Complications and/or death occur only very rarely.

Escherichia coli O157:H7

One of several strains of *E. coli* that can cause human illness

- Undercooked beef, especially hamburger
- Unpasteurized milk and juice
- Contaminated raw fruits and vegetables, and water
- Person-to-person
- Severe diarrhea that is often bloody, abdominal cramps, and vomiting. Usually little or no fever.
- Can begin 1 to 8 days after food is eaten; lasts about 5 to 10 days.
- Some, especially the very young, have developed hemolytic-uremic syndrome (HUS) that causes acute kidney failure or even death.

Listeria Monocytogenes

Can grow slowly at refrigerator temperatures

- Contaminated hot dogs, luncheon meats, cold cuts, fermented or dry sausage, and other deli-style meat and poultry
- Soft cheeses and unpasteurized milk
- Fever, chills, headache, stiff neck, backache, sometimes upset stomach, abdominal pain, and diarrhea. May take up to 3 weeks to become ill.
- At-risk patients (including pregnant women) may later develop more serious illness from this bacteria that could result in death.
- Pregnant women who think they have eaten contaminated food should seek medical advice.

Noroviruses (and other caliciviruses)

- Shellfish and fecally contaminated foods or water
- Ready-to-eat food touched by infected food workers, e.g., salads, sandwiches, ice, cookies, fruit
- Nausea, vomiting, stomach pain, fever, muscle aches, and some headache usually appear within 1 to 2 days and may last 1 to 2 days.

- Diarrhea is more prevalent in adults, and vomiting is more prevalent in children.

Salmonella (over 2,300 types)

- Raw or undercooked eggs, poultry, and meat
- Raw milk or juice
- Cheese and seafood
- Contaminated fresh fruits and vegetables
- Stomach pain, diarrhea, nausea, chills, fever, and headache usually appear 8 to 72 hours after eating; may last 4 to 7 days.
- A more severe illness may result if the infection spreads from the intestines to the bloodstream. Without treatment, death may result.

Staphylococcus aureus

- Contaminated milk and cheeses
- Salty foods; e.g., ham
- Sliced meat
- Food made by hand that require no cooking; e.g., puddings, sandwiches
- Foodworkers who carry the bacteria and contaminate food
- Nausea, vomiting, stomach cramps, and diarrhea usually occur within 30 minutes to 6 hours after eating contaminated food.
- Symptoms typically last 1 to 3 days; the young and the elderly may have a more severe illness.

Toxoplasma gondii

- Accidental ingestion of soil contaminated with cat feces on fruits and vegetables; raw or undercooked meat
- Flu-like illness usually appear 5 to 23 days after eating; may last months. Those with a weakened immune system may develop more serious illness.
- Can cause problems with pregnancy, including miscarriage.

Vibrio vulnificus

- Undercooked or raw seafood, such as fish and shellfish

- Diarrhea, stomach pain, and vomiting may appear within 1 to 7 days and last 2 to 8 days. May result in a blood infection; can result in death for those with a weakened immune system.

SHOPPING FOR FOOD

For consumers, food safety most likely begins in the supermarket aisle. Whether you're doing a quick trip to pick up dinner ingredients...or tackling a week's worth of grocery shopping all at once, there are a few easy steps you can follow to ensure that the food you bring home will arrive there safely.

At the Store

- **Select cold food last.** Picking up perishable food like meat, poultry, and eggs at the end of your shopping trip ensures that they stay refrigerated until right before checkout.
- **Read the label.** Don't buy food that is past the "Sell-By," "Use-By," or other expiration dates. (See About Food Labels.)
- **Check the packaging.** Never choose meat or poultry with packaging that is torn or leaking. Make sure frozen food is frozen solid and refrigerated food feels cold.
- **Buy clean eggs.** At the store, choose refrigerated Grade A or AA eggs with clean, uncracked shells before the "Sell-By" or "EXP" (expiration) date on the carton. When purchasing egg products or egg substitutes, look for containers that are tightly sealed.
- **Inspect fresh produce:** Don't buy fresh fruits or vegetables that are bruised or damaged. Make sure fresh-cut fruits and vegetables are displayed in refrigerated cases at the store. If not...don't buy them.
- **Place meat, poultry, and seafood in plastic bags.** By bagging these foods before placing them in your cart, you'll guard against cross-contamination - which can happen when raw meat or poultry juices drip on other food, spreading bacteria from one food to another.
- **Separate foods in your grocery cart.** Keep raw meat, poultry, seafood, and their juices away from other food to

further prevent the possibility of cross-contamination. Keep them separated during checkout and in your grocery bags, too.

Cross-Contamination Cross-contamination is the transfer of harmful bacteria to a food from other foods, cutting boards, utensils, surfaces, or hands. It is prevented by keeping food separated and by keeping hands, utensils, and food handling surfaces clean.

Transporting Groceries

Once your groceries are packed for the trek home, there are some easy "timing" tips you should follow to continue to maintain their safety.

- **Go straight home.** Plan to drive directly home from the grocery store. Don't leave groceries in the car while you run other errands. The key is to *always refrigerate perishable food within 2 hours*. This is true of all perishable food and in all situations — and is known as the "2-Hour Rule."
- **Do a "Weather Check."** When the outside temperature reaches 90 °F, you should refrigerate your purchased perishables more quickly — *within 1 hour*. If your grocery store is more than a half hour away from home, bring a cooler when you go shopping. Pack your meat, poultry, seafood, and eggs in a cooler for the drive home.

Arriving Home

When you get home, don't get caught up reading the mail! Unload your groceries right away to keep them safe, and refrigerate or freeze all perishables.

Focus on: The "Danger Zone" Throughout the *Kitchen Companion*, there are references to keeping food out of the "Danger Zone." Understanding the "Danger Zone" is critical — because bacteria can multiply rapidly in any perishable food that is left in the "Danger Zone" (between 40 and 140 °F) for more than 2 hours. (See Remember the 2-Hour Rule.) The "Danger Zone" is a potential risk for cold food that goes above 40 °F and hot food that falls below 140 °F. However, it's easy to avoid the "Danger Zone": just keep hot food hot and cold food cold!

(Tabular version of Danger Zone graphic)

The Danger Zone

165 °F : **Minimum Internal Temperature for Safety** Poultry, stuffing, casseroles, reheat leftovers

160 °F: Ground Meats; Beef, Lamb, Veal (medium); Pork; Egg Dishes

145 °F: Beef, Lamb, Veal steaks and roasts (medium rare), Seafood

140 °F: Ham, fully cooked (to reheat) **Holding Temperature for Cooked Foods**

In the Danger Zone

125 °F: Some bacterial growth may occur

60 °F: Some bacterial growth may occur

Out of the Danger Zone

40 °F: Refrigerator Temperatures

0 °F : Freezer Temperatures

ABOUT FOOD LABELS

Product Dating

The dates on labels have different meanings. Here's how to decipher them:

- **"Sell By" date:** Tells the store how long to display the product for sale. You should buy the product before the date expires.
- **"Best If Used By" (or Before) date:** Recommended for best flavor or quality. It is not a purchase or safety date.
- **"Use-By" date:** The last date recommended for the use of the product while at peak quality. The date has been determined by the manufacturer of the product.
- **Closed or Coded dates:** Packing numbers for use by the manufacturer. If a product is not "dated," consume perishable ready-to-eat food soon after purchasing it, and no more than 3 to 5 days after opening it.

Ready to Eat — or Not?

Check labels carefully. Some products may appear to be precooked or browned, but are raw and not ready to eat. These foods must be fully cooked for safety. Unless a product is labeled as "fully cooked," the food should be handled and prepared no differently than raw products.

Safe Handling Instructions

These guidelines on raw meat and poultry provide specific information for handling and preparation. Following these instructions is particularly important for consumers in at-risk groups.

What is "Organic"?

- **Organic meat, poultry, eggs, and dairy products** come from animals that are given no antibiotics or growth hormones.
- **Organic foods:** To be labeled "organic," a Government-approved certifier must inspect the farm where the food is grown to make sure all the rules necessary to comply with USDA organic standards are met.

STORING FOOD

The food you store falls into three basic "storage categories."

- *Perishable food:* in the refrigerator (read the label if you're not sure)
- *Frozen food:* in the freezer
- *Shelf-stable food:* in a clean, dry place

Refrigerated Perishable Food

Food safety is the best reason ever to "chill out"! Follow these basic guidelines to protect your perishables — and yourself and your family. And remember: always refrigerate perishable food within 2 hours (1 hour when the temperature is above 90 °F).

- **Raw Meat, Poultry, and Seafood:** Place in containers or sealed plastic bags to prevent their juices from dripping onto other food in the refrigerator. This could cause cross-contamination (see inset box). If you're not planning to use the food within a day or two, freeze it.
- **Cooked, Whole Stuffed Poultry:** See Storing Cooked Poultry.

- **Eggs:** Store in the original carton and place in the main compartment of the refrigerator - not in the door. When ready to use, do not wash them. (Read more about Eggs.)
- **Produce:** Store perishable produce in the refrigerator. Throw away fresh fruits and vegetables that have not been refrigerated within 2 hours of cutting, peeling, or cooking. If any fruit or vegetable has touched raw meat, poultry, or seafood and will not be cooked immediately, do not eat it. Throw it away.
- **Leftovers:** Refrigerate (or freeze) leftovers within 2 hours in clean, shallow, covered containers to prevent harmful bacteria from multiplying. (See more on Leftovers.)

It's a Date!

- As you store your food, *check dates* on the labels.
- If a product does not have a date on it, *write the purchase date on it* before you refrigerate or freeze it.
- Place newer items in the back of the refrigerator or freezer. That way, you'll *use the older ones first*.

Frozen Food

For long-term storage of many perishable foods, rely on the freezer. Food stored constantly at 0 °F or below will always be safe. Only the quality suffers with lengthy freezer storage.

Freezer Facts

- **Preventing Freezer Burn:** Freezer burn — white, dried-out patches on the surface of meat — won't make you sick, but it does make meat tough and tasteless. Here's how to avoid it:
  - o Wrap freezer items in heavy freezer paper, plastic wrap, freezer bags, or foil.
  - o Date all freezer packages. Use the oldest food first.
  - o Place new items toward the back of the freezer - that way, older items are easier to access and you'll use them first.
- **Refreezing Thawed Food:** If food is thawed in the refrigerator, it is safe to refreeze it without cooking. (See

Thawing section.) However, there may be a loss of *quality* due to the moisture lost through defrosting.

- **Freezing Cooked Food:** After cooking raw food that was previously frozen, it is safe to freeze the cooked food. In addition, if previously cooked food were frozen and then thawed in the refrigerator, you may refreeze the unused portion.
- **Prevent Moisture Loss:** To maintain quality when freezing meat and poultry in its original packaging, overwrap the package with foil or plastic wrap that is recommended for use in the freezer.

Your Refrigerator and Freezer: Take Their Temperatures! It's common to assume that your refrigerator's temperature control dial keeps food cold enough — but this isn't necessarily true. "Built-in" temperature control dials may not be effective, and if your refrigerator isn't cooling to 40 °F or below, you're providing a haven for bacteria to grow.

- Instead, use a separate appliance thermometer to check the internal refrigerator temperature and help keep food safe. They are available in grocery, hardware, and kitchen specialty stores.
- If the refrigerator thermometer shows a temperature that's too high (above 40 °F), adjust the refrigerator's control dial.
- Use the thermometer to check the freezer, too. It should read 0 °F or below. If not, adjust the dial.

Shelf-Stable Food

Food that doesn't need to be refrigerated or frozen must still be stored with care. Follow these basic guidelines and you'll have food safety in the bag (or can)!

- **Where:** Store canned food and other shelf-stable products in a cool, clean, dry place. Never put them above the stove, under the sink, in a damp garage or basement, or any place exposed to high or low temperature extremes.

- **How Long:** In general, you can store high-acid food such as tomatoes and other fruit for 12 to 18 months; low-acid food such as meat and vegetables, 2 to 5 years.
- **Care and Cautions for Cans:** Discard cans that are dented, leaking, bulging, or rusted. Can linings might discolor or corrode when metal reacts with high-acid food such as tomatoes or pineapple — but as long as the outside of the can is in good shape, the contents should be safe to eat. Keep in mind, though, that the taste, texture, and nutritional value of the food can diminish over time. (Also see In Case of Flood.)

Botulism Alert

The greatest danger in canned goods is a toxin produced by the *Clostridium botulinum* bacteria. Never use food from containers that show possible "botulism" warnings:

- Leaking, bulging, or badly dented cans
- Cracked jars or jars with loose or bulging lids
- Canned food with a foul odor
- Any container that spurts liquid when opened.

Play it safe — and *never* taste it. Even a tiny amount of *botulinum* toxin can be deadly. Double bag the cans and jars in plastic bags that are tightly closed. Then place in a trash receptacle for non-recyclable trash outside of the home. Keep out of reach of humans and pets.

Common Sense Caution

If you're not sure how old a food is, or fear that it may not have been properly refrigerated or has been left out too long, don't taste it! Instead, remember the "golden rule" of food storage: When in doubt, throw it out!

FOOD PREPARATION

Food safety doesn't end with buying, transporting, and storing food safely. In fact, once you have food home...the safety of your food is, literally, in your hands. Follow these basic guidelines — and remember, safe food preparation always begins with "clean."

Keeping It Clean

Handwashing

- Always wash hands with soap and warm water for 20 seconds before beginning food preparation, after handling food, and after using the bathroom, changing diapers, or touching pets.
- Use gloves to handle food if you have a cut or infection. Do not sneeze or cough into food.

Surfaces and Utensils

Harmful bacteria can spread throughout the kitchen and get onto cutting boards, utensils, and countertops — causing "cross-contamination." (See inset box.) Keep raw meat, poultry, fish, and their juices away from other food — especially ready-to-eat food.

- Wash cutting boards, dishes, and countertops with hot, soapy water *after* preparing each food item and *before* you go on to the next item.
- After cutting raw meat, poultry, and seafood, wash cutting boards, knives, and countertops with hot, soapy water.

Cutting Boards

Proper cutting board "care-and-feeding" is a key component of preventing cross-contamination. Here's how:

- Always use a clean cutting board for food preparation.
- Try to use one cutting board for fresh produce — and a separate one for raw meat, poultry, and seafood.
- Sanitize cutting boards with a freshly made solution of 1 tablespoon of unscented, liquid chlorine bleach in 1 gallon of water.
- Once cutting boards become excessively worn or develop hard-to-clean grooves, replace them.

Kitchen Cleanup

- Use hot, soapy water and a clean dishcloth (or paper towels) to clean kitchen surfaces and wipe up spills.
- Wash dishcloths often in the hot cycle of your washing machine.

Preparation Tips for Produce

Fresh fruits and veggies are nutritional mainstays. Here's how to make sure they're safe:

- Before eating or preparing, wash fresh produce under cold running tap water to remove any lingering dirt. This also reduces bacteria that may be present. Firm produce (like apples or potatoes) can be scrubbed with a brush.
- Don't wash fruits and vegetables with detergent or soap. These products are *not approved* for use on food. You could ingest residues from soap or detergent absorbed by the produce.
- Remove and throw away bruised or damaged portions of fruits and vegetables when preparing to cook them or before eating them raw.

Thawing

Going from "frozen to thawed" needs to be accomplished safely!

There are three ways to thaw — and because bacteria can multiply rapidly at room temperature, none of these methods involve the kitchen counter.

In the Refrigerator: This is the safest way to thaw meat and poultry.

Take the food out of the freezer and thaw it in the fridge. Place it on a plate or in a pan to catch any juices that may leak. Normally, it will be ready to use the next day.

In Cold Water: For faster thawing, put the frozen package in a watertight plastic bag and submerge it in cold water; change the water every 30 minutes. The cold water slows bacteria that might be growing in the thawed portions of the meat while the inner areas are still thawing. Once thawed, cook it immediately.

In the Microwave: Follow instructions from the oven's manufacturer or owner's manual. Cook immediately after thawing in the microwave.

Refreezing Tips:

- Meat and poultry that have been fully defrosted in the refrigerator may be refrozen before or after cooking.

- If thawed in cold water or in the microwave, always fully cook before refreezing. (Also see Storing Food: Frozen Food.)

COOKING FOOD SAFELY

Cooking food to a safe temperature is the best way to ensure safety.

That's because when food reaches a *safe minimum internal temperature,* bacteria that may be lurking are destroyed. Sound complicated? It's not. It's as easy as using a *food thermometer.*

About Food Thermometers

Food safety experts agree: food is safe to eat when it is cooked or reheated to a high enough temperature to kill the harmful bacteria that cause foodborne illness.

The only accurate way to know if food is cooked safely is to measure the internal temperature of cooked meat, poultry, and egg products with a food thermometer.

You can't tell by looking — use a food thermometer to be sure. Color and texture are not reliable indicators of safely cooked food.

How to Use a Food Thermometer

1. Place the food thermometer in the **thickest part of the food.**
   - o Make sure it's not touching bone, fat, or gristle.
   - o For whole poultry, insert the thermometer into the innermost part of the thigh and wing and the thickest part of the breast.
   - o For combination dishes, place the thermometer in the center or thickest portion of the food. Egg dishes and dishes containing ground meat or poultry should be checked in several places.
2. Wait the amount of time recommended for your particular type of thermometer (See Food Thermometers and Temperature Indicators).

3. Compare your thermometer reading to the Safe Minimum Internal Temperature Chart to determine if your food has reached at least a safe internal temperature.
4. Clean your food thermometer with hot, soapy water before and after each use!

Tasting Tips

- Don't taste food while it's cooking. To ensure safety, food should not be tasted until it reaches a safe minimum internal temperature.
- No double dipping. Use a clean utensil each time you taste food; otherwise, you may contaminate the batch.

Food Thermometers and Temperature Indicators	
Dial Oven-Safe (Bimetal)	• Reads in 1-2 minutes • Place 2 to 2-½" deep in thickest part of food • Best used in roasts, whole poultry, casseroles, and soups
Digital Instant-Read (Thermistor)	• Reads in 10 seconds • Place at least ½" deep • Use in thick *and* thin foods
Dial Instant-Read (Bimetal)	• Reads in 15-20 seconds • Place 2 to 2-½" deep in thickest part of food
Disposable Temperature Indicators (Single-Use)	• Reads in 5 to 10 seconds • Place approximately ½" deep (follow manufacturer's directions)
Pop-up	• Commonly used in turkeys and roasting chickens • Pops up when food reaches final temperature for safety and doneness • Recommendation: Use an additional food thermometer to check temperature in other parts of the food

Done Versus Safe: What You Need to Know Webster's Dictionary defines "doneness" *as the condition of being cooked to the desired degree.* This includes subjective qualities, like a food's appearance, texture, and optimum flavor.

But whether a food is cooked to a "safe" degree is another story. The standard that ensures "safety" is not subjective at all. It's a simple matter of cooking food until the internal temperature reaches the level that ensures destruction of any potential pathogens, as measured with a food thermometer.

Visual signs of doneness should only be taken into consideration after the food has reached a safe temperature.

And if you're thinking about leaving the food thermometer in the drawer, consider this: According to USDA research, **1 out of every 4** hamburgers turns brown before it reaches a safe internal temperature!

Safe Minimum Internal Temperature Chart

Safe Minimum Internal Temperature Chart

Food	°F
Ground Meat & Meat Mixtures	
Beef, Pork, Veal, Lamb	160
Turkey, Chicken	165
Fresh Beef, Veal, Lamb	
Steaks, roasts, chops	145
Poultry	
Chicken and Turkey, whole	165
Poultry breasts, roasts	165
Poultry thighs, legs, wings	165
Duck & Goose	165
Stuffing (cooked alone or in bird)	165
Fresh Pork	160
Ham	
Fresh (raw)	160
Precooked (to reheat)	140
Eggs and Egg Dishes	
Eggs	Cook until yolk and white are firm
Egg dishes	160
Leftovers and Casseroles	165

For oven roasting guidelines, see the roasting charts for turkey and meats and other poultry.

Avoid the "Danger Zone" — Keep Hot Food Hot After Cooking

The possibility of bacterial growth is greater when food cools because the drop in temperature allows bacteria to thrive. There are two ways to keep cooked food from entering the "Danger Zone":

- **Don't Interrupt Cooking:** Interrupted cooking allows partially cooked food to cool down...and may encourage bacterial growth before cooking is complete. To avoid this, make sure to cook food all the way through the first time.
- **Keep Food at Holding Temperatures:** If you aren't going to serve food right away, it's important to keep it at 140 °F or above. Once food is safely cooked on the stovetop, in the oven, or in a microwave oven, keep food hot by using a heat source. Place food in chafing dishes, on warming trays, or in slow cookers. Check the temperature frequently to make sure food stays at or above 140 °F.

SPECIAL GUIDELINES FOR CERTAIN FOOD

In addition to the basic cooking guidelines (see Cooking Food Safely) — there are some food-specific tips that can help you take special care with your culinary favorites.

Ground Meat and Poultry

Ground meat and poultry receive more handling than any other cut of meat or poultry. This means that hamburger has the opportunity for the introduction of more foodborne bacteria, too. Be diligent with general safe food handling guidelines, and keep these **buying tips** in mind:

- When you purchase ground beef, it should be **cherry-red** (or purple-red, if in vacuum packaging).
- Return any package that has an unusual odor when you open it.

Ham

Even though it is *cured* — for example, smoked, aged, or dried— ham can still contain foodborne bacteria. Follow these tips to keep it safe:

Storing:

- *Refrigerator:*
  - o Store sliced or whole ham in the coldest part of the refrigerator.
  - o Use slices within 3 to 4 days; whole ham within a week.
  - o Most canned hams should be refrigerated. Be sure to check the label!
  - o Observe "Use-By" dates on hams sealed at the plant; use store-wrapped cooked ham portions within 3 to 5 days.
- *Freezer:* Ham tends to lose flavor and texture when frozen. If you do need to freeze it, wrap it tightly in freezer paper or plastic freezer bags and use it within 1 or 2 months.

Cooking: First and foremost, read the label.

- "Fully cooked" ham can be served "as is" — hot or cold. If reheating, cook to 140 °F.
- Fresh ham (labeled "Cook before eating") and other fresh pork must be cooked to 160 °F.

Roasts

Sit-down dinners and special occasions aren't only about turkey! There are many other types of roasts that become the stars of the dinner table. Use these guidelines to "make the most of your roast"...safely.

Cooking Your Roast

Roasting is the recommended method for cooking tender meats.

To roast, meat is placed on a rack in a shallow, uncovered pan and is cooked by the indirect, dry heat of an oven. To keep the meat tender and minimize shrinkage due to the evaporation of moisture, an oven temperature of 325 °F should be used.

- Boned and rolled meat require more cooking time per pound than bone-in cuts because it takes longer for the heat to penetrate through the solid meat. Rolled, tenderized, or scored cuts of meat should be cooked to 160 °F.

- USDA does not recommend cooking meat and poultry at oven temperatures lower than 325 °F. This can cause food to remain in the "Danger Zone" (temperatures from 40 to 140 °F) too long, allowing bacteria to multiply rapidly.

Watch Temperatures Closely Fat content (or a lack of it) affect the cooking times of a variety of meats — so keep a close eye on your roast to avoid overcooking, and use a food thermometer. And remember — regardless of the size of the roast, it still must be cooked to a safe internal temperature.

Roasting Chart

Meat	Oven Temp. (°F)	Timing (Approx.)	Safe Minimum Internal Temp. (°F)
BEEF, FRESH			
rib roast, bone in 4 to 6 pounds	325	23 to 25 minutes per lb.	145
rib roast, boneless, rolled 4 to 6 pounds	325	28 to 33 minutes per lb.	145
round or rump roast 2 ½ to 4 pounds	325	30 to 35 minutes per lb.	145
tenderloin, whole 4 to 6 pounds	425	45 to 60 minutes total	145
LAMB, FRESH			
leg, bone in 5 to 7 pounds	325	20 to 25 minutes per lb.	145
leg, bone in 7 to 9 pounds	325	15 to 20 minutes per lb.	145
leg, boneless, rolled 4 to 7 pounds	325	25 to 30 minutes per lb.	145
VEAL, FRESH			
shoulder roast, boneless 3 to 5 pounds	325	35 to 40 minutes per lb.	145
leg rump or round roast, boneless 3 to 5 pounds	325	35 to 40 minutes per lb.	145

CHICKEN, FRESH (Turkey Cooking Charts can be found here.)			
whole roasting hen 5 to 7 pounds	350	2 to 2 ¼ hours	165
breast, halves, bone-in 6 to 8 ounces	350	30 to 40 minutes	165
breast, halves, boneless 4 ounces	350	20 to 30 minutes	165
legs or thighs 4 to 8 ounces	350	40 to 50 minutes	165
PORK, FRESH ***(Tip: When cooked to safe temperatures, fresh pork may still be pink inside – but it will be safe.)***			
loin roast, bone-in or boneless 2 to 5 pounds	325	20 to 30 minutes per lb.	160
crown roast 4 to 6 pounds	325	20 to 30 minutes per lb.	160
tenderloin ½ to 1 ½ pounds	425	20 to 30 minutes total	160
HAM, SMOKED			
fresh, cook-before-eating, bone-in whole, 10 to 14 pounds	325	18 to 20 minutes per lb.	160
half, 5 to 7 pounds	325	22 to 25 minutes per lb.	160
fully cooked, bone-in whole, 10 to 14 pounds	325	15 to 18 minutes per lb.	140
half, 5 to 7 pounds	325	18 to 24 minutes per lb.	140
fully cooked, spiral cut, whole or half 7 to 9 pounds	325	10 to 18 minutes per lb.	140
country, dried, whole or half	Soak 4 to 12 hours in refrigerator. Cover with water, then boil 20 to 25 minutes per pound. Drain, glaze, and brown at 400 °F for 15 minutes.		

For reasons of personal preference, consumers may choose to cook the above meats and poultry to higher temperatures.

Turkey and Other Poultry

No doubt about it, millions of Americans view holiday time as "turkey time." Of the millions of turkeys produced every year,

30 percent are served at Thanksgiving and Christmas. But no matter when you are preparing and serving your turkey — gobble up these important facts first!

Choosing Your Turkey

When selecting your turkey, allow **1 pound of turkey per person** for fresh or frozen; 1¼ pound per person for frozen pre-stuffed.

- *Frozen*: Make sure you have adequate space in your freezer.
- *Fresh:* Purchase it 1 to 2 days before cooking. Refrigerate on a tray or in a pan to catch any juices that may leak.
- *Frozen Pre-stuffed:* Check packaging for the USDA or State mark of inspection, which ensures that it has been processed under controlled conditions. Follow package directions carefully for storage and cooking. DO NOT THAW before cooking. Cook from the frozen state.
- ***Safety Alert:* Do not buy a fresh pre-stuffed turkey,** as bacteria spreads easily from the bird to the stuffing.

Thawing Your Turkey

For basic food thawing recommendations, see the Thawing section. In addition, keep these turkey-specific timelines and tips in mind:

- *In the Microwave:* Check the manufacturer's instructions for the size turkey that will fit into your oven, the minutes per pound, and the power level to use for thawing. Remove any outside wrapping and place on a microwave-safe dish to catch any juices that may drip. Cook immediately after thawing.
- *For Frozen Turkeys:* Forget to thaw? It's safe to cook a turkey from the frozen state. Keep in mind that cooking will take *at least 50 percent longer* than with a fully thawed turkey.
- *About refreezing:* Decide not to cook? A turkey that has been safely thawed in the refrigerator can be refrozen safely.
- After thawing, poultry may be left in the refrigerator for up to 2 days before cooking.

Turkey Thawing Chart: Approximate Timelines Allow approximately 24 hours for every 4 to 5 pounds		
Turkey Size	**In the Refrigerator (Approximately 24 hours for every 4 to 5 pounds.)**	**In Cold Water (Approximately 30 minutes per lb.)**
4 to 12 pounds	1 to 3 days	2 to 6 hours
12 to 16 pounds	3 to 4 days	6 to 8 hours
16 to 20 pounds	4 to 5 days	8 to 10 hours
20 to 24 pounds	5 to 6 days	10 to 12 hours

Stuffing Your Turkey

- For more even cooking, cook your stuffing outside the bird in a casserole dish. Use a food thermometer to check the internal temperature of the stuffing. The center should reach 165 °F.
- If you choose to stuff your turkey, keep wet and dry ingredients separate and combine just before stuffing.
  - o If preparing ahead of time, chill all of the wet ingredients (butter/margarine, cooked celery and onions, broth, etc.).
  - o Mix wet and dry ingredients just before filling the turkey cavities. The stuffing should be moist, not dry, since heat destroys bacteria more rapidly in a moist environment. Fill the cavities loosely.
  - o **Cook the turkey *immediately*.** Use a food thermometer to make sure the center of the stuffing reaches 165 °F.

Stuffing Other Poultry

Just as with turkey, it's important to take special precautions with other stuffed poultry to ensure they reach a safe minimum internal temperature.

Bacteria grow particularly well in starchy or "bready" foods. In raw poultry, it can get into the stuffing, which in turn may not heat to safe temperatures when deep inside the bird. See Stuffing Your Turkey.

Got Giblets?

Remember to remove the giblets from the turkey cavities after thawing. Cook them separately.

Prevent Cross-Contamination!

Always wash hands with soap and warm water before and after contact with raw poultry or its juices. Wash cutting boards, dishes, utensils, the sink, and countertops with hot, soapy water.

Roasting Your Turkey

- Set your oven temperature no lower than 325 °F. Place your turkey or turkey breast on a rack in a shallow roasting pan, and use the Turkey Roasting Chart as a guide.
- If you're using an oven roasting bag, make sure to follow the manufacturer's instructions!
- Cook to a safe minimum internal temperature of 165 °F throughout the bird.
- Check the internal temperature in the innermost part of the thigh and wing and the thickest part of the breast.
- For reasons of personal preference, you may choose to cook to higher temperatures.
- If your turkey has a "pop-up" temperature indicator, also check the internal temperature of the whole poultry in the innermost part of the thigh and wing and the thickest part of the breast to make sure it has reached at least 165 °F.
- Let the turkey stand for 20 minutes before carving to allow juices to set. The turkey will carve more easily.

Leftover Turkey

Storing Leftover Turkey

Turkey connoisseurs agree: the leftovers are the best part! Here's how to store them safely:

- Cut the turkey into small pieces. Refrigerate stuffing, turkey, and gravy separately in shallow containers within 2 hours of cooking (or 1 hour in temperatures above 90 °F). If left out longer, discard.

- Use leftover turkey, stuffing, and gravy within 3 to 4 days; or freeze these foods. Use frozen leftovers within 2 to 6 months for best quality.

Reheating Leftover Turkey

If you choose not to go the "cold turkey" route, use these guidelines for reheating.

- In the Oven
  - o To keep the turkey moist, add a little broth or water and cover.
  - o Set the oven temperature no lower than 325 °F. Reheat to an internal temperature of 165 °F — use a food thermometer to check.
- In the Microwave
  - o Cover and rotate the turkey for even heating. Allow standing time.
  - o Check the internal temperature with a food thermometer to make sure it reaches 165 °F.

A Note About Other Cooking Methods

Turkey isn't just about roasting anymore. There are several other ways to prepare the bird — use the chart for at-a-glance guidelines.

Turkey Roasting Chart: Approximate Times		
Fresh or Thawed Turkey - Set oven at 325 °F - Cook to 165 °F		
Size of Turkey	**Unstuffed**	**Stuffed**
4 to 6 pounds (breast)	1½ to 2¼ hours	Not usually applicable
6 to 8 pounds (breast)	2¼ to 3¼ hours	2½ to 3½ hours
8 to 12 pounds	2¾ to 3 hours	3 to 3½ hours
12 to 14 pounds	3 to 3¾ hours	3½ to 4 hours
14 to 18 pounds	3¾ to 4¼ hours	4 to 4¼ hours
18 to 20 pounds	4¼ to 4½ hours	4¼ to 4¾ hours
20 to 24 pounds	4½ to 5 hours	4¾ to 5¼ hours

Cooking a Frozen Turkey: The cooking time will take at least 50% longer than recommended for a fully thawed turkey (see above chart).

For chicken roasting instructions, see chart.

Alternate Ways to Cook Turkey			
Note: Always make sure whole turkeys reach a safe minimum internal temperature of 165 °F as measured in the innermost part of the thigh and wing and the thickest part of the breast.			
Method	**Size**	**Estimated Cooking Time**	**Notes**
Electric Roaster Oven	8 to 24 lbs.	Generally same times as for oven roasting (see above).	Minimum oven temperature 325 °F. Check appliance manual.
Grilling: Covered Charcoal Grill or Covered Gas Grill	8 to 16 lbs.	15 to 18 minutes per pound. DO NOT STUFF.	Air in the grill must maintain 225 to 300 °F; use drip pan.
Smoking	8 to 12 lbs.	20 to 30 minutes per pound. DO NOT STUFF.	Air in the smoker must maintain 225 to 300 °F; use drip pan with liquid.
Deep Fat Frying	8 to 12 lbs.	3 to 5 minutes per pound. DO NOT STUFF.	Oil must maintain 350 °F. Follow manufacturer's instructions.
Microwaving	8 to 14 lbs.	9 to 10 minutes per pound on medium (50%) power. DO NOT STUFF.	Use oven cooking bag. Rotate during cooking.

Eggs and Egg-Rich Food

Eggs can be part of a healthy diet. However, they are perishable just like raw meat, poultry, and seafood — and just like these foods, they must be properly refrigerated in the store and at home and cooked for safety. So get cracking!

Storing:

- **Refrigerate Eggs.** Take eggs straight home and store them in their original carton in the refrigerator. Follow the 2-Hour Rule: Never allow eggs to be unrefrigerated for more than 2 hours.
  - Place them in the coldest part of the refrigerator — not in the door, where they'd be exposed to warmer air every time the door is opened.
  - If any eggs cracked on the way home from the store, break them into a clean container, cover tightly, refrigerate, and use within 2 days.
- **Keep Easter/Decorated Eggs Refrigerated, Too.** Even with egg hunts, the 2-Hour Rule still applies — make sure your "hide-and-seek" activities occur within 2 hours (1 hour when the temperature is above 90 °F), and then re-refrigerate the eggs.
- **Freeze Beaten Eggs for Longer Storage.** Eggs should not be frozen in their shells. To freeze whole eggs, beat yolks

and whites together. Egg whites can also be frozen by themselves.

Cooking:

- **Cook Thoroughly.** To ensure safety, eggs must be cooked until **yolks are firm**. Scrambled eggs should *not* be runny.
  - o Raw eggs and other ingredients, combined according to recipe directions, should be cooked immediately or refrigerated and cooked within 24 hours.
  - o Casseroles and other dishes containing eggs should be cooked to 160 °F as measured with a food thermometer.
  - o Serve cooked eggs and dishes containing eggs immediately after cooking, or place in shallow containers for quick cooling and refrigerate at once for later use. Use within 3 to 4 days.
  - o If eggs crack during hard cooking, they are safe.

Egg Storage Chart

Product	Refrigerator	Freezer
Raw eggs in shell	3 to 5 weeks	Do not freeze. Instead, beat yolks and whites together; then freeze.
Raw egg whites	2 to 4 days	12 months
Raw egg yolks	2 to 4 days	Yolks do not freeze well.
Raw egg accidentally frozen in shell	Use immediately after thawing.	Keep frozen; then refrigerate to thaw.
Hard-cooked eggs	1 week	Do not freeze.
Egg substitutes, liquid ***Unopened***	10 days	12 months
Opened	3 days	Do not freeze.
Egg substitutes, frozen ***Unopened***	After thawing, 7 days, or refer to "Use-By" date	12 months
Opened	After thawing, 3 days, or refer to "Use-By" date	Do not freeze.
Casseroles with eggs	3 to 4 days	After baking, 2 to 3 months.
Eggnog ***Commercial***	3 to 5 days	6 months
Homemade	2 to 4 days	Do not freeze.
Pies **Pumpkin or pecan**	3 to 4 days	After baking, 1 to 2 months.
Custard and chiffon	3 to 4 days	Do not freeze.
Quiche with filling	3 to 4 days	After baking, 1 to 2 months.

- **Never Eat Raw Eggs.** This includes "health-food" milk shakes with raw eggs, Caesar salad, Hollandaise sauce, and any other food, like homemade mayonnaise, ice cream, or eggnog, made from recipes in which the raw egg ingredients are not cooked.

- All egg products (such as liquid eggs) distributed for consumption are pasteurized and may be used in products that will not be cooked. However, egg products are best used in a cooked product, especially if serving high-risk persons (pregnant women, newborns, young children, older adults, and people with weakened immune systems).

Egg Recipes: Playing it Safe

- **Egg mixtures** are safe if they reach 160 °F.
- **Homemade ice cream and eggnog** are safe if made from a cooked egg-milk mixture. Heat it gently and use a food thermometer to ensure that it reaches 160 °F.
- **Dry meringue shells, divinity candy, and 7-minute frosting are safe** — these are made by combining hot sugar syrup with beaten egg whites. However, avoid icing recipes using uncooked eggs or egg whites.
- **Meringue-topped pies** should be safe if baked at 350 °F for about 15 minutes. But avoid chiffon pies and fruit whips made with raw, beaten egg whites — instead, substitute pasteurized dried egg whites, whipped cream, or a whipped topping.
- **Adapting Recipes:** If your recipe calls for uncooked eggs, make it safe by heating the eggs in one of the recipe's other liquid ingredients over low heat, stirring constantly, until the mixture reaches 160 °F. Then, combine it with the other ingredients and complete the recipe.
- **Use a Food Thermometer:** To determine safety in egg dishes such as quiche and casseroles, the center of the mixture should reach 160 °F when measured with a food thermometer.

Hot Dogs and Luncheon Meat

Hot dogs and luncheon meat are processed to last longer than other meat, but they can still spoil — or harbor foodborne bacteria. Here are tips for keeping them safe.

Storing:

- Keep **unopened hot dogs and prepackaged luncheon meats** in the refrigerator in their original vacuum-sealed package for up to 2 weeks.

   - o Once opened, rewrap well and use luncheon meats within 3 to 5 days and hot dogs within 1 week.
- **You can freeze** hot dogs and luncheon meat, but there may be flavor and texture loss after 1 to 2 months.

A Note for Those Most "At Risk": Those at increased risk of foodborne illness should reheat hot dogs and luncheon meat until steaming hot before eating, due to the threat of listeriosis.

Leftovers

Leftovers are a staple in the kitchen. But they also need special care to ensure safe storage and reheating. These guidelines will help ensure their safety the "second time around."

Storing:

- **Hot food** can be placed directly in the refrigerator, or it can be rapidly chilled in an ice or cold water bath before refrigerating. Cover food to retain moisture and prevent it from picking up odors from other food in the fridge, and use shallow containers for rapid cooling.
- Divide a **large pot of food,** like soup or stew, into shallow containers before refrigerating.
- **A large cut of cooked meat or whole poultry** should be divided into smaller pieces and wrapped separately or placed in covered, shallow containers before refrigerating.
- Discard perishable food if it has been left at room temperature for more than 2 hours (1 hour if it's above 90 °F). This includes leftovers that were **mistakenly left out** overnight.

Reheating:

- Heat leftovers to **165 °F** — use a food thermometer to check!
- Bring gravies and sauces to a **rolling boil** before serving.
- **Cover leftovers** to reheat. This retains moisture and ensures that food will heat all the way through.
- **In the microwave,** use a lid or vented plastic, and rotate food for even heating. Beware of "cold spots"; use a food thermometer to check the temperature in several places.

"Take-Home" Leftover Alert: Doggie Bags are leftovers, too! Follow the same rules for storing and reheating.

SPECIFIC PREPARATION AND COOKING METHODS

"Making dinner" can go far beyond simply putting a roast in the oven. These basic guidelines will keep your food safe as you use a variety of cooking and preparation techniques.

Marinating

Marinades can enhance the flavor of meat, poultry, or seafood. Follow these tips for marinating safely.

- **Marinate in the Refrigerator.** Marinating at refrigeration temperatures is the only option for keeping bacteria at bay. Meat and poultry can be marinated for several hours or days to tenderize or add flavor.
- **Don't "Cross-Contaminate."** Sauce used to marinate raw meat, poultry, or seafood should *never* be used on cooked foods unless it is boiled just before using.
  - o Sauce used to marinate contains raw juices — which can, in turn, contain dangerous bacteria.
  - o If some of the marinade is to be used as a sauce on the cooked food, reserve a portion of the marinade before putting raw meat or poultry in it.
- **Don't Use Metal.** Marinate in glass or plastic. The process may take several hours, so you need a tray or bowl that won't be affected by acid.

Microwave Cooking

On a hungry night after a long day, a microwave oven can be a cook's best friend. While saving time in food preparation, it's still critical to make sure food reaches a safe minimum internal temperature throughout.

- **Prep and Cover:** Arrange food items evenly in a covered dish and add some liquid if needed. Cover the dish with a lid or plastic wrap; loosen or vent the lid or wrap to let steam escape. The moist heat that is created will help destroy harmful bacteria and ensure uniform cooking. Cooking bags also provide safe, even cooking.

- **Avoid Cold Spots:** While microwaving is quick, it doesn't always cook food evenly. Stir or rotate food midway through the microwaving time to eliminate cold spots and for more even cooking.
- **Defrost in the Microwave *Only* if Cooking Immediately.** Cover foods with a lid or a microwave-safe plastic wrap to hold in moisture and provide safe, even heating.
- **Use Partial Cooking With Care:** Partial cooking may be done in the microwave *only* if the food is to finish cooking immediately, either on the stovetop, grill, or in a conventional oven.
- **Observe Standing Times:** These are stated in recipes, and they are important for ensuring that the cooking process is completed.
  - Standing times allow internal cooking to continue after the food is cooked in the microwave. They are necessary in order to kill possible foodborne bacteria that may be present in meat and poultry.
  - Try covering food with foil during standing time to retain heat (but don't use foil in the microwave!).
- **Use a food thermometer.** Check the temperature in several places to ensure a safe minimum internal temperature has been reached. (For safe temperature guidelines, see the Safe Minimum Internal Temperature Chart.)
- **No, You Can't "Can"!** *Do not* use your microwave for home canning. As liquid inside the sealed glass jar heats and expands, pressure can build up, causing the jar to explode.

If you have any questions about proper microwave use, check the **manufacturer's instructions.**

Grilling and Barbecuing

Grilling and summer sometimes seem synonymous—even though many cooks use their grills year round, whatever the weather. Whenever or wherever you're grilling, keep these hot tips in mind. (Traveling to the cookout? Don't miss Transporting Food.)

Grilling Guidelines:

- **Remember your food thermometer!** Meat and poultry cooked on a grill can brown quickly on the outside — use a food thermometer to be sure the food has reached a safe minimum *internal* temperature. (See Safe Minimum Internal Temperature Chart, and Food Thermometers and Temperature Indicators.)
- **Consider partial precooking.** Partial cooking in the microwave, oven, or on the stove is a good way to reduce grilling time. Just make sure that the food goes **immediately** onto the preheated grill to complete cooking. **Never** partially grill meat or poultry and finish cooking it later.
- **Use a clean platter for cooked food.** Don't put the grilled food on the same platter that held raw meat or poultry because any harmful bacteria present in the raw juices could contaminate safely cooked food. (See also: Cross-Contamination, Marinating, and Serving Food Safely: General Guidelines on page 35.)

Smoking

Smoking is cooking food *indirectly* in the presence of a fire. Smoking is done much more slowly than grilling, so *less tender meats* benefit from this method — and result in a natural "smoke" flavoring permeating the meat. As with any method of cooking, follow the basic steps for safety before smoking:

- **Preparation:** Defrost meat entirely — and safely — before smoking. Marinate meat in the refrigerator. (See Thawing and Marinating.)
- **Partial Cooking:** If you decide to cook food partially in a microwave oven or on the stove to reduce smoking time — make sure that the food goes *immediately* from the microwave or stove to the hot smoker.
- **Two Thermometers:** To smoke meat and poultry safely, you'll need **two types of thermometers**. Cooking time depends on many factors, and since it can take anywhere from up to 8 hours or longer to smoke meat or poultry, the *only* way to monitor the safety and doneness is to use the two thermometers.

- o *Smoker Thermometer:* These are often built in. The smoker thermometer enables you to ensure that the **temperature in the smoker** stays between 225 and 300 °F for safety.
- o *Food Thermometer:* Once **food** is in the smoker, cook until it reaches a safe internal minimum temperature as determined with a food thermometer. (See Safe Minimum Internal Temperature Chart, and Food Thermometers and Temperature Indicators.)

- **Prompt Chilling:** If you aren't taking your smoked food straight to the dinner table, refrigerate meat and poultry within 2 hours after cooking is complete (1 hour when the temperature is above 90 °F). Cut the meat or poultry into smaller portions or slices, place it in shallow containers, cover, and refrigerate. Use it within 4 days, or freeze for later use.

Slow Cooking

In today's multitasking world, there's nothing like having dinner cooked for you while you go about your day. That's the beauty of a slow cooker. As you take advantage of this time-saving wonder, here are tips for keeping your "crock o' dinner" safe.

- **How Slow Cookers Work:** As the name implies, the countertop "slow cooker" cooks foods slowly and at a low temperature — generally between 170 and 280 °F.
  - o The direct heat from the pot, lengthy cooking time, and steam created within the tightly covered container work in combination to destroy bacteria and make the slow cooker a **safe process** for cooking foods.
  - o While food is cooking and once it's done, food will stay safe as long as the cooker is operating.
- **Preparation:** Since the slow cooker may take several hours to reach a safe bacteria-killing temperature, keep perishable ingredients refrigerated right up until preparation time. This keeps bacteria from getting a "head start."
  - o Always defrost meat or poultry *before* putting it into a slow cooker.

  - o If you cut up meat and vegetables in advance, store them separately in the refrigerator.
  - o Keep the lid in place, removing only to stir the food or check for doneness.
- **Choose Appropriate Recipes:**
  - o Prepare foods with a high moisture content such as chili, soup, stew, or spaghetti sauce.
  - o If using a commercially frozen slow-cooker meal, prepare according to manufacturer's instructions.
  - o Fill the cooker to between half full and two-thirds full.
- **Slow-Cooker Leftovers:** Store leftovers in shallow, covered containers and refrigerate within 2 hours after cooking is finished. Reheating leftovers in a slow cooker is **not recommended**. However, cooked food can be brought to steaming on the stove top or in a microwave oven and then put into a preheated slow cooker to keep hot for serving.
- **If the Power Goes Out:**
  - o If you are not at home and the power goes out, throw away the food even if it looks done.
  - o If you *are* at home, finish cooking the ingredients immediately by some other means: on a gas stove, on the outdoor grill, or at a house where the power is on. If the food was completely cooked before the power went out, the food should remain safe up to 2 hours in the cooker with the power off.

SERVING FOOD SAFELY

"Dinner is served!" More than ever, this happens in a wide variety of places, both indoors and out. But no matter where your meal is taking place...safety must still be the first item on the menu.

General Guidelines: Whatever or Wherever You're Serving!

- **Keep Hot Food Hot & Cold Food Cold.** Whether you are in your kitchen or enjoying the great outdoors, there are some food safety principles that remain constant. The first is "Keep hot food hot and cold food cold" to keep foods out of the "Danger Zone." (See Focus on: The "Danger Zone".)

- **Keep Everything Clean.** It's a fact that bacteria from raw meat and poultry products can easily spread to other foods by hands, utensils, or by juices dripping from packages.
  - When **transporting raw meat or poultry,** double-wrap or place the packages in plastic bags to prevent juices from the raw product from dripping on other foods.
  - Always **wash your hands** before and after handling food, and **don't use the same platter and utensils** for raw and cooked meat and poultry.
  - **Soap and water are essential** to cleanliness, so if you are going somewhere that will not have running water, bring water with you or have disposable wipes on hand.
- **Remember the 2-Hour Rule:** Perishable food should never be left in the "Danger Zone" for more than 2 hours. This includes both hot food and cold food. If it's been more than 2 hours (or 1 hour in temperatures above 90 °F) - discard the food.
- **Be Cool:** If you are traveling with cold food, bring a cooler with a cold source. It is difficult to keep food hot without a heat source when traveling, so it's best to cook food before leaving home and refrigerate and transport cold. (See Transporting Food.)

Buffets...Cooking for Groups

Food sitting out for extended periods of time is a recipe for potential disaster. In addition to the basics for temperature and cleanliness, follow these guidelines when cooking for and/or serving groups:

- **Safe Advance Prep:** If you're getting ready ahead of time, be sure to cook food to a safe minimum internal temperature. (See Safe Minimum Internal Temperature Chart.) Divide cooked food into shallow containers to store in the refrigerator or freezer until serving. This encourages rapid, even cooling.

- o Reheat hot food to 165 °F and maintain at a safe temperature of 140 °F or above.

o Don't risk cross-contamination: place food on clean platters. Arrange on several small platters rather than on one large platter, and keep all platters cold in the refrigerator until serving time.

- **Remember the "Temperature Rules": Keep hot food hot** (140 °F or above) with chafing dishes, slow cookers, and warming trays. Cold food should be held at 40 °F or below, so keep food cold by nesting dishes in beds of ice. Or use a series of small serving trays and replace them often.
- *o Replace* empty platters — don't *refill* them. Discard food that has been sitting out and may have been handled by many people.

- **2-Hour Rule:** As always, perishable food should not be left out for more than 2 hours at room temperature (1 hour when the temperature is above 90 °F). Be sure to keep this in mind as the party rocks on — and when in doubt, throw it out. (Also see Transporting Food.)

Take-Out and Delivered Food

With take-out or delivered food, the cook gets to take a shortcut with meal preparation — but not with food safety. Basic guidelines still apply.

Hot Take-Out or Delivered Food

- **Hot Food Hot...**Hot food must be kept out of the "Danger Zone" — and that means that just keeping it "warm" is not enough.

o If you aren't going to eat it right away, **use a food thermometer** to monitor the internal temperature of the food — and don't let it drop below 140 °F. A preheated oven, chafing dishes, preheated warming trays, or slow cookers may be used to keep food hot.

o If you plan to eat at a later time, take-out or delivered food should be **divided into smaller portions or pieces,** placed in shallow containers, and refrigerated. Reheat to 165 °F as you would any leftover.

Cold/Refrigerated Take-Out or Delivered Food

- **...And Cold Food Cold.** Cold food should be kept at 40 °F or below. Refrigerate perishable food as soon as possible, always within 2 hours after purchase or delivery.
  - o If the food is in air temperatures above 90 °F, refrigerate within 1 hour.
  - o When take-out or delivered food is purchased cold for an outdoor event-like a picnic, sporting event, or outdoor buffet-a cooler with ice is a practical alternative to a refrigerator. The cooler should be packed with plenty of ice or frozen gel packs. Keep the cooler in the shade when possible.

Take-Out

- Refrigerate within 2 hours (1 hour in temperatures above 90 °F)
- Use within 3 to 4 days
- Reheat to 165 °F using a food thermometer

TRANSPORTING FOOD: COOLERS, PICNICS, AND BAG LUNCHES

When it comes to food, you can take it with you — but you need to do it safely, too. Whether you're tailgating, picnicking, or just packing your lunch, start with a clean cooler or lunch pack and begin by preparing food using standard "clean" practices. In addition, follow these special guidelines to keep your packed food safe...wherever your travels take you.

Bag Lunches

Bag lunches aren't just for school kids! No matter where you're carrying to, pack only the amount of perishable food that can be eaten at lunch to avoid worrying about the storage or safety of leftovers.

Cold Food:

- Prepare cooked food, such as turkey, ham, chicken, and vegetable or pasta salad, ahead of time to allow for thorough chilling in the refrigerator. Try preparing it the night before!

- Freezing sandwiches helps them stay cold — but for best quality, don't freeze sandwiches containing mayonnaise, lettuce, or tomatoes; add these ingredients later.
- In your lunch bag: once the cold source thaws, perishable food is no longer safe. Discard it.
- Types of Lunchboxes: Insulated, soft-sided lunchboxes or bags are best for keeping food cold, but metal or plastic lunchboxes and paper bags can also be used — just remember that an ice source (such as a gel pack or frozen juice box) should be packed with perishable food in any type of lunch bag or box. If using paper lunch bags, create layers by double-bagging to help insulate the food.

Hot Food:

- Use an insulated container to keep food like soup, chili, and stew hot. Fill the container with boiling water, let it stand for a few minutes, empty the water out, and then put in piping hot food. Keep the insulated container closed until lunchtime to keep the food hot. For safety, it needs to stay at 140 °F or above.
- If you're reheating lunch in a microwave onsite, cover food to hold in moisture and promote even heating. Reheat leftovers to at least 165 °F; food should be steaming hot. Cook frozen convenience meals according to package instructions.

Coolers

The cooler is the key to keeping cold food out of the "Danger Zone!" Use an insulated cooler with sufficient ice or ice packs to keep the food at 40 °F or below.

Packing:

- As you prepare, **divide large amounts of food** into shallow containers for fast chilling and easier use. Keep cooked food refrigerated until it's time to leave home.
- **Pack food right from the refrigerator** into the cooler immediately before leaving home.
  - o For your cold source: use **frozen gel packs or ice**. A block of ice keeps longer than ice cubes. Or, in advance,

freeze clean, empty milk cartons filled with water to make **blocks of ice.** Add the ice first, then the food.

- Pack smart! **Pack usable quantities in reverse order:**
    - o The *first* foods packed should be the *last* foods to be used. (There is one exception: **Pack raw meat or poultry below ready-to-eat foods** to prevent raw meat or poultry juices from dripping on the other foods.)
    - o Take foods in the smallest quantity needed (e.g., a small jar of mayonnaise).
- Consider **packing drinks in a separate cooler** so the food cooler is not opened frequently.
- It is important to pack an **appliance thermometer** in your cooler. Since the food in the cooler should be kept at 40 °F or below, you need to be able to monitor it.
- Before you leave home, find out if there's a **source of clean water** at your destination. If not, bring water for preparation and cleaning. Or, pack clean cloths and moist towelettes for cleaning surfaces and hands.

Placement:

- At your destination, keep the cooler **in the shade,** and try to **insulate it** with a blanket, tarp, or poncho. Keep the lid closed and avoid repeated openings. Replenish the ice if it melts.
- Remember that the rule for keeping food safe changes during warmer weather. While food can be kept out of the cooler for 2 hours at normal temperatures, if the weather is **above 90 °F outside,** food should be returned to a cooler or refrigerated after only 1 hour. (See Focus On: The Danger Zone.)

Party's Over?

- Discard all **used food packaging** and bags — they could contaminate other food and cause foodborne illness, so don't reuse them.

Discard all perishable foods if there is no longer ice in the cooler, or if the **gel packs** are no longer frozen. (See also: Serving Food Safely, and Grilling and Barbecuing.)

Slow Cookers and Food Safety

Opening the front door on a cold winter evening and being greeted by the inviting smells of beef stew or chicken noodle soup wafting from a slow cooker can be a diner's dream come true. But winter is not the only time a slow cooker is useful. In the summer, using this small appliance can avoid introducing heat from a hot oven. At any time of year, a slow cooker can make life a little more convenient because by planning ahead, you save time later. And it takes less electricity to use a slow cooker rather than an oven.

Is A Slow Cooker Safe?

Yes, the slow cooker, a countertop appliance, cooks foods slowly at a low temperature—generally between 170° and 280° F. The low heat helps less expensive, leaner cuts of meat become tender and shrink less. The direct heat from the pot, lengthy cooking and steam created within the tightly-covered container combine to destroy bacteria and make the slow cooker a safe process for cooking foods.

Safe Beginnings

Begin with a clean cooker, clean utensils and a clean work area. Wash hands before and during food preparation. Keep perishable foods refrigerated until preparation time. If you cut up meat and vegetables in advance, store them separately in the refrigerator. The slow cooker may take several hours to reach a safe, bacteria-killing temperature. Constant refrigeration assures that bacteria, which multiply rapidly at room temperature, won't get a "head start" during the first few hours of cooking.

Thaw Ingredients

Always thaw meat or poultry before putting it into a slow cooker. Choose to make foods with a high moisture content such as chili, soup, stew or spaghetti sauce. If using a commercially frozen slow cooker meal, prepare according to manufacturer's instructions.

Use the Right Amount of Food

Fill cooker no less than half full and no more than two-thirds full. Vegetables cook slower than meat and poultry in a slow cooker so if using them, put vegetables in first, at the bottom and around sides of the utensil. Then add meat and cover the food with liquid such as broth, water or barbecue sauce. Keep the lid in place, removing only to stir the food or check for doneness.

Settings

Most cookers have two or more settings. Foods take different times to cook depending upon the setting used. Certainly, foods will cook faster on high than on low. However, for all-day cooking or for less-tender cuts, you may want to use the low setting.

If possible, turn the cooker on the highest setting for the first hour of cooking time and then to low or the setting called for in your recipe. However, it's safe to cook foods on low the entire time — if you're leaving for work, for example, and preparation time is limited.

While food is cooking and once it's done, food will stay safe as long as the cooker is operating.

Power Out

If you are not at home during the entire slow-cooking process and the power goes out, throw away the food even if it looks done.

If you are at home, finish cooking the ingredients immediately by some other means: on a gas stove, on the outdoor grill or at a house where the power is on.

When you are at home, and if the food was completely cooked before the power went out, the food should remain safe up to two hours in the cooker with the power off.

Handling Leftovers

Store leftovers in shallow covered containers and refrigerate within two hours after cooking is finished. Reheating leftovers in a slow cooker is not recommended. Cooked food should be reheated on the stove, in a microwave, or in a conventional oven until it reaches 165 °F.

Then the hot food can be placed in a preheated slow cooker to keep it hot for serving—at least 140 °F as measured with a food thermometer.

Use A Food Thermometer

Safe Temperature Chart Included!

Why Use a Food Thermometer?

"I want to keep my family safe."

"I used to overcook my food. Now my food is juicier - not dry as a bone."

People all over the country are taking Thermy's™ advice. They're using a food thermometer to check the temperature of everyday foods — like hamburgers, pork chops, and chicken breasts.

Most people think they know when food is "done" just by "eyeballing it." They look at it and trust their experience.

Experience is good, but it sometimes can be misleading. For instance, cooking by color is definitely misleading. Meat color — pink or brown — can fool you!

How do you know when your hamburger is cooked? Because it's brown inside?

Think about this ... 1 out of every 4 hamburgers turns brown in the middle BEFORE it has reached a safe internal temperature, according to recent USDA research.

Use a food thermometer.

Keep your family safe.

Be a better cook.

Digital, Dial, & Disposable!

Thermometers are turning up everywhere in today's kitchens in all shapes and sizes — digitals, instant-reads, probes for the oven and microwave, disposable indicators and sensor sticks, pop-ups, and even barbecue forks. They're high-tech and easy to use.

Some thermometers are meant to stay in the food while it's cooking; others are not. Some are ideal for checking thin foods, like the digital. Others, like the large-dial thermometer many people use, are really meant for large roasts and whole chickens and turkeys.

Choose and use the one that is right for you!

- Dial Instant-Read
- Digital Instant-Read
- Disposable Temperature Indicators
- Fork
- Dial Oven-Safe
- Pop-Up

Why Is It Important?

These are the facts!

- Millions of people get sick from dangerous bacteria in food every year.
- Public health data in 2000 show that there are more than 5 times the number of dangerous bacteria in our food than we were aware of in 1942.
- Many people don't link their illness to foodborne bacteria. They think they have a case of the flu.
- You can become sick anytime from 20 minutes to 6 weeks after eating food with some types of harmful bacteria.
- Infants and young children, pregnant women, and older adults are at greatest risk for foodborne illness, as are all people with weakened immune systems caused by cancer treatment, AIDS, diabetes, kidney disease, and organ transplants.

IT'S SAFE TO BITE WHEN THE TEMPERATURE IS RIGHT!

Using a food thermometer is the only sure way of knowing if your food has reached a high enough temperature to destroy foodborne bacteria.

Is it done yet?

Where is your food thermometer?

TEMPERATURE RULES!

Food	°F
Ground Meat & Meat Mixtures	
Beef, Pork, Veal, Lamb	160

Turkey, Chicken	165
Fresh Beef, Veal, Lamb	
Medium Rare	145
Medium	160
Well Done	170
Poultry	
Chicken & Turkey, whole	165
Poultry breasts, roast	165
Poultry thighs, wings	165
Duck & Goose	165
Stuffing (cooked alone or in bird)	165
Fresh Pork	160
Ham	
Fresh (raw)	160
Pre-cooked (to reheat)	140
Eggs & Egg Dishes	
Eggs	Cook until yolk & white are firm
Egg dishes	160
Leftovers & Casseroles	165

Thermy™ is the messenger of a national consumer education campaign of the USDA/FSIS designed to promote the use of food thermometers.

Additives in Meat and Poultry Products

People have been using food additives for thousands of years. Today about 2,800 substances are used as food additives. Salt, sugar, and corn syrup are by far the most widely used additives in food in this country.

History of Food Additives

In prehistoric times, cavemen may have smoked meats to make them taste better. In coastal regions, early man probably soaked foods, including meat and poultry, in seawater for better flavor and for preservation. The spice trade between Asia, the

Middle East, and Europe flourished because the public demanded the flavors that spices added to foods. Early explorers went in search of salt and spices, and wealthy Romans were kidnaped for ransom of salt and spices. Our ancestors discovered that large amounts of sugar helped preserve fruits.

What is a Food Additive?

"Food additive" is defined by the Food and Drug Administration (FDA) as any substance used to provide a technical effect in foods. The use of food additives has become more prominent in recent years, due to the increased production of prepared, processed, and convenience foods. Additives are used for flavor and appeal, food preparation and processing, freshness, and safety. At the same time, consumers and scientists have raised questions about the necessity and safety of these substances.

Who Monitors the Safety of Food Additives?

Before any substance can be added to food, its safety must be assessed in a stringent approval process. The Food Safety and Inspection Service (FSIS) of the U.S. Department of Agriculture (USDA) shares responsibility with FDA for the safety of food additives used in meat, poultry, and egg products. All additives are initially evaluated for safety by FDA.

When an additive is proposed for use in a meat, poultry, or egg product, its safety, technical function, and conditions of use must also be evaluated by the Labeling and Consumer Protection Staff of FSIS, as provided in the Federal Meat Inspection Act, the Poultry Products Inspection Act, the Egg Products Inspection Act, and related regulations. Although FDA has overriding authority regarding additive safety, FSIS may apply even stricter standards that take into account the unique characteristics of meat, poultry, and egg products. Several years ago, for instance, permission was sought to use sorbic acid in meat salads. Although sorbic acid was an approved food additive, permission for use in meat salad was denied because such usage could mask spoilage caused by organisms that cause foodborne illness.

Additives are never given permanent approval. FDA and FSIS continually review the safety of approved additives, based on the best scientific knowledge, to determine if approvals should be modified or withdrawn.

Why Are Food Additives Regulated?

During the early part of the first century in America, people lived off the land. They grew their own foods or bought them from someone they knew and trusted. There was no need for food safety laws. As the country grew and became more industrialized, the number of people who produced their own foods decreased drastically. Therefore, the nation depended on the newly emerging food industry to produce and distribute its food. Unfortunately, during the 1850's, there was much dishonesty concerning adding substances to foods.

The first efforts to pass laws to govern foods were state laws (1850 and beyond). These laws were difficult to enforce. The first major Federal law governing food was the 1906 Federal Food and Drug Act. It set the framework for the regulation of foods and stated that it was illegal to sell misbranded or adulterated foods and drugs in interstate commerce. It listed chemicals that were illegal to add to foods, such as borax or formaldehyde. The law was weak in that there was no method of enforcement and no punishment.

In 1938, the Federal Food and Drug Act was revised to account for changes in medical science and food technology, and was renamed the Federal Food, Drug, and Cosmetic Act. Among the many provisions of the law was a requirement for truthful labeling of additives.

When Did Food Additives Regulations Begin?

The 1958 Food Additives Amendment to the Federal Food, Drug, and Cosmetic Act provided for the first specific regulations of food additives. Approval of new food additives was required before they could be marketed, and the responsibility for proving their safety was placed on the manufacturer.

To use or market a substance to be used as a food additive, a company must first file a petition with the FDA outlining the tests that prove the substance to be safe under the proposed conditions of use. If it is approved as safe under the proposed conditions of use, FDA prescribes in its regulations, the types of foods it may be used in, and how it may be used.

Are Any Additives Exempt from the Approval Process?

The Food Additives Amendment exempted two groups of food additives from FDA's testing and approval process. One is the list of substances known as "generally recognized as safe" (GRAS). This group includes a variety of substances, from commonly used flavorings and spices to phosphates and carrageenan. These substances are considered harmless under prescribed conditions of use. Past extensive use of these substances has produced no known harmful effects. The other group of additives known as "substances with prior sanction" was approved by USDA and FDA for use in foods prior to the passage of the 1958 Food Additives Amendment. Examples of these types of substances include potassium nitrite and sodium nitrite. Additives can be removed from the lists if tests indicate the substances are not safe for human consumption.

When Were Color Additives Addressed?

The 1960 Color Additives Amendment brought all colors, natural and synthetic, under the Food, Drug, and Cosmetic Act. Color additives may not be used to deceive consumers or to conceal blemishes or inferiorities in food products. Colors used in foods, drugs, and cosmetics must be approved by the FDA before they can be marketed.

The Food Additives Amendment and the Color Additives Amendments include the Delaney Clause, which prohibits the approval of an additive "if it is found to induce cancer when ingested by" people or animals, or "if it is found, after tests which are appropriate for the evaluation of the safety of food additives, to induce cancer in" people or animals. Any substance found to cause cancer is regulated under the general safety provisions of these laws, as well as by the Delaney Clause.

What are Labeling Requirements for Additives?

The statutes and regulations to enforce the statutes require certain information on labels of meat and poultry products so consumers will have complete information about a product. In all cases, ingredients must be listed on the product label, in the ingredients statement in order by weight, from the greatest amount to the least. Substances such as spices and spice extractives may be declared as "natural flavors," "flavors," or "natural flavoring" on meat and poultry labels without naming each one. This is because they are used primarily for their flavor contribution and not their nutritional contribution.

Substances such as dried meat, poultry stock, meat extracts, or hydrolyzed protein must be listed on the label by their common or usual name because their primary purpose is not flavor. They may be used as flavor enhancers, binders, or emulsifiers. They must be labeled using the species of origin of the additive, for example, dried beef, chicken stock, pork extract, or hydrolyzed wheat protein.

Color additives must be declared by their common or usual names on labels, e.g., FD&C Yellow 5, or annatto extract, not collectively as colorings. These labeling requirements help consumers make choices about the foods they eat.

GLOSSARY OF COMMONLY USED MEAT AND POULTRY ADDITIVES AND TERMS

ANTIOXIDANT - substances added to foods to prevent the oxygen present in the air from causing undesirable changes in flavor or color. BHA, BHT, and tocopherols are examples of antioxidants.

BHT (butylated hydroxytoluene), BHA (butylated hydroxyanisole), TOCOPHEROLS (VITAMIN E) - antioxidants that help maintain the appeal and wholesome qualities of food by retarding rancidity in fats, sausages, and dried meats, as well as helping to protect some of the natural nutrients in foods, such as vitamin A.

BINDER - a substance that may be added to foods to thicken or improve texture.

BROMELIN - an enzyme that can dissolve or degrade the proteins collagen and elastin to soften meat and poultry tissue. It is derived from pineapple fruit and leaves, and is used as a meat tenderizer.

CARRAGEENAN - seaweed is the source of this additive. It may be used in products as binder.

CITRIC ACID - widely distributed in nature in both plants and animals. It can be used as an additive to protect the fresh color of meat cuts during storage. Citric acid also helps protect flavor and increases the effectiveness of antioxidants.

CORN SYRUP - sugar that is derived from the hydrolysis of corn starch. Uses include flavoring agent and sweetener in meat and poultry products.

EMULSIFIER - substance added to products, such as meat spreads, to prevent separation of product components to ensure consistency. Examples of these types of additives include lecithin, and mono- and di-glycerides.

FICIN - enzyme derived from fig trees that is used as a meat tenderizer.

GELATIN - thickener from collagen which is derived from the skin, tendons, ligaments, or bones of livestock. It may be used in canned hams or jellied meat products.

HUMECTANT - substance added to foods to help retain moisture and soft texture. An example is glycerine, which may be used in dried meat snacks.

HYDROLYZED (SOURCE) PROTEIN - flavor enhancers that can be used in meat and poultry products. They are made from protein obtained from a plant source such as soy or wheat, or from an animal source, such as milk. The source used must be identified on the label.

MODIFIED FOOD STARCH - starch that has been chemically altered to improve its thickening properties. Before the starch is modified, it is separated from the protein through isolation techniques; therefore, the source of the starch used is not required on the label.

MONOSODIUM GLUTAMATE (MSG) - MSG is a flavor enhancer. It comes from a common amino acid, glutamic acid, and must be declared as monosodium glutamate on meat and poultry labels.

PAPAIN - an enzyme that can dissolve or degrade the proteins collagen and elastin to soften meat and poultry tissue. It is derived from the tropical papaya tree and is used as a meat tenderizer.

PHOSPHATES - the two beneficial effects of phosphates in meat and poultry products are moisture retention and flavor protection. An example is the use of phosphates in the curing of ham where approved additives are sodium or potassium salts of tripolyphosphate, hexametaphosphate, acid pyrophosphate, or orthophosphates, declared as "phosphates" on labels.

PROPYL GALLATE - used as an antioxidant to prevent rancidity in products such as rendered fats or pork sausage. It can be used in combination with antioxidants such as BHA and BHT.

RANCID/RANCIDITY - oxidation/breakdown of fat that occurs naturally causing undesirable smell and taste. BHA/BHT and tocopherols are used to keep fats from becoming rancid.

SODIUM CASEINATE - used as a binder in products such as frankfurters and stews.

SODIUM ERYTHORBATE - is the sodium salt of erythorbic acid, a highly refined food-grade chemical closely related to vitamin C, synthesized from sugar, and used as a color fixative in preparing cured meats. (Note: Erythorbate is **NOT** earthworms. Perhaps the spelling or pronunciation has contributed to this misconception because the Hotline receives many calls related to this concern.)

SODIUM NITRITE - used alone or in conjunction with sodium nitrate as a color fixative in cured meat and poultry products (bologna, hot dogs, bacon). Helps prevent growth of *Clostridium botulinum,* which can cause botulism in humans.

SUGAR (SUCROSE) - used as sweetener in an endless list of food products.

TEXTURIZERS/STABILIZERS/THICKENERS - used in foods to help maintain uniform texture or consistency. These are substances that are commonly called binders. Examples are gelatin and carrageenan.

WHEY, DRIED - the dried form of a component of milk that remains after cheese making. Can be used as a binder or extender in various meat products, such as sausage and stews.

MEAT AND POULTRY LABELING TERMS

"What does `mechanically separated meat or poultry' mean?"

"If chicken is labeled 'fresh,' how can it be so rock hard?"

"Does 'natural' mean 'raised without hormones'?"

These are just some of the questions consumers have asked USDA's Meat and Poultry Hotline about words which may be descriptive of meat and poultry. Can they be legally used on labels and, if so, what are their definitions?

Here from USDA's Food Safety and Inspection Service (FSIS) is a glossary of meat and poultry labeling terms. FSIS is the agency responsible for ensuring the truthfulness and accuracy in labeling of meat and poultry products. Knowing the meaning of labeling terms can make purchasing of meat and poultry products less confusing.

BASTED or SELF BASTED: *Bone-in* poultry products that are injected or marinated with a solution containing butter or other edible fat, broth, stock or water plus spices, flavor enhancers and other approved substances must be labeled as basted or self basted. The maximum added weight of approximately 3% solution before processing is included in the net weight on the label. Label must include a statement identifying the total quantity and common or usual name of all ingredients in the solution, e.g., *"Injected with approximately 3% of a solution of* ____________ (list of ingredients)."

Use of the terms "basted" or "self-basted" on *boneless* poultry products is limited to 8% of the weight of the raw poultry before processing.

CERTIFIED: The term *"certified"* implies that the USDA's Food Safety and Inspection Service and the Agriculture Marketing Service have officially evaluated a meat product for class, grade, or other quality characteristics (e.g., "Certified Angus Beef"). When used under other circumstances, the term must be closely associated with the name of the organization responsible for the *"certification"* process, e.g., *"XYZ Company's Certified Beef"*.

CHEMICAL FREE: The term is ***not allowed*** to be used on a label.

FREE RANGE or FREE ROAMING: Producers must demonstrate to the Agency that the poultry has been allowed access to the outside.

FRESH POULTRY: In August, 1995 USDA/FSIS published a rule attempting to modify the definition of "fresh" to refer to poultry whose internal temperature has never been below 26 °F. That rule said poultry whose internal temperature is between 26 °F and 0 °F cannot be called "fresh" but must be called "hard-chilled" or "previously hard chilled." In January, 1996 the final rule was published in the Federal Register. However, Congress did not appropriate money for enforcing the rule. On August 8, 1996, Congress asked FSIS to revise the final rule. FSIS has now amended the poultry product inspection regulations to prohibit the use of the term "fresh" on the labeling of raw poultry products whose internal temperature has ever been below 26 °F. Also, labels of raw poultry products whose temperature has ever been below 26 °F, but above 0 °F, will not be required to bear any specific, descriptive labeling terms, including "hard chilled" or "previously hard chilled." To be in compliance with the revised rule, raw poultry products that are labeled as "fresh" but have ever had an internal temperature *below 26 °F will have* to have the "fresh" designation deleted or removed from labeling on the package. The final rule also sets a temperature tolerance for raw poultry products. The temperature of individual packages of raw poultry products labeled "fresh" can vary as much as 1°F below 26 °F within inspected establishments or 2 °F below 26 °F in commerce. This revised final rule appeared in the December 17, 1996, Federal Register and became effective 1 year later – December 17, 1997.

FROZEN POULTRY: Temperature of raw, frozen poultry is 0 °F or below.

FRYER-ROASTER TURKEY: Young, immature turkey usually less than 16 weeks of age of either sex.

HALAL and ZABIAH HALAL: Products prepared by federally inspected meat packing plants identified with labels bearing references to *"Halal"* or *"Zabiah Halal"* must be handled according to Islamic law and under Islamic authority.

HEN or TOM TURKEY: The sex designation of *"hen"* (female) or *"tom"* (male) turkey is optional on the label, and is an indication of *size* rather than the tenderness of a turkey.

KOSHER: *"Kosher"* may be used only on the labels of meat and poultry products prepared under Rabbinical supervision.

Bibliography

Anderson, Kenneth: *International Dictionary of Food & Nutrition*. New York: Wiley, 1993.

Asiedu, J.J.: *Processing chicken*, MacMillan Press Ltd, London, 1989.

Axtell, B., Kocken E., and Sandhu, R., *Fruit Processing*, IT Publications, London, 1993.

Barlow K: *Ecology of Food and Nutrition*, Oceania, New Guinea, 1984.

Bindon JR: *Food and Foodways*, Oceania, Samoa, 1988.

Bowes, Anna De Planter: *Bowes and Church's Food Values of Portions Commonly Used*. Philadelphia: J.B. Lippincott, 1994.

Casado, Matt A: *Food and Beverage Service Manual*. New York: Wiley, 1994.

Coultate, T.P.: *Food in Kitchen Safety*, Burlington House, London, 1984.

Fellows, P. and Hidellage, V.: *Making Safe Food*, IT Publications, London, 1992.

Hays, Judi Radice: *Restaurant & Food Graphics*. Glen Cove: PBC International, 1994.

Hobbs, B. and Roberts, D.: *Food Poisoning and Food Hygiene*, Edward Arnold Ltd, London, 1987.

MacDonald, I. and Low, J.: *Fruit and Vegetables*, IT Publications, London, 1984.

Pollock NJ: *The Concept of Food in Pacific Society: A Fijian Example*, Oceania, Fiji, 1985.

Sims-Bell, Barbara: *Career Opportunities in the Food and Beverage Industry*. New York: Facts on File, 1994.

Zaccarelli, Herman E.: *Food Service Management by Checklist: A Handbook of Control Techniques*. New York: Wiley, 1991.

Index

C

Canning Fruits, 41, 49.
Canning Meat, 90, 91.
Canning Procedures, 30, 50, 51, 53.
Chopped Meat, 11, 94, 97.
Cooking Food Safely, 252.
Cooking Ham, 158.
Cooking Methods, 128, 172, 210.
Cooling Jars, 34, 48, 92.
Cream Style, 38, 43, 44.

E

Egg Products, 193, 194, 195, 196, 197, 203, 279.

F

Food Preparation, 246, 247, 264, 274, 279.
Food Safety, 1, 59, 134, 155, 163, 168, 173, 214, 219, 222, 226, 227, 233, 245, 284, 286.
Food Safety Guidelines, 1, 59, 162.
Foodborne Bacteria, 139, 235, 236, 252, 262, 265, 277.
Freezing Fruits, 73, 76.
Fruit Products, 18.

G

Governments, 199.
Guidelines, 1, 31, 46, 51, 52, 66, 78, 97, 149, 178, 184, 228, 235, 247, 253, 262, 269, 271, 272, 276, 277, 278, 282, 284, 285, 286.

J

Jams, 18, 19, 21, 22, 23, 24, 144.
Jellies, 18, 19, 20, 22, 23, 24, 142, 144.

N

Nutrition Information, 29, 197.

P

Pickled Fish, 15.
Pickled Smelt, 15.
Preserving Fruit, 120.
Proteins, 129, 132, 149, 165, 181, 282, 283.

S

Sausage Formulations, 2, 60.
Serving Food Safely, 266, 273.
Spreads, 18, 19, 23, 145, 223, 239, 256, 283.
Sugar Spreads, 19.

T

Transporting Food, 265, 269, 270.

V

Vegetables, 30, 31, 38, 39, 40, 43, 44, 96, 99, 102, 110, 111, 112, 113, 223, 236, 238, 239, 240, 244, 248, 268, 274, 275.

♦♦♦